NO RETURN ADDRESS

NO RETURN ADDRESS

A Memoir of Displacement

Anca Vlasopolos

COLUMBIA UNIVERSITY PRESS

NEW YORK

Columbia University Press
Publishers Since 1893
New York   Chichester, West Sussex
Copyright © 2000 Columbia University Press
All rights reserved
Library of Congress Cataloging-in-Publication Data
Vlasopolos, Anca, 1948–

    No return address : a memoir of displacement /
Anca Vlasopolos.

    p. cm.

    ISBN 0–231–12130–X (acid-free paper)

    1. Vlasopolos, Anca, 1948– 2. Literary historians—United
States—Biography. 3. English teachers—United States—Biography.
4. Romanian Americans—Middle West—Biography. 5. Romania—
Social conditions—1945–1989. 6. Middle West—Social life and
customs. 7. Jews—Romania—Biography. 8. Jewish families—
Romania. I. Title.
PE64.V57 A3 2000
973.'049240498'092—dc21
[B]   99-098189

Casebound editions of Columbia University Press books are printed
on permanent and durable acid-free paper.
Printed in the United States of America
c 10 9 8 7 6 5 4 3 2 1

FOR MY DAUGHTER,
Olivia Vlasopolos Ambrogio

IN MEMORY OF MY PARENTS,
Hermina Grünberg Vlasopolos and Paul Vlasopolos

CONTENTS

While writing this story of exile, I characterized it as a "fictionalized" autobiography. The quotation marks emphasize the vexed question of the difference between fiction and autobiography, a question I recollect Grace Paley dismissing as a concern only booksellers might have with shelf labeling. Yet where does the truth of an individual's history reside in a narrative labeled autobiographical? Is *Mrs. Dalloway* more fictional than *To the Lighthouse*? Is *A Portrait of the Artist as a Young Man* more autobiographical than *Ulysses*? Did Dante really meet Beatrice in the streets of Florence? Did everything that Maxine Hong Kingston related in her memoir of a girlhood among ghosts really happen? Is Marcel Proust?

I use these literary contexts as a diversionary tactic from the uneasy awareness that whenever we re-collect, re-member our past, we fashion it out of threads, scraps, disparate pieces that for reasons fathomable or not have been taken along in the mental trunks that hold our past selves. Were these shreds ever whole? Is there a continuity of time that remains seamless, unrent by the violence of loss, displacement, or the insidious wearing thin of daily circumstance? Memory is fragmentary, and we like to think that imaginative re-collection can assemble the pieces, whether in the crazy quilt of a postmodern refusal to believe in the integrity of self and history or in the deceptively organic patterns of a method that testifies to its user's faith in ends, and endings, and thus beginnings and middles.

In this book I have tried to be faithful to my historical experiences and my remembrances, distorted though they inevitably are, first and foremost by the very dislocation of language effected in the translation from native to other tongue, by distance in space and time, by personal animus, and by the mutability of that very history that had tried so hard to escape its own condition.

Of necessity the principle of selection lifts episodes into disclosure and leaves others, sometimes the context, in the obscurity of the barely hinted at or the unsaid. My selections function along the axis of places, large cities for the most part, for mine is fundamentally the story of an urban dweller. The narrative thread, the leitmotif through these various displacements, is the fear and delight generated by food and speech that those who have lived under repression—theocratic, ideological, familial—will, I hope, recognize. But my most deeply felt impulse to write has been to keep alive my mother's spirit, indomitable through ill chance, bleak history, and peregrinations that would have crushed or maimed a lesser being.

I must come clean about departures from strict truth that neither serve aesthetic purposes nor result from involuntary suppressions. I have changed many names. I took pains to blur incidents involving people who took risks on my family's behalf and mine; unlike us, who live in the West as we presently know it, where books don't much matter, some of these brave people still live in regimes where a change in the wind might make the literary text the bearer of literal truth to be used for persecution. And while this book might hurt a few people's feelings, I want no one to suffer for it, for I alone am accountable for my story.

ACKNOWLEDGMENTS

I wish to thank Michigan State University Press for its kind permission to reprint chapter 16, "Where All the Lights Were Bright," excerpted in *Pen/Insula: Essays and Memoirs from Michigan,* ed. Michael Steinberg (East Lansing, Mich.: Michigan State University Press, 2000). I am grateful to Wayne State University for granting me a course release through the Humanities Center Fellowship and a semester sabbatical to complete this book. My agent, Julie Popkin, kept the faith much longer than I had any right to expect. My editor, Jennifer Crewe, made the process of publishing a delight. Leslie Kriesel restored my trust in manuscript editors; may other writers be equally blessed. My colleague and friend, Charles Parrish, helped me enhance the visions captured in old and damaged photographs.

The Detroit Writers' Guild—Anthony Ambrogio, Olivia V. Ambrogio, Carol Campbell, Claire Crabtree, Helen Franklin, Larry Levine, Patrick O'Leary, Jane Schaberg, and Robin Watson during the years when I read the book to the group—have sustained me with their encouragement and astute critiques for over twenty years of fruitful exchanges. I look forward to many more years of shared work with them and the newer members, John Gallagher, Kathe Koja, Suzanne Scarfone, Peggy Stack, and Melanie Van Der Tuin.

My daughter, Olivia V. Ambrogio, for whom I recorded these memories, read the manuscript with enthusiasm and her fine critical eye. She did her best to keep me honest.

Three people went to great lengths to promote this book.

Patrick O'Leary spoke of it to his agent, his publisher, his connections in the publishing business; Jane Schaberg championed it to her overseas publisher and to U.S. editors. The book, however, might have remained in manuscript indefinitely had it not been for the untiring efforts, on many fronts, of Ralph Freedman, who recommended it to Julie Popkin. In him—as well as in his long-time companion, Lore Metzger, whose death diminishes us and whom we will miss for the rest of our lives—I found what every writer dreams of: the ideal reader.

To my husband, Anthony Ambrogio, goes the greatest share of thanks. In a writerly household, he gave me the space, the computing technical help, the critical insights, and most of all the faith to proceed with a narrative that was often harrowing to recall and express. His generosity and love speak volumes about his merits and my luck.

Romania

1914—Birth of Paul Vlasopolos, son of a Greek immigrant father and a Hungarian mother, in the Danube port town of Braila.

1919—Birth of Hermina (Mimi) Grünberg, daughter of a Jewish father of Sephardic origin whose family emigrated through Germany and Russia and a Jewish Romanian mother, in Bucharest.

1921—Death of Clara Pollock Grünberg, Hermina's mother, of typhoid.

1944—Transylvania, a province of Romania since the Treaty of Versailles, reverts to Hungary during the Nazi conquest. The border between Transylvania and Romania proper closes; the Nazis order the deportation of all Jews in Hungarian territories.

Hermina Grünberg is deported to Auschwitz, where she remains three months before being transported to three successive labor camps.

Death of Aron Grünberg of pneumonia.

May 2, 1945—The event to which Hermina Grünberg always refers as her second birthday: the liberation by the Soviet Army of the slave-labor camp in which she has been held.

c. 1943–44—Death of Harilaus Vlasopolos, father of Paul, in a German bombardment of Athens, where Harilaus had fled from the Romanian Iron Guard's persecution of minorities.

1947—Hermina and Paul meet at a labor-resolution negotiation in the Romanian film industry; in August, they marry.

1948—Birth of Anca Vlasopolos.

Romania elects a communist government. Election fraud is widely suspected. Soviet overseers move in to supervise all key operations of business, industry, and government.

1952—Paul Vlasopolos is arrested in the night; he is held without charges.

1953—Paul Vlasopolos is tried for disseminating antigovernment propaganda. He is condemned to a year in prison, time served. He is released almost a year to the day of his imprisonment.

1956—Death of Paul Vlasopolos by cardiac failure during a bout of Asian flu.

1958—Along with most of Romania's Jewry, Hermina Vlasopolos applies for permission to exile herself permanently from Romania. Within two months, she is fired and forbidden to participate in the People's Workforce—i.e., she is blacklisted from all legitimate employment.

1958–62—Hermina Vlasopolos supports herself and her daughter by doing literary work sub rosa and substituting for women workers on maternity leave.

1962—Hermina and Anca Vlasopolos are granted permission to become permanent exiles; they are required legally to renounce their citizenship. Death of Helen Ethel Vlasopolos, Paul's mother.

Western Europe

1962–63—Hermina and Anca Vlasopolos are in transit: six months in Paris, five months in Belgium, one month in Germany. While in Belgium, Hermina Vlasopolos marries Avram Bril.

The United States

1963—Hermina and Avram Bril and Anca Vlasopolos arrive in Detroit, Michigan, U.S.A.

1963–65—Hermina and Avram Bril find jobs as high school teachers in a village in Michigan.

1965—Hermina and Avram Bril find new teaching jobs and move to a suburb of Detroit.

1966—Hermina Vlasopolos divorces Avram Bril.

1972—Anca Vlasopolos marries Anthony Ambrogio, son of first-generation Italian American parents.

1980—Birth of Olivia Vlasopolos Ambrogio, Detroit, Michigan.

1989—Death of Hermina Vlasopolos of cardiac failure, Detroit, Michigan.

ONE: *Mouthfuls*

I am not Philip Roth, and this is not Portnoy speaking to his therapist. I hate therapy. Even without it I know, as I rapidly pass my mid-forties, that I will not be the voice of the age or one of its foremost poets, critics, novelists, or colorful characters. So why bother to speak? Certainly not to "get better"; what distinguishes talking to a therapist from addressing our old friend the reader is that in the first case the talker pays to be listened to and in the second, as we all hope, the reader will pay to hear. And beyond that delusional hope, why speak? The old clichés, I suppose: I've known interesting people in my time, in a culture that has begun to vanish, none the voice of the age, most of them dead. But then our past always vanishes behind us, and I don't intend to resurrect it through any fortuitous meeting of buttery confection and linden tea. The foods of my childhood are forever gone from the world, not just my world, and besides for me the past comes back more through smell than the other senses. I remember returning to Paris after an absence of seven years, Paris not the city of light but the site of my first acute consciousness of cultural displacement; I stood on a metro platform, and as the train made its breakneck approach, the fumes from the tracks, loaded with strangulating memories of my first encounter with the West, rushed upon my whole being with greater speed and more impact, more lasting impact at any rate, than the bullet-shaped locomotive would have had. Yet I cannot evoke such smells until I find a way of trapping them inside little inserts that would fall out of these pages at appropriate intervals, like perfume samples from glossy magazines.

So I'm left with the voices I'm trying on, stilled yet resounding inside the walnut shell of my moveable domain. But are these their voices? It isn't their language in which I speak their stories; the stories aren't perhaps even theirs but the precipitate of words I remember imperfectly or invent to cover the silences, the stirred sediment of feelings these memories evoke. And being a transcription, the crude text unadorned by modulations of speech or the lightning-quick pointer of gesture, is this also an act of betrayal—the "creative" departure from the original?

I hate therapy, even if people I respect tell me it's helped them. I see it in the same way I see religion in this time and place, as a mere economic transaction. Which reminds me of Herczog, my father's friend, newly landed on Long Island, innocently attempting to exercise his religious freedom. His skills had gotten rusty after so many years of concealment and disuse, but come his first American fall he went to the synagogue on Yom Kippur to say kaddish for his father. I'd known him since I was a child, so I'd never thought of him as having had a father. Now in the town of Roslyn, as he entered the lobby of the synagogue, he was asked for his ticket. "You're putting on a play," he said. He'd remained a naive guy, Herczog, despite his survivor's cunning. "What do I need a ticket for? I just came to say a prayer for my father." They were a little embarrassed, not so much by their rules as by his greenhorn ignorance, reminiscent no doubt of the very people for whom they would offer prayers on the Day of Atonement. They told him that seating, particularly at the High Holy Days, was at a premium. Not everyone had room. The House of God had to maintain itself. He drove off, feeling a little heartburn and regretting having drunk the fresh-squeezed grapefruit juice his wife handed him each morning since she'd come to America. She was making up for the many winters without citrus fruit back in Romania. As he passed the Anglican church around the block from his apartment house, his mind made that qualitative leap Marx had so fondly expounded on: ecumenically, he decided that a house of worship was a house of worship, and he'd offer a prayer for his father inside the church. Its heavy doors were both locked. It was a weekday, after all. He went back to his car, which he'd parked under a huge elm that shaded half the parking lot. It was the kind of crisp autumn day when you feel the undertow of winter beneath the sunny breeze, but your car still gets hot as an oven under the cloudless sky. The elm leaves shone like Hanukkah geld in the sun. He got in the car and said kaddish, right there in the parking lot, without a minyan. He found himself sobbing so hard that he jumped when his forehead bumped the horn and made it honk absurdly loud in the quiet early afternoon.

Once home, he raved on and on about the synagogue and the tickets and extortion, his Hungarian speech habits—all neutral pronouns—taking over as usual when he was excited, so that his story in Romanian sounded like an invective against the bitch rabbi and her fucking notion of masculine religion. His wife became suspicious—this kind of barely believable excuse was nothing new. They had been married for over thirty years, and their mutual and repeated betrayals predated the marriage. At the time when my father was courting my mother during walks that traced the periphery of Bucharest, he referred to the young Herczog as a very good friend about to marry a whore. Not that my father was a prude by any means. Hadn't he told my grandmother, when she called on him as head of the family to straighten out his younger sister, who'd taken up with a man fifteen years older, "She's eighteen and vaccinated"? But, having been trapped into marriage himself, only to find that his first wife had advanced syphilis before he himself had been infected, my father worried about Herczog's innocence.

Now, on this High Holy Day, Herczog's wife began accusing him of having spent the morning with another woman, religious fraud that he was. While she was yelling, he sank into a sense of wellbeing not unlike what he felt when he took off his dress leather shoes and stretched the gray fabric of the socks with his toes.

So, I hate therapy. I know, that's the third time I've mentioned it. I hold it in contempt because its authority derives from the fee. Take the intelligent people who insist on going. It's like coming back from the hairdresser or the cosmetic makeover—we talk ourselves into liking what's been done to us; otherwise, we've been fools to have spent the money and time. As for the quality of the advice, sure, you pay a hundred dollars for it per session, you feel obligated to do what the man or woman says, even though your Aunt Amelia told you exactly the same thing four years ago at the family picnic, when you burst into tears at something your mother said and your aunt took you to the food table ostensibly to cut the strawberries over the angel-food cake.

Food and talking remind me of a story my father used to tell about his parents. At Easter time, my grandmother would bake dozens of yeast cakes, some covered with poppy seeds like freckles on a golden face, others looking plain but hiding within folds rich with melted butter the plump sultana raisins my grandfather would bring back from his Mediterranean wanderings. For Easter dinner, the family always had roast lamb. My grandfather would take the carving knife, wipe it on a kitchen cloth, and slice himself a large helping of cake, which he would dip in the succulent, herb- and rum-perfumed pan drippings from the roast. This mixing of dessert and main course would make my grandmother see red. "Pagan!" she'd scream at him. My grandfather, who after better than twenty years in the country still spoke Romanian with a pronounced Greek accent, would say, "Moira . . ." I asked my father what that meant; he said it was a term of endearment, but I later read that *Moira* means Fate. Did my grandfather really see his wife Helen as his fate? Her, not the fascist government that would send him fleeing alone to Greece, not the Nazis who would drop the bomb that would kill him in Athens? At Easter, my grandfather would call his stiletto-tongued wife "Moira," and tell her that God doesn't mind what people put in their mouths, only what they let out. At the time my father told me this story, my grandfather's *bon mot* struck me as a riposte to my grandmother, and it made me laugh. Years later I learned to appreciate his unorthodoxy, at least on one count, since in every religion with which I'm acquainted God seems to do little else than police what people put in and take out of their mouths. I am a postwar baby, so my grandfather had been dead for three years before I was born, but my grandmother was still around, the only one of the optimal set of four. She would point to his picture in a small silver frame and say, "Greeks. They always desert their families," the same Homeric sentence she passed on my father's disappearances when they lied to her about his imprisonment and, later, his death.

Ah, my grandmother. One day in my third year, I learned her phone number. When my mother came home from work, she got a call from my grandmother, who was so furious she could barely speak. "Do something about that child," she said. "She's been calling me every ten minutes." My mother found the story very funny, but thinking back I believe I know why my grandmother, whom my uncle, her saintly son-in-law, called "the Hun," couldn't scare me off. I wanted something she wouldn't give me, so I called again and again, expecting to hear at the other end of the line the voice of grandmotherly affection I had a right to, according to all the fairy tales.

She had a green thumb, my grandmother; she willed plants to grow, not for their beauty but for their utility in her kitchen. There was the potted laurel, slim and unobtrusive like a shy Daphne, giving up waxy bay leaves for the roasts, spreading branches tentatively as if conscious of the economy of space, close to the daybed in the dining room of my aunt's house, where my grandmother slept. Each spring on her sill a garden of Adonis would magically appear, the green tight cluster of fragile, succulent, semitransparent shoots of new wheat entrancing me, then soon after, tied with a red string of yarn, it would just as magically disappear. When I asked where the wheat had gone, my grandmother would suck her thin lips over her gums—she refused dentures—and glare at me, saying nothing. Yet she fed me wheat, the wheat boiled with sugared milk and sprinkled with silver candy that they gave out at funerals, a delicacy pleasing to my palate, which had not yet tasted irremediable loss, the bitterness in the lying symbolism of swollen grains, big with their own death and not the germination of life to come.

She would also dole out to me, her only grandchild, one tiny, oval hard candy per visit—as if, had she given me more or even, God forbid, the whole 100-gram little paper bag hidden in a drawer of the vast china cabinet, she would exhaust her limited supply of love in a single stroke. When I was little I thought it hard, and also a little pathetic, that she would not relent. I didn't care about the candy. I was a strange child who liked olives and pickles better than sweets, and being an only child I would be paraded by relatives and friends, though mostly by my mother, before the glass cases of pastry shops where rows of confections stood for my cool inspection like colorful troops in brown and lilac and lemon and pink uniforms, and when asked to choose, I would look for an exasperatingly long time. If I spied my favorites, a chocolate-mousse cylinder glazed in bittersweet crust and named for a triumphant French general or a squat home-ly truffle dusted in cocoa called a potato, I would acquiesce. If not, I turned my back indifferently on all that marvelous art, that gusta-tory pleasure that my adult self hardly ever resists. So how could my grandmother's little milk candy compete? The contents of her pantry, her domain, the seemingly hundreds of jars of perverse industry—fetal walnuts, adolescent green apricots, rose petals, all sunk and changed into gleaming viscous concentrates to be served in a teaspoon on a porcelain saucer accompanied by a glass of cold water to visitors between dinner and evening meal—she never offered me, unless I chanced to be there when other people came.

I regretted this, not for the sake of the preserves among which I had equally exclusive and unshakable preferences: only black cherry and rose-petal preserves, the latter so fine in their texture and so fra-grant that I felt I could achieve, long before I knew the word, synes-thesia as I crushed and tasted against my palate the perfume of the flowers. My grandmother was so attuned to my tastes that when she gave me a jar of rose-petal preserves to take home because, she told me, they had not turned out as well as she expected and I told her they were my favorite, she said, "Too bad I didn't know. The dog almost got sick from eating them since I couldn't serve them to guests." Yet, despite my lack of interest in the contents themselves, I sorrowed about being barred from the pantry, since I was intrigued by the variety of seemingly unnatural things my grandmother would trap in her jars; that forbidden room loomed for me like a laborato-ry with specimens from the deep sea.

IF by now you discerning, post-Freudian reader have begun to per-ceive the thread of food and speech, both given and withheld, that holds together this narrative, forebear just yet from attributing it to childhood trauma in the dysfunctional family. As I was growing up, the scarcity and the exorbitant price of food were a constant in everyone's life, even for those people who had relatively more money than the rest. All the grown-ups carried with them nets and precious paper bags, just in case. We children were put on alert—if you saw a line (actually, in Romania, this meant a murderous crowd) forming, you had to find out what was for sale (meaning without exception what foodstuff had miraculously and briefly, like manna but not as plentifully, descended from the will of whoever in the government was in charge of distribution) and rush home or even to the office of one or both parents, so they could drop whatever they were doing and join the throng for a chance at fresh fish or marmalade.

Imagine, if you will, such an intimate relationship to food. I use the word advisedly—little in the adults' lives commanded such exertions, fatigue, attention, and expense as food. It had to end up in a love affair. Imagine waking up, as my father used to do after he came out of jail, at four o'clock on a November morning—it has to be November, mind you, summer mornings are too easy, and summer's bounty even in those times made for better pickings. In November, all the summer vegetables are gone and if you didn't have the money and foresight to buy your fifty kilos of potatoes for the winter you're out of luck, since at the outdoor market you can find only wrinkled carrots and aborted cabbages. You go to stand in line in front of the butcher shop because the night before a rumor swept the neighborhood that meat might be sold the next day. As a rule, the butcher shops were a pleasure to the eye: empty hooks, gleaming counters, a cutting block of pristine surface, *le dernier cri* in minimalism. But occasionally, as my father hoped while he pulled on his clothes in the dark so as to allow my mother another couple of hours' rest, meat appeared. How much of the designated quantity made it to the shop after the supplier, the transporter, the inspector, a chance policeman, the butcher, and his assistants had had their cuts, literally, was anybody's guess; it provided hours of amusement for the people in line, who as they advanced, if they moved at all, would wonder how soon the meat would run out. The lucky ones who got to make contact with the object of their desire at the counter had to contend with the butcher's extremely limited stock of good will, likely to have been used up on the first three customers or not to have been in store at all. Which meant that, whereas by law the butcher could give you with every purchase 20 percent suet and 30 percent bones not generally from your own cut, he ordinarily made sure that you went home with a kilo of beef that contained perhaps 300 grams (a little over a half pound) of edible meat, for which you had paid a day and a half's wages. How could you not obsess about the little bundle swinging back and forth at the bottom of your otherwise empty net? How could you not see that the people going home with their nets still folded in their pockets, meat having run out long before their turn, would at best shove their way to a seat in the streetcar at the risk of fracturing the other passengers' ribs, at worst take it out, often with fists and heavy shoes, on mates and children who'd dare to register disappointment on their return?

But then the line for meat generated its own satisfactions, at least for people like my father, who used it as an underground source of news. I remember him coming home, empty-handed but exalted, from one of these trips, and announcing to my mother over ersatz coffee that Miron Constantinescu—the Minister of Education—was dead. He told her that when he first heard the news—not to be announced officially for at least a day longer so the proper Marxist construction could be put upon the minister's departure for a much hotter world, or so my father the atheist and many others firmly hoped—he turned so pale with joy that the people around him feared he'd been taken ill. Then they feared that he was sorrowing over the news. When he ejaculated "Hallelujah," people cheered. It was my mother's turn to pale beneath the news. "You never learn, do you?" she said, shaking her head. "That year in jail wasn't enough to teach you to keep your mouth shut." It was true. Only my father's early death prevented him from being condemned again, sooner or later, as an enemy of the people for what he let out of his mouth.

TWO: *Gatekeepers*

It was only when I went to an arts fair with my own child that I understood my mother's violent frustration with my refusals to delight in sweets, those compensations she was offering me for all that she had no control over, such as my father's absence. All my friends fantasized about the pastry shops, sneaking in, being locked in overnight, eating trays after trays of exquisitely decorated gâteaux. And here I am now in the land of plenty, my daughter holding my hand, offering her this or that, cotton candy, hot dogs, a translucent slice of agate, and she adamantly says, *no, thank you.* For me it started with a sincere lack of interest, or perhaps with a precocious specialization in chocolate, this habit of denial. After my mother saw her occupation gone as punishment for having expressed her desire to leave the country, then through our years as emigrants then immigrants, I cultivated denial as a virtue. Why ask for what I could not have, why accept what I was offered when it was gotten by sacrifice? But, with my daughter's hand in mine and her words in my ear, *no, it's too expensive, I don't want it,* I feel a surge of rage I recognize as rising from the maternal well. I want to give it to you, I don't care if it's expensive, I'll barter something else for your pleasure. And I realize that in circumstances incomparably easier than my mother's when I was a child I have raised an inflexibly reasonable successor. How can I undo what I have done and teach her self-indulgence, that lovely vice that keeps the heart going ever so much longer than denial, regardless of bacon and eggs consumed or perhaps only if you do eat them whenever you feel like it?

My grandmother's parsimonious offerings of small hard candy bring to mind another type of sweets and a different setting, this one theatrical in the extreme. Across the street from the huge building where I occupied a two-bedroom apartment with my parents and simultaneously a succession of other people, including the Herczogs, there was a cream-colored villa. An American couple working at the U.S. Embassy two streets over lived in the upper quarters, and several Romanian families lived below. In retrospect I assume that the embassy people had been housed in that particular dwelling because at the end of a long gravel drive starting behind the forged-iron gate was a garage. At the time neither the garage nor the proximity of the Americans seemed strange. Our own apartment house had a huge underground garage, not for the residents, none of whom had cars, but for the storage of vehicles used to transport the high and mighty or to arrest people in the night. The cars were brought in and out by chauffeurs, men who occasionally amused themselves by talking to us kids and from whom I picked up subjects of conversation and turns of phrase that never failed to create a sensation among my family. But private residences with garages were rare.

The yard across the way had many attractions, especially in late summer, when the trees overhanging the brick wall on the right side tempted us with small round plums. We used to squeeze through two widened bars in the fence and climb up on the wall to steal plums. There was no rational need for this. In fall, floods of plums overran Bucharest's markets, the supply for once exceeding the demand so that the prices fell, but somehow the taste of barely ripe, inferior plums from the top of the wall, gotten with risk to life and limb and liberty, was better, more real. The comings and goings of the Americans affected us very little, although we children were as fascinated as the adults with whatever it was they were doing or saying in their hilarious accents. They were so utterly removed from our daily life that even though we accepted their presence matter-of-factly, we would have had the same attitude toward them if they had been visitors from another galaxy.

One day the intergalactians, for some reason that moved their mysterious brains and would not connect with human thought, came out on the wrought-iron balcony, watched us on the gravel below, and, like actors in Shakespearean dramas that we had seen at theater matinees, threw us, the unwashed hordes in the low court, plastic bags full of color. We took them, making exaggerated stage bows, and retreated, screaming with delight and curiosity. In our own courtyard, we opened the bags. Mine smelled atrocious, an artificial scent that had something metallic in it. One of my friends said, "Candy." We looked in disbelief, tentatively brought the garishly colored bits to our tongues, and had to concur—whatever it was, it tasted sweet. But not just sweet. Mixed with it were flavors and colors that reminded us of asphalt and blood, and the texture against our teeth felt, we concluded, just like tar: hard, yielding, sticky, impossible to extricate without pulling the molars along with it. We had never experienced such vile stuff. We ended up not wasting it, though. It made excellent projectiles for our homemade slingshots.

We built our own slingshots from thin copper wire, which we wrapped around a thicker wire frame. We then laboriously knotted at each end pieces of elastic that we managed to pull out of our underwear through a loose seam. As a result of this ingenuity, we were often in danger of having our underpants slide down our hips. My friends were at least immune to embarrassment if not discomfort since they wore pants, while I was required to wear skirts in school and at so many social occasions that it hardly seemed worth it to my mother to have pants made for me. To arm our slingshots, which had delicate frames and even more ethereal elastic bands, we never used stones; we used spitballs, small dried blobs of mud, even, for a brief time, straight pins bent like horseshoes. It only took one grown-up to notice what we had devised before we all had private conferences with our respective parents, during which our slingshots were taken away and promises exacted that we would never dare to shoot pins at people. Over time, we built a more powerful slingshot, but the materials were so scarce that we had only one. This one, however, took stones, and one evening, about three years after the pin episode, we entertained ourselves by trying to shatter the light bulbs of the street lamps on our block. I think we only managed to put out a couple, but our glee was extreme.

When my mother found out what we'd done by piecing together the rumors—the whole block was talking about the vandals—with my expression of perfect satisfaction, she sat me down and asked me if I remembered the young boy my father had talked about when he'd come out of prison. I immediately understood that I'd done something terrible, for in those days my mother avoided mentioning my father. On the advice of pediatricians and friends, she had lied to me about his death, and we both worked hard to sustain her story that he was away at a sanitarium for rheumatic patients, a place called Herculane after the spa dating back to the time of the Romans, who first discovered the curative properties of the hot springs. The year my father was jailed he was for me in Herculane, at least for the purposes of open discussion. I knew he was in jail, just as my cousin knew her father was in jail, and we both pretended to believe our mothers' stories and would fantasize about our fathers returning like *dei ex machina* bringing helicopter loads of toys to make up for their absence.

I've always wondered why my mother would move my father to Herculane those times he disappeared so suddenly and radically from our lives. In the stairwell of my house is a picture of my parents at a restaurant table with wine glasses on it. The time is New Year's, 1948, approximately two weeks before my conception. They were on their honeymoon in Herculane, a beautiful region nestled among the older Carpathians, a town where my father and two of his friends would follow the hot-springs regime for their rheumatic aches and my mother could indulge her love of luxurious hotels and late nineteenth-century architecture. She told me of the carriage rides they took, of the "countesses," as the two old ladies who had seen better times were called, who knocked at their door every late morning with trays of fresh-baked pastries, of the finches that hopped about the window sill to peck at the pastry flakes my father carefully sprinkled out of the damask napkin for them. So while my father's bones rotted in the damp prison cell, while his flesh decomposed beneath the earth, my mother effected his cure and then his resurrection by transporting him to the one place where they had briefly escaped history.

I knew, then, that when my mother uttered the words *Tata* and *prison* in the same sentence, I was in for it. I remembered him talking about the boy, at sixteen so very much older than I, who had been one of six or seven cellmates. My father would tell my mother how he'd tried to keep the child uncorrupted by the men who, though all political prisoners, had few scruples about a boy's innocence. At the time I understood practically nothing of what my father was saying other than that he'd told the boy stories from Greek mythology and taught him math by scratching equations with a pebble on the cement floor. Yes, I remembered, I told my mother. "That boy was in jail for half a year because, like you, he fooled around with a slingshot and knocked off the nose from Stalin's statue in the park," she said. "Do you have any idea what you're doing? You're destroying state property," she added, and I gasped, recognizing the slogan that got people condemned without trial. I nodded. I shed a few tears of repentance. I've never held a slingshot in my hand since that evening. A year or so after my father came out of jail, Stalin was dead and his statue hauled off in the night, leaving an empty pink-marble pedestal at the park entrance.

Amused but also horrified by my seeming penchant for what the state called hooliganism, my mother did ask me how we had cooked up the idea of putting the street in the dark. I was obliged to tell her of a little caper that we had embarked on, my friends and I. Several evenings in a row, just as our games got really animated, something would fall from the sky and pop in our midst. It was a light bulb, and it shattered spectacularly. The effect made such an impression on us that we tried to duplicate the thrill by shooting at the street lamps. In some dim way we figured out, however, that the person throwing the light bulb was doing it not for aesthetic reasons but because he didn't like us, and that flying shards might not be harmless. We drew up a list of suspects, devised an elaborate plan right out of *Emil and the Detectives* for following them, and in time discovered the culprit, who was humiliated enough by being caught that he desisted for a long time. It was our building porter, a hugely overweight man with a drinking problem. He was also an informer for the Security Police.

His entire extended family lived in the building as part of his perks. His wife, a portly and not always unkind woman, sometimes took over his surveillance job when he was indisposed. It was he who taught me the meaning of abjection.

The grown-up tenants called him by his first name, Ion, though they prefaced it with the obligatory "Comrade," while he addressed them by their last name, the "Comrade" in this way reduced to mere façade of equality. But Ion, whom to show respect we children called "Uncle," was not an inferior—he was the building tyrant, before whom all quaked whenever they returned home after ten at night and had to ring the bell to be let in through the heavy front door, like truant children. He would ask them where they'd been, and they all told him, whether the truth or the story they'd rehearsed since getting off the tram two blocks away. No one ever said, "None of your business," although my mother would occasionally get evasive, as if to hint at it. Instead of distributing the mail into mailboxes, Ion would hand certain tenants their mail and say, dangerously, "Another one from Paris in three months. I wonder what they're writing you now," or summarize the contents of postcards for them. My father, who adored absurdity and thus not only suffered gladly but went out of his way to draw out fools and knaves, would dissolve in laughter telling one of his friends that Ion had complained about the friend's illegible writing on a postcard he'd sent my father from vacation.

With us children, Ion was invariably brutal, and we knew that there was no escape from his undisguised hatred—none of our parents was powerful enough to take him on. This knowledge freed us from even the thinnest civilized veneer our parents had imposed upon our instincts—with him, we felt easy about giving way to our wildest impulses and, because he paid us mind, we tormented him as much as we could without getting caught. From April to October he would water the thin strips of earth along the rectangular courtyard, where indestructible perennials put out tiny blue flowers with bright yellow stamens every morning, and the two plots of weeds growing above the level of the courtyard in immense, waist-high cement containers against which people leaned to chat all summer long. Why he watered these tough growths that were clearly surviving better than a large portion of the population I can't figure out to this day. I think he liked to play with the hose, a kind of male extension the way he held it, and certainly a weapon against us children, especially on really brisk spring and fall evenings, when Ion seemed to take special delight in drenching us. Our greatest fun, in turn, was to devise intricate diversions to attract his attention elsewhere; that these plots against him never failed must have had something to do with his blinding hatred of us and the alcohol-sodden cells of his brain. He'd leave his post close to the outdoor faucet, carrying his weapon crotch level, and pursue several of us, while another of us would travel from one back stairs and inner court to another, emerge behind him from a different entrance, and turn off the hose. These diversions went on all summer, with most of us soaked to the skin and shivering on some nights and on others Ion apoplectic about the temporary impotence of his hose.

Before these vicious rituals became firmly entrenched, Ion had loomed large over one aspect of our lives. None of us was allowed to use the elevators alone until we were eight or so years old, and in a building with high ceilings and high steps, seven to eight floors are not easy to climb. For me especially, the interminable stairs and hallways had held a Kafkaesque terror. Once, when I was about four, my mother had taken me down to the courtyard to play with my friend Teddy. He left early, and I bravely started my climb to our floor. Each landing looked exactly the same. I was too short to see the names above the doorbells. I climbed stair after stair till I got to a point where the stairs began to curve. I realized I had overshot my mark—I had never been on a spiral staircase in our building before—and started back down. I went up and down, back to where the stairs no longer looked familiar, then down again where they were recognizable but indistinct from one another, a series of landings parading before me in grotesque uniformity, till I began to sob violently, invoking the magic presence that resolved all crises, "Mama, Mama." My mother heard me—I was very close to my floor after all—and she came out to rescue me from the labyrinth. Then she showed me how to tell one floor from another and particularly how to look for the small embossed plaque with our name. Thereafter the halls became less terrifying, and I managed to make myself heard when I got home by kicking against the door since the doorbell remained out of my reach for some time to come.

After kindergarten or school, we children often hung around the spacious but bare entrance hallway of the building, where Ion stared malignantly from behind his huge desk atop a granite pedestal in a recessed alcove fronting the door, and we took bets about the incoming people. Would they go right, to wing F, and perhaps take with them the three of us who lived on different floors there, or would they turn left and thus be likely to push the number 7 button to my floor in wing E? As soon as they had made their fateful turn, the adults would immediately be accosted by one child or a group, pleading, "Would you please take me to the eighth (or whatever) floor?" Occasionally, the front door would rest undisturbed upon its hinges for what seemed to us an eternity. We would then tentatively approach the great mountain of a man glowering behind his desk and ask him, defeat already in our voices, "Would you take us to our floor?" He always said no and added, "Get lost" or "Get away from here."

I shouldn't say "always" because in my first year of school, when I regularly returned home without my parents and needed adult company to take the elevator, I noticed a change had come over Ion, a change so shocking that I asked my parents to explain it. For several days Ion would see the bunch of us coming home and would rush to greet us, his large belly trembling, and would actually offer to take us up to our respective floors. We were so stunned as to be suspicious, but we went, frightened by the unnatural distortion that a wide smile carved under his thin mustache. When I asked my parents what had made Ion turn nice, they both burst out laughing and exploded the mystery, leaving me with a pattern to watch for, which repeated itself up to our emigration and no doubt beyond. Every year about five or six days before Christmas, Ion would grin, run to open the front door, greet everyone enthusiastically, and generally behave as if possessed by some spirit of kindliness that had gotten firm hold of his body but not his soul. On Christmas morning he would ring the doorbells of more than three hundred apartments to wish everyone a happy season (Christmas was not a proper greeting) and receive his yearly tip, which often consisted of a bottle of liquor.

The liquid consumed over the next couple of days kept him afloat in relatively good humor, although he no longer offered anyone help. Then, as suddenly as the transformation had occurred, it went, leaving us with a sense of order restored and faith in human nature unredeemed. I think a world of reformed sinners would be terribly hard on us all, but especially on children, who depend on a certain consistency of character from their elders.

With the usual egoism of children, we believed that Ion had it in for each of us in particular, although he did not seem to differentiate along class or gender lines. We could see that he treated his own granddaughter altogether more lovingly than he did anyone else, and the little girl was consequently held in abhorrence by us all as the heir apparent. My mother would invite her to my birthday parties, over my protests, with the curt explanation that she had no choice. At the time, my father had been demoted and then disappeared, and she felt especially vulnerable under Ion's eyes. I remember one time when the porter's granddaughter came to visit me while my mother was away, and I, in the spirit of good hosting, offered her a small square of chocolate, the same size as the square I was allowed for dessert to make the 100-gram package last. When I told my mother, she flew into a panic at what Ion might surmise about our finances from our being well-off enough to offer chocolate to guests. Much later, my mother told me that she was torn between a desire to commend my generosity and good manners and the necessity to teach me subterfuge. I can't recall learning much from the episode except the terror of seeing my mother afraid and more hatred for the girl whose visit had triggered it.

The little girl, who was a couple of years younger than the youngest of our gang and whom everyone called Baby, made herself thoroughly obnoxious for several years, until her brother's birth. Suddenly and ruthlessly, she was overthrown. Ion's brutality, inherited by his daughters, who delighted in slaughtering chickens for the building's residents, descended fiercely upon Baby. Utterly dethroned, a girl in a family yearning for a male, she became an abject creature, hanging at the edges of her family and not quite daring to approach us, whom she had helped her grandfather persecute by ratting on every plan that she had overheard. About a year after her brother was born, I occasionally began talking to her on the way home from school, and she hinted at the hardships she endured as the displaced princess. People take *Cinderella* to be a fairy tale, but Baby had the truth of childhood slavery stamped on her prematurely depressed features. She could never play—she had to watch her brother. All gifts and attentions from the tenants now shifted to the little prince since they soon saw the change in Ion's family dynamics. Her clothes grew more ragged and she herself more pale as time passed.

And we, although suspicious at first about the change in Baby, soon bonded to her through our common loathing of the boy, whose unpleasant little face I have before me but whose name through some trick of aggressive repression I cannot recall. To this day I wonder what became of him, whether he gained the ascendance his grandfather's spying had prepared for him, whether he fell when Ceauşescu fell or managed to hang on as had the World War II fascists when the Communists took over, and as did the Communists when the supposed freedom fighters brought down the Communist regime in 1989. Somehow, if he's survived, I don't think he'll become a candidate for the Nobel Peace Prize. For me, a moment when his life intersected with mine captures the creation of an arrogance devoid of moral qualms. Children are not born napoleonic, yet by the age of three he had already developed the napoleonic gait, pacing his domain, the courtyard, where he was immune from fault or guilt. We of course rebelled in the few ways we could. In winter he wore a woolen pointed cap with a tassel on a string swinging behind. The tassel was an irresistible temptation on anyone, as I, who for a while wore a similar hat to school, knew too well. On his head, it became a magnet for our derring-do missions—how to sneak up behind the little tyrant and pull off his cap. His outrage at the *lese-majesté* only prompted us to try again. His grandmother patrolling behind him only spurred us on to greater ingenuity and daring. As long as he wore that hat, we could challenge his sovereignty.

Then, one day, his grandmother cornered us and herded us together in the courtyard, forcing us against the cement wall of one of the grass containers, now desolate brown in the frosty air. With her grandchild beside her, she lectured us at nauseating length about our cruelty and evil nature, about how none of us would come to any good, about how we were all doomed partly because, she hinted, of our accursed race (most of us were Jewish) and partly because of our accursed class—we were almost all children of intellectuals. "The future is his," she ended her peroration, pointing to the little prince, who had a finger up his nose at the moment. My friend Benny burst out in a short laugh. The child glared at him and announced the guilty verdict, "Benny laughed." In a second we were all laughing, our relief let out in sharp bursts of hilarity that sounded almost like sobs in the echoing courtyard. We doubled over with laughter. We kept it up till tears rolled down our cheeks. Maria, the porter's wife, spat at our feet and left, taking her grandson with her, leaving the field to us.

But what price victory? Where are the friends who that day shared with me the knowledge that laughter, oh so momentarily, deflates tyranny? Scattered on at least three continents, of the six of us only two really keep in touch, so to speak, touch reduced to invisible fingerprints on yearly cards or to voices distorted by travel over hundreds of miles of wires, to remind each other that we did have a childhood, that there was a place such as I describe, that it's not all a trick of creative memory, but also that there is no longer such a place, just as there are no longer people like us there; that, ultimately, Maria was right—our future in that place was doomed, and our future elsewhere could only be bartered for at the cost of our past.

THREE: *Out of the Mouth*

I was always told too much when I was still too young to bear the weight of implacable reality, but what choice was there, really? One spring afternoon my friend Teddy started to brag about his parents' new radio.

"Is it new or newly bought?" I asked.

"New," he exclaimed.

"Oh," I said, disappointed.

"What?" he wanted to know, acute and inquisitive as only children can afford to be in matters of self-interest.

"New is not as good as old," I informed him. "Made before the war, I mean," I added, though we couldn't have been more than six and the war, which had ended three years before either of us was born, was strictly a rhetorical marker for us, an arbitrary barrier between before and after, like noon or the Greenwich time we occasionally heard about on BBC shortwave emissions.

This conversation took place in the courtyard of the apartment building, within my parents' hearing. Horrified, my mother took me aside and admonished me never, but never, to repeat what I had heard at home. Her warning veered into that abyss of fear that not infrequently seized me: "If you don't want your parents to be taken away." Could she have used a less terrifying means of convincing me to be careful? Keeping a child politically innocent, as in my friend Cornel's case, meant sitting on a time bomb. He and his father were in a streetcar one evening when the child announced, seconds before they were to get off, "Ladies and gentlemen, Radio London wishes you good night." His father almost dislocated the precocious son's arm as he whisked him off the streetcar and ran with him aimlessly into the night, hoping no one had followed them. Listening to shortwave radio from the West was punishable by a long prison term.

Another time my father and I found ourselves on a side street connecting two main avenues, large, beautifully laid-out roadways flooded with sunshine. The massive late nineteenth-century build-ings on the side street provided a dense shade that made even the air we breathed feel cool and refreshing. My father shuddered. "Are you cold?" I asked, although it was the middle of summer and my father, out of lifelong habit, was wearing a long-sleeved shirt; he had been born without a right forearm.

"Whenever I'm on this street I feel as if I were walking on souls in agony," he said dreamily, almost lost in a private vision. At home he told my mother that we'd taken such-and-such a street as a short-cut from the park. She said, "Ah."

"What's wrong with the street?" I burst out. My mother was silent. My father said, "You're old enough to know. The security police have prisoners down there, in their tunnels. Some they tor-ture." Since my father died before my ninth birthday, how old must I have been at the time? Was I old enough to know that underneath the streets of Bucharest lay a hell more accessible to the reasoning mind than the one with which my Anabaptist sitter, one in a series of young women who took pleasure in abusing me in some way or another, had blighted my early childhood? She had done it for the highest of motives—she wanted to save the soul of the little pagan girl whose parents were leading her to perdition. She had told me there were two roads, the right and the wrong, and those who took the wrong way would forever be burned in pits filled with tar. In my short life I had seen pitch and tar, had smelled the stench and felt the heat rising from the containers on huge wheels pushed about by roadwork crews. That seemed bad enough, but through a linguistic association that dates back at least to Latin the right and wrong became for me the right and left roads. Since I was about four and still unable to tell right from left with great certainty, I lived in fear that I would plunge into hell every time I turned the corner of a street whose ethical significance I could no more discern than I could tell my left from my right. The Anabaptist's high moral lesson became in my confused mind a cruelty showing the irrational and random nature of God. That's why I surprised my mother with the glee I exhibited when I told her I'd discovered a swelling at the base of one of my teeth. I felt I had been granted a period of reprieve when the abscessed baby molar had to be pulled by the dentist, and I acquired a hole on the left side of my mouth into which I would stick my tongue in order to determine my next moral choice: right or left. By the time I grew my permanent teeth I had learned my right from my left, and perhaps it's to this early fright about the consequences of getting lost that I owe my almost unfailing sense of direction.

That lower hell at which my father hinted didn't have the fanciful and heart-arresting devils that had begun to stare at me every night through the crisscross patterns of our bathroom window since the Anabaptist took charge of my soul. It was a mundane place, underneath streets I knew by name, populated by people I knew, torturers and victims. "Security colonel," I'd hear neighbors whisper behind another neighbor's suited back. "Security informant among us—watch what you say," they'd whisper as you entered a crowded room at a friend's apartment. As for the souls in agony, hadn't I seen one come to our apartment during my father's disappearance, thin as a wraith and as secretive, sliding in and out of the front door, careful not to be seen, slithering along the hallway to the kitchen from which my mother then utterly banished me? I heard them talk in tones that remained indistinguishable despite all my efforts to eavesdrop and heard him swallow the food my mother put before him.

"Who is he?" I would nag my mother. "Is he good?" I would ask, confused by his furtive and ghostlike air. My mother would sigh. "He's part good, part bad, like most people, but he's very brave and is being very good to us." After my father returned, wraithlike himself, I learned that the man had been my father's cell companion and had taken an enormous risk in smuggling out a note my father had written my mother on a piece of cigarette paper. What could he have written? I wonder to this day. (Of course the precious tiny square was burned as soon as read.) *I'm alive? I hope you're well? I love you?* I never found out, although I did hear my parents speak of the messenger as a former Iron Guard and renowned anti-Semite. Yet he knew my mother was Jewish and came nevertheless, not once but many times, to tell my mother stories from hell, to present himself as evidence that some hells do let their victims out. "People are so contradictory," my mother would say, then illustrate with a story from Auschwitz, which would once more confirm for me not so much the contradictory nature of people as the arbitrariness of a world in which right and left led to such different fates.

When did I begin hearing stories about Auschwitz? It was certainly after an incident that I place sometime in my fifth year. Whereas the adult world was fraught with thousands of unsuspected dangers, we children lived like privileged savages, able to roam the neighborhood on our own at an early age and the whole city from the time we were eight or nine. It was summer, a sultry evening, and my mother in one of her few moments of leisure had scooped out the sweet insides of two small, round watermelons for our dessert and was now carving intricate, lacelike patterns in their shells with the curved end of one of my pen nibs. Soon, both watermelon hulls looked like Chinese lanterns, and my mother found two candle ends to stick inside and illuminate them. I knew my mother could make magic—she could bring a cardboard ballerina to life and make her dance—and here was another instance. We turned the lights off in the kitchen and let the tiny patterns of circular dots shed droplets of golden rain all over, miraculous and sensuous like Zeus's coming to Danae. She told me I could see if any of my friends were about and go down into the courtyard to display my magical jack-o'-lanterns.

I shot out the door carrying the two magic globes, one under each arm like volleyballs, and went downstairs, glowing nearly as much as the candles. I found my friend Benny, who was only too happy to relieve me of one of the melons. We began holding them aloft and swinging them, perilously for the candle flames, making light patterns dance against the pebble-cement of the court and the granite of the walls so that all the mineral chips trapped inside paving and building blocks answered our lanterns and the whole yard

became a whirl of lights calling to one another. Several adults passing by remarked on the beauty of our light show; then, suddenly,
from the shadows, Costa, a teenaged boy, loomed huge over us,
snatched the lanterns from our hands, and smashed them over our
heads till they were reduced to mushy garbage. Benny and I howled
from pain, humiliation, and rage.

After we'd spent our tears and before we sought retribution by
calling on our parents to talk to the boy, we sat down on the step
leading to the building entrance and tried to figure out why such a
thing would happen. I was at a loss. Benny, however, surmised that
Costa had attacked us because he was Christian and we were Jews.
"What does that mean?" I asked, genuinely bewildered. I had never
heard the words before, or if I had, I hadn't registered them. This is
not as odd as it may seem in a state that shortly after my birth became
militantly secular, at least in its rhetoric and declared policies.

"Christians hate Jews," he told me.

"Why?" I asked.

"I don't know, but that's how it's always been."

So here I was, at five, faced with an immutable natural order of
things that put me in the category of the hated. Later on that night,
after Costa had been duly chastised by our parents, I asked my father
what Jews were. He looked at me in surprise and then said, "Ask
your mother," which in turn alarmed me, for there had never been
a question that he either couldn't answer or to which he wouldn't
reply, "I'm not sure. Let's take out the encyclopedia and see." But I
suppose he decided to delegate the task of my maternal heritage to
my mother, to let her tell me as much or as little as she wanted. The
strange thing is that I don't remember her explanation, except for
her confirming my Jewishness, so I knew Benny to have been right
about that anyway. But I think I began to hear the Auschwitz stories
shortly thereafter.

In vain I try to reconstruct what I thought and felt when I first
heard the concentration-camp stories. The context was sometimes
so pleasant that I listened to them as to adventure tales, with a sense
of excitement as the plot rose and with sorrow or relief at the
denouement, but I believe on the whole with emotions not unlike
those elicited by my reading of *The Three Musketeers* or *The Count of*

Monte Cristo. Sometimes there would be passages whose meaning I simply could not grasp, but then there were such descriptions in *Huckleberry Finn*, especially toward the end, about Jim, and I assumed I would either grow into understanding or have to accept the unfathomable gaps between past and present or between transatlantic ways.

The marathon storytelling sessions generally took place at the house of my mother's friend from before the war, a woman who had been deported from Transylvania along with my mother and who spent most of that year, 1944 to 1945, at Auschwitz and at two of the three labor camps to which they were marched at various times, as part of the general German retreat before the Russian army and as much-needed slaves in hazardous war industries. Her home in Bucharest was an anomaly—a single house with a little garden. Her silver-haired husband and I would play a board game while Ritzi and my mother would pour forth reminiscences, adding to and amplifying each other's stories, digressing, going over the same ground again and again, occasionally bursting out in laughter, very rarely weeping briefly over a name one mentioned, a name alone, flashing out of nowhere like an asteroid, crashing into their joint memory. I liked going to Ritzi's. They didn't have children and they spoiled me with delicacies and little presents, but mostly with a triumphant kindliness: "Look how well she's turning out," as if I were a point they were scoring in an argument with something or someone invisible. And then I got to hear the stories, these outlandish events that held for me no greater tangibility than trolls devouring passersby beneath old bridges. How much did I absorb without knowing it? Three times in my life I did my best to learn German, only to have the hard-won knowledge pass through my brain as if through the proverbial sieve. On German soil my foremost instinct is to depart. But do these reactions come from later processing, from the cumulative effect of story after story, from photographic evidence that gives gray grainy texture to my mother's words?

So often in my adulthood my mother feared that I was about to forget or neglect what she'd told me. At a gathering at my house she'd wrestle for control of the after-dinner talk and launch into monologues of the year of her metaphoric death. Like the Ancient

Mariner, she'd mesmerize the guests and leave them sadder if not wiser. I was torn by so many conflicting feelings that I fell mute or clumsily tried to change the course of the indomitable flow of my mother's reminiscences. What could they mean, I'd wonder, for people comfortably seated and well fed, some of whom would retort with their own deprivations, paltry tales of missed rations during the war? What did they mean to me anymore other than an interruption in social ease? How wearying the acrobatics between allegiance to my mother's history, in so many ways beyond access even to me, and my yearning for the lotus of normality.

When I tried to argue with my mother that everyone's tragedy is deeply tragic to the individual, she'd say, "Well, maybe the loss of a child. But no, not really, what about the loss of all the children? Can you picture a neighborhood where every child under thirteen dies a violent death? Every *one*, no exceptions." And I'd have to concede, always, the limits of my imagination. I remember the happier stories she used to tell me of her youth, her first job away from home, after which I learned to stop asking, "Whatever became of your roommate? Of your star student? Of your fiancé? Of the little boy you babysat for?" because the answer almost inevitably was, "She didn't come back. She made a run for it and they shot her. They took him first. The little ones were taken right away."

Because of Romania's "friendship with the great Union of Socialist Republics to the East," as the slogan went, my mother and her friend Ritzi could give full vent to their war stories. Here was a piece of history that, like any other episode of group victimization—especially religious or racial—became under Communist ideology emblematic of capitalist and church corruption. My mother stopped writing feature stories about her experiences the moment she caught on that what she wrote was used in the campaign, as she put it, "to bad-mouth the past." "If you make it look bleak enough," she'd say, laughing, "by comparison they think they'll look better."

Even we children learned to read the marginal and the absent and to pay scant attention to the center. A tiny news story, buried on the back page, about the redecoration of the Romanian Academy's foyer was immediately decoded as news that someone must have defaced one of the posters of the Great Fathers, Marx, Engels,

Lenin, and Stalin, that hovered over every entrance like household gods. A day without newspapers meant a lapse, intentional or not, in spelling that might have mocked the regime, and we knew the silence of print shouted of arrests and cruel prison terms. Radio speakers whose diction slipped on certain proper nouns would never again be heard. Large portions of history, like Yugoslavia on the map of Europe, remained a blank. Roman history consisted mostly of Dacian resistance and Spartacus's rebellion, although the movie with Kirk Douglas was not allowed into the country because it had been made in the United States and might dilute the image of anti-democratic, imperialist America. Which meant, of course, that we watched all the more intently for slippages, for gaps, for everything that the regime dismissed, and that we were all in stupefied love with the West.

With my training in skewed reading, the textual attentions of deconstructive theorists strike me as almost touching in their pride of primacy—no one ever read like this before, no one dismantled ideology's palpable design. I suspect the same sad amusement might have seized the first wave of Jewish academicians confronted with the discoveries of New Criticism, its scrutiny of syntax, nuance, ambiguity, in the context of six millennia of Talmudic textual inter-pretation. But then being there first remains a matter of being seen and heard when you get there, and I for one would rejoice in a life less shaded in historic ironies.

FOUR: *The Vocabulary of Faith*

Yet for all the stories told me, many of which I stored away as if in shepherd's purses neatly tied up and stacked at the back of my mind, waiting to be opened or carried away in flight, my childhood was full of silences. There were subjects about which my mother would not speak unless forced by circumstances. Why did I have to wait for Benny to tell me that I was Jewish? How did he, only a year older than I, know not only his origins but mine? Even later, my mother would elide anything to do with Jewish tradition, although she was delighted one afternoon when I asked her whether I could go to the synagogue with my friend Simon. It was Simhat Torah, of which I knew nothing.

When Simon saw me look longingly at the little hand-sized flag inscribed with scriptural verse in the living room of his parents' apartment that also served as bedroom for his grandmother, he thought I was pretending not to understand what it meant, as part of the general effort of all Jews not to disclose their identities in a hostile culture. I went home to ask my mother permission to go with him, feeling depressed in advance about her forbidding me. She was reluctant to let me attend any observance smacking even remotely of religion. The couple of times I went to Easter midnight mass with my father, I remember my mother's restlessness, her starting to speak and stopping herself, visibly torn. But for her tenseness, those times would have been untroubled and happy for me: my father's splendid tenor rising over everyone else's voice in the church, making people turn and look admiringly at him; the orange wax candles, coiled like snails to slow down their burning, that people lit and carried into the night like fireflies.

Later, my memory gradually layered the stories I heard of cities like prewar Bucharest and Iaşi with rare literary examples, like Caragiale's famous story "The Easter Candle," into an intelligible stratum that disclosed the uses of midnight mass as incitement for believers to make forays into the Jewish quarters and maim and kill so as to avenge Christ's death. And only as an adult did I begin to fathom my mother's fear that I would somehow be sucked into that whirlpool, that somehow my father and I would betray her through our common Christianity. No doubt her fears rose from a rather daffy idea of my father's that since anti-Semitism was becoming more and more overt I should be baptized, as if a baptismal certificate, even at the age of 6, would erase my maternal ties. My aunt his sister, who by some quirk of her parents' highly unusual marriage arrangement was Catholic while my father was Greek Orthodox, took up the thought of my baptism with copious enthusiasm. For her, it was not a formality but a confirmation of my being my father's child as opposed to a little Jewess. As her plans for the festivities got more grandiose, my mother's theophobia increased, and one day she ordered me to go outside and play. When I returned, nothing seemed to have changed between her and my father, but I found out soon enough that my baptism was not to be. "Besides," my pagan father would remind whomever he had occasion to, "at my baptism I wailed in protest, but no one paid attention."

So, to my astonishment, my mother seemed thrilled that I wanted to go to Simhat Torah. For that reason alone, the event would have stayed with me. Little did I know that my first visit to the synagogue would be as dramatic as it turned out. On this holiday centered on children, the young celebrants march around in a circle carrying a little flag with an apple on top. The apple in turn has a lit candle on it, or at least that was what we carried around on that October evening. I was taller than many children my age, and since Simon and I were at the upper range in age as well, we rather towered over the little ones. The girl behind me held her flag aloft and set my hair on fire. Suddenly, I saw a rush of women coming toward me screaming. In a second the sparks were out, but I can't recall to this day what was more frightening: realizing that my hair had caught fire or finding myself smothered by a crowd of alarmed Jewish mothers.

In later years, my mother would recall with bitterness that at an early age I had been schooled by my paternal relatives to tell my Jewish great-aunt that religion is determined by the father, not the mother. Since I recalled neither words nor context for such assertions, I asked my mother if she was sure I had said such things. "Why would Aunt Emma lie?" she'd reply, silencing me with my own bitter remembrances of the many times in my childhood when adults used me strictly as a field of combat in their own wars about religion or class or personal enmity, when they either attributed to me sentiments they did not dare express directly or used some story about my misbehaving as a pre-emptive strike against any possible report of mine after I'd seen them in compromising circumstances. Bucharest was, like all great cities, only a small town in some ways.

After my father's death, my mother hired a woman about her own age to clean house once every two weeks. Most of the household help she'd had, either for child care or cleaning, were very young women who came and went rapidly, either because my mother discovered that they abused me or because the brighter and more ambitious ones, whom my mother liked best, found greater opportunities elsewhere. Victoria was a married woman, settled in her own apartment, a long-time resident of Bucharest, and for the first time in my life I saw my mother sitting down with the cleaning woman at the end of their respective work days to share a cup of coffee and talk. One day, when Victoria left before I returned from play, I came home to find my mother in a rage that to my young self seemed as unappeasable as natural disasters. Nothing she shouted at me helped clarify what I had done. She reproached me for having left to play before she got home, but I did that practically every afternoon. At some point in the maelstrom of her fury and my intense misery, it came out that Victoria told her she had asked me to wait for my mother to come home from work before going to play, and that I had replied, "Let her go to hell." The phrase itself, especially in relation to my mother, was so utterly removed from my mental universe that I stared at her dumbstruck, a picture of unmasked guilt. "Why would she lie?" my mother would ask over and over as I shrugged, saying in helpless abjection, "I dunno." And I didn't at the time. How could I? Only much later, when these occurrences had shaped themselves in a predictable pattern, did I begin to fathom why Victoria, who seemed to bear me no malice, would plunge me into the desert of my mother's displeasure. It's painful to realize that one is not the center of anyone else's existence, that for Victoria I was only the most effective weapon in wounding my mother, whose crime was to be so unwittingly unlike her.

I remember other times when in my walks with friends I would come upon women I knew as my mother's colleagues or as neighbors on park benches with men I didn't know, and would come home to face my mother's rage about stories they had phoned her with, regarding my unseemly behavior with boys in public parks. I would defend myself in the same idiotic way and only convince my mother that I compounded my sins with lies. Twenty years or so after the fact, I managed to surmount my embarrassment and tell my mother what, as I pieced it together later on, had really happened. By then it was too late. My mother had formed the habit of relying on my integrity and of course believed me—why would I lie, at this late date?—but she sank under horrible feelings of guilt, of having failed me when I was a child, so I relearned to keep my own counsel. She had trusted me implicitly for so many years; why did I need this latter-day vindication at the price of her peace of mind?

From the beginning of my adolescence onward, my mother would reproach me for my silences. "You never confide in me," she'd say. In a way it was true. I had learned to protect her from her own omissions, from violences I endured about which she could do nothing but despair. But on the other hand, what was there to tell? In my thirties I would call long-distance from as far away as Europe and pronounce a cheery hello into the phone, and my mother would instantly ask, "What's wrong? What happened?" honing in at nearly the speed of light on the fact that something indeed was wrong, something that I would nevertheless hide from her because she could do nothing to remedy it, although she always knew about it. And now, thinking back, I wonder—was I punishing her for her silences? Understandably, given the dangers of the time and my age, she did not tell me my father was arrested. She said he'd been taken ill with rheumatism and gone to the spa at Herculane. I remember how I stopped asking about him when the answers seemed so vague and troubled. Four years later, when he died while I was away, my mother told me the same story to explain his absence, but this time I didn't ask for details, for explanations why he never wrote. I knew what had happened, and the complicity of silence I entered into with the adults around me left me free to fantasize about my father's eternal return. In fact, everything surrounding his death seemed so shrouded in mystery that when the news spread that my mother and I were to leave for America, many children and not a few grown-ups in the neighborhood were convinced we were going to meet my father, who had somehow escaped over the border five years earlier. And I triumphantly fed those rumors, nodding my head discreetly whenever anyone asked me whether we had news of my father from the United States.

Both my parents taught me my way around language, and each did so in order to spare the other in a tenderness of anticipated and deflected hurt that to this day makes me honor their love. One time, after one of my prolonged conversations with the men who tended the rulers' cars parked in the underground garage of our building, I came home and began playing with my bear and my doll. I was under the dining-room table, and, as usual, I spoke in voices for my characters. My mother was above me, deep in proofreading her film titles. She would often hear nothing at these times, so I was startled when she interrupted me with, "What was the last word you used?" I was very proud of my expanding vocabulary under the tutelage of my newfound friends, the chauffeurs downstairs. I explained to her that the doll was "my little roll-in-the-hay" and the bear "the gimp." "What do those words mean?" my mother asked socratically. "They're friends, and they like each other," I replied unhesitatingly. My mother put her pen down and took off her glasses. She took me on her lap and instructed me not to use those terms, especially *gimp*, especially in my father's presence. I needed to know why, and she told me they were not nice words, and they didn't mean love. Why not in front of Daddy, I needed to know. " 'Gimp,' " my mother said, "is something cruel people call people who don't have a limb."

Why would they say things like that? I asked, but what I wanted to know was why the men who knew whose child I was would teach me a word like that. "Because people are cruel and stupid," my mother said, and gently disengaged me from her lap.

I thought of my father and his missing right arm, which had never seemed a liability to me before, but rather something that made him the immensely interesting person he was. After he'd been in jail, he could occupy no government post, which meant no post since the government was sole employer. It was the happiest time of my childhood. He stayed home to take care of me; even later, when he began to make good money tutoring privately and illegally, he took me along to lessons. I reveled in his new role. On my first day of elementary school, when the teacher, unmindful of anyone's right to privacy, asked us to declare our parents' occupations, I announced that my father was a housekeeper. The hateful mornings when my sitter would tie me up because I would not get dressed fast enough, the one month spent in a government day-care center that loomed like years in my childhood memory, all faded in my father's presence, which I look upon as recompense, though paltry, for my then losing him so soon again. What would I have remembered of him if he had not come back or if he had resumed insane hours of work?

My mother later told me that I had seen little of him since I'd been a baby, when he used to snatch me from the cradle and hide with me in an armchair behind the door, where he'd talk and sing to me. He became caught up in the economic reforms the country was undergoing; he sat on the Economic Council; he worked so late try-ing to fight the five-year plan that was being pushed by the Soviets' lackeys that he ended up being brought home on a stretcher one night. My mother, who had become skeptical about the regime long before my father, was exasperated by what she saw as his excesses for a lost cause. But my father kept insisting that this was the dawn of a new age in which reason and good will would prevail.

What made my mother see the light so much sooner? She'd tell me that when she came back from concentration camp, she joined the demonstrations on Boulevard Brăteanu. "A sea of people stretched for miles, and I, despite my horror of crowds, marched with them. When they started singing 'The International,' I walked with tears streaming down my cheeks, so moved I was at the thought of a world without prejudice and exploitation. But then," she said, "they started making me sell papers for them. They were rags too, just slogans and stupid distortions. Being a journalist myself, I was embarrassed. I'd buy the whole lot and go home. The last straw was when they started coming to my room to pick me up for meetings at eight o'clock on Sunday mornings. Can you believe it?" She'd explode with indignation some thirty years after the fact. "That's the respect they had for working people, disturbing their only day of rest. I was working like a dog at the time, having come back with nothing, not even a change of clothes, and I didn't have the time to rinse out my underwear, let alone take a walk or go to see a play. And they'd want to drag me to their dumb meetings where all they did was listen to themselves talk. Your father, now, he could cope. He took along a little notebook and he'd write down all the malapropisms and stupidities people uttered, and he'd keep himself amused."

But my mother, like Emma Goldman, wanted a joyful revolution. She'd have no truck with a system too dour to let people dance. After the Communists, with my parents' assistance, stuffed the ballot boxes and won the election in 1948, my father, who'd gotten quite a reputation as a labor negotiator, was quickly enlisted as Marxist economic consultant. Soon, however, Marxism "evolved" into Leninism, then Stalinism. The Communists dubbed "genuine" (because they had been Communist in the long period before and during the war when the party was outlawed and they suffered constant searches and arrests and tortures) began to be edged out, rather gently at first, then more and more brutally, till within a few years the entire leadership contained not one of the founding members of the party. They were all in jail or exiled or in the grave, shot by military squads after secret trials. No one inquired about their absence, although they remained vividly imprinted on the national consciousness.

I remember one time when my mother returned from a theater matinee with a group of friends, all of them in a high degree of excitement. "She was there." "Did you see her?" "She's so aged you can hardly recognize her." "You think she gave in?" "She's a broken woman, anyhow." SHE was Ana Pauker, one of the leaders of the CP in its outlawed days, a legend of courage and daring. She had been under house arrest for some five years before her extraordinary, one-time public appearance. Did they let her out so rumors of her having been done away with would stop? Who could fathom the motives of the new brand of leaders, many of whom (as it turned out when Bucharest, shaken by one of its periodic earthquakes, opened up the ground under a razed apartment building and revealed a safe containing records of the Nazi Iron Guard) were the same leaders who had persecuted the genuine Communists all along, in a reassuring continuum of actions against true revolutionaries?

Sponsored by one of the leading "genuine" Communists, my father was about to be appointed ambassador to Greece when one of the frequent minor coups took place. His mentor, Pătrășcanu, who would be "rehabilitated" thirty years after his execution, had had my father's dossier on his desk at the time of his arrest; my father's fate in the still-forming government was sealed. Whether the new leaders planted spies in his university classes or whether a zealous student reported him on his own initiative is hard to know. In any case, several weeks after Pătrășcanu's disappearance my father was arrested for having spread antistate propaganda—i.e., for having told two jokes in his classes, one about the chronic problems with food distribution in the country and one about the state of Soviet technology. Jail didn't cure him of his love of jokes. Unrepentantly Marxist, whenever confronted with news of abysmal corruption and evil-doing in the regime he'd worked so hard to bring to power, he'd shout gleefully, "The material base," and add, "Ah, Papa Marx, what a genius."

Miraculously, I was spared the trauma of men pounding on the door in the middle of the night and whisking my father away with warnings that no one should breathe a word about it. I was staying overnight with one of my mother's friends. My mother, in her recurrent musings about human nature, said, "You know, not everyone is the same, even when they perform unconscionable acts: one of the men was a real pig, tore through the wardrobe and made nasty remarks about high living. He enjoyed what he was doing. The other looked through the desk drawers and picked up what could have been a very incriminating postcard from one of your father's friends. He saw me watch him, and he took it and shoved it under the lining of the drawer. That postcard could have added two more years to your father's sentence, and he surely would have died before being freed."

But I still remember practically nothing of my father before his disappearance, perhaps because of the trauma of his return. I know I missed him; I also recall his return as if it happened yesterday. I was pedaling my tricycle madly around and around the sparsely furnished room now occupied by the first person in a series who shared our two-bedroom apartment. He was the son of a friend of my mother's who had died at Auschwitz, and my mother was happy to have him take over what the government had decreed was the inexcusable luxury of too much living space for a single family. Eric was a mixed-up young man who would forget to turn off faucets and pressing irons and thus caused innumerable household disasters during his short stay with us. But he gave me permission to ride my tricycle in his room while he was away. I thought of him as a child in grown-up disguise, which wasn't far from true; one time my mother came home with a tree ornament advertised as unbreakable, a shapely silver glass swan, and showed it to Eric, who promptly tested it by banging it against the door frame and shattering it to pieces. "It's not unbreakable," he calmly declared.

Now, still dazed by the speed and gyres of my ride, I found myself in my mother's arms. "Daddy's come home," she said. I'd had no intimations of his coming. I suppose my mother thought it best not to prepare me, should the government reverse itself on the sentence of a year and time served. "He's lost a lot of weight," she said. "Please don't mention it when you see him." I thought my mother for once was being silly; in the rush of joy at the news, why on earth would I care about my father's weight? I ran into my parents' bedroom, where first my view was blocked by a number of people standing around the bed; then I saw my father lying in bed in the middle of the day, his hand stretched toward the nightstand, on which there was a glass of lemonade. The afternoon light shot right through his hand like x-rays, revealing only bones, so thin had he grown. I, pierced to the heart by a premonition, rushed to him and tried to give him the glass that I thought he couldn't possibly have the strength to lift, saying, of course, "Oh, Daddy, you're so skin-ny." He refused my help, gently, and smiled his sideways smile. "You think I got as clumsy as someone we know?" he said, and held my head against his breast. He was so unchanged in spirit, or so I thought, and recovered so quickly, so everyone believed, that for the next three years I was allowed to draw a curtain over that vision of his skeletal hand.

For those three years between his release and his death, we were together most of the time. And all that time, he never asked for my help. I would watch, deeply fascinated, as he tied his leather strop to the back of a chair and stuck the other end in the desk drawer, then deftly and dangerously moved the razor across the red, green, black colors of the strop in a pattern whose significance I could not guess. When the razor was sharp enough, he'd let me watch him shave. Invariably, the steam in the bathroom would defeat his austere hair discipline, and a curl would drop over his forehead. Then, before he rinsed out his brush, he'd touch the tip of my nose with it, and I'd lift myself on tiptoe to look in the mirror and admire my clown dis-guise. For snacks, he'd take out a freshly bought loaf of bread and hold it down with his upper right arm while he sliced it with his left hand. On streetcars, where he needed to hold on, he'd taught me to grab his empty sleeve so as not to be thrown around by the jerky movements. He sharpened pencils for me with razor blades. The time I slipped trying to get a drink at the fountain in the Botanical Gardens and fell on a pile of cactus prunings, he used tweezers to remove thorn after thorn from my mangled knees. A Danube-taught swimmer, he used the sidestroke to cross the large lake at the edge of Bucharest and often raced and defeated challengers. One time, when my mother, instead of furtively beckoning someone aside, naively announced in front of a movie theater showing Olivier's *Hamlet* that she had extra tickets and was beset by a mob, my father plunged into the crowd and flipped over a man who'd threatened to beat my mother. His absent arm was truly absent from my percep-tion of him, his right stump another adorable feature, somewhat like the black curl dangling over his forehead wrinkled in annoyance, that made him unlike anyone else.

My father believed that practically nothing should be hidden from me except his nakedness. He would begin reading books to me, then leave them open, knowing that each plot was a baited hook I'd take sooner or later, and so I did, finding myself rushed through then left struggling for breath, dazed and often slightly wounded by the passage through that other, subterrestrial realm. Thus began my compulsive relation to fiction. I'm afraid of novels in a way I'm never afraid of a box of good chocolates. I can pace my eating so that the chocolates last, but with a novel I begin my little two-step of deferred desire, circling, circling around the bait, until inevitably I bite and I'm in for the haul. Often, during vacations, my husband would find me still on the couch at four in the morning, face tear-stained, the book closed beside me. He would ask, horrified, "What's wrong?" but now he knows—"You finished it." "Yes, and it was so sad," I say, because it so often is.

It was a book of Greek mythology that provoked my first literary discussion with my father. I was seven. In another year I would flunk a math exam because I'd been reading *The Odyssey* under my school desk during class. In the book I came upon the story of Hephaistos, his marriage to Aphrodite, her affair with Ares, and the indestructible, almost invisible net Hephaistos forged in the depths of his crater, the smoldering heart of the volcano. The net fell on the lovers, catching them *in flagrante delicto*, exposing them naked to the mockery of the other gods. "That was a terrible thing to do," I ventured to my father, who said, "He thought what they had done to him was a terrible thing."

"But," I insisted, "wasn't it cruel? And it couldn't have made him feel any better to have everyone see his wife naked."

"To tell you the truth," my father admitted, "it never bothered me before." Later that evening, I overheard my father telling my mother, "She's an attentive reader," which pleased me immensely, until I heard my mother say, "I told you she was too young for these stories. They disturb her. I wish you wouldn't." They were right and wrong, both of them, of course.

Only now, as I record my first unease about men's punishments of women (and in my awakening I cared far more about Aphrodite than Ares being tangled in that unbreakable net), do I think my way back to my father. Handsome with the unflinching severity of a

hawk, he nevertheless bore the double mark of foreignness and infirmity. He must have played the lame, soot-covered Hephaistos often
enough in his imaginings. When I was nearly grown, my mother told
me, "You can't imagine the trouble I had convincing your father to
stop wearing a suit jacket in the heat of summer. He kept saying the
sight of his empty sleeve would repulse people. I finally had to tell
him, 'It's empty either way. Why don't you just wear the long-
sleeved shirt? Why suffer more?' " And when I look at the handful of
pictures I have of him, the few that made it out, smuggled like dangerous goods, I see him placed in each so as to hide his missing arm.
I imagine the source of surprise first my mother, then her family,
must have been to him, whose own mother, sister, brother, first wife
couldn't love him without preening themselves on their generosity.
Even his father tried, perhaps a bit clumsily, to compensate. In my
mother and her extended family, he found people ready—once they
got over his not being Jewish—to love beyond, around, inside that
empty sleeve, people long ago smitten by love of good talk, on
whom my father's tongue, which could change the color of the sea-
sons and make a gustatory feast of bad weather, easily cast its spell.

There was one time when I came home with another word in my
treasury, a word spat out, not taught me by guile, so I wanted to test
it carefully, lest it should prove wounding. But my mother wasn't
home yet, and despite my apprehension about my father's feelings,
I needed to know the word's power. I told my father about the
drunk who looked just like the illustration of the "*ivrogne*" in my
French primer and who kept shouting about *kikes*. "What does that
mean?" I asked.

"Don't let your mother hear it," my father said. And he had his
turn at teaching me, reluctantly, about how people spend their time
devising evil names for one group or another, names that, he said,
didn't mean anything if people did not believe in them. It was a
word I was to hear almost routinely. Perhaps I had heard it before
and paid no attention, but my knowledge of its meaning became
equivalent to faith: I now believed in that word and in the word my
mother told me not to utter before my father, and therefore looked
up in terror each time they were pronounced, lest one of my parents
should hear and wince from the sting of these hollow words.

FIVE: *Mud Miracles*

Perhaps because of Benny's categorical distinction between Jews and Christians or, who knows, because we recognized the slant glance of the Other as we met in shops that sold coffee or odd assortments of buttons or sweets, I always felt closer to Mohammedans in Romania than to other minorities, with the possible exception of the Armenians. Whatever horrors had taken place and were to divide our ethnic interests in Asia Minor and the Fertile Crescent somehow failed to touch us, weighed down as we all were by the pressure of a virulent, historically belated Romanian nationalism. At some point in my transcontinental teenage meditations I should have made the connection between that ugly growth and American patriotism, but I was so taken with my utterly fabricated image of America as the land of the free that I resisted being plunged once more into the bog of political cynicism. In Romania, not only I but other Others— Greeks, Jews, Armenians, Turks—drew together in a kind of huddle of the prideful wounded.

I particularly remember the summer before my father's death, a perfect vacation as far as I was concerned (and one that has made me fear perfection, for we happened to have another dream season by the sea the summer before my mother's death). My father suffered from chronic attacks of rheumatism after his year in a jail called Jilava—the Damp One—built, it was said, under a river, somewhat like the Inquisition's cells in Venice under the Bridge of Sighs, where the water seeps through the walls and no salubrious ray ever penetrates to burn off the mildew. The doctor, who unlike so many doctors in the United States had not been paid off by pharmaceutical companies to drug his patients and thus mask their symptoms, told him to go for therapeutic baths at the Black Sea, especially in Lake Techir-Ghiol. The word *lake* may be redundant for all I know, as in Grasmere Lake; the name is Turkish. The lake itself is a prehistoric leftover from a retreating sea, separated from the shoreline by a mere couple of miles and with so few freshwater tributaries that its salinity almost rivals the Dead Sea's. Except that in Techir-Ghiol there is life, tiny microorganisms that survive in the rich black sediment on the bottom.

The mud is considered a miracle cure for practically every disease. Since it smells awful, we children made horrible faces when pressed by the adults to smear it on ourselves, as if we had suddenly grown fastidious about dirt and smells. I was fascinated by people taking mud treatments: many had physical problems, came in crutches or wheelchairs, smeared mud on huge cicatrices; others came, as my mother did, for prevention's sake. The women especially gave themselves mud facials and even smeared mud in their hair. I thought this went beyond disgusting, but then the women would go into the shower and wash away the mud, which rinsed off easily, and a cascade of luminously shiny hair would pour out. In the course of three weeks, I watched a man who could barely drag himself on crutches move with greater assurance every day till by the time we were to return to Bucharest he had begun walking without crutches. There were, of course, physical problems beyond the mud's restorative power. At the farmhouse where we rented a room that summer was an Armenian family, also come for their vacation. They had two little girls, one my age, the other about four. The younger had had polio the year before, and her affected leg was already distinctly shorter and thinner than the other. Her frail mother carried her, an otherwise healthy and hardy child, part of the way to the baths since limping fatigued the little girl. The mud treatments worked no wonders for them.

I struck up a fast friendship with the older girl, whose misfortune became a cautionary tale in my family. She had a cataract that completely covered one eye as a result of an injury. Children perhaps show greater kindness in their directness; everyone at the farmhouse wondered what was wrong with the girl's eye but asked no questions, while they looked upon the mother as the most tragic of creatures, having to bring up two children crippled in different ways. I wondered too, but determined to ask my new friend why there was a cloud in her eye. It was clear that she found relief in telling, for she did so in great detail: alone at home and thirsty, she had tried to open a soda bottle with scissors. The scissors slipped and struck her eye. They rushed her to the hospital, but too much of the liquid in the eye had drained out, and there was nothing they could do to save it. She told me, ruefully, "My mother told me not to open things toward me, only away from me, but that day I didn't listen." Nothing my own mother could have ever said about the wisdom of following parental instructions would have had the same impact.

The place where we were all staying was at the top of a small incline and looked like a picture-book farmhouse. It had a red-tile roof and was painted a brilliant white. On the slope in front were hundreds of dahlias of sunny hues. The courtyard was paved with flagstones, and the verandah wound around the house. Potted hanging geraniums mirrored the red roof. It looked particularly striking in contrast with neighboring houses and others, more distant, that we had seen in our search for a place that rented rooms.

When we first got off the train from Bucharest, my father remained at the Techir-Ghiol train station with the luggage while my mother went seeking a decent place to stay and I tagged along for company. My mother, never an easy woman to please, was almost obsessive when it came to hygiene. I suppose it came of having grown up in a family that kept kosher and brought a German style of housekeeping to Romania. Our search for rooms was not only instructive but proved a prototype for many a similar quest we were to undertake together in our peregrinations. My mother would point to the front yard and say, "Filthy. Look where they keep the chickens," as I let myself be entranced by visions of chickens feeding at my feet. She'd go inside, examine the bed, and say, "Look, bed-bug stains on the mattress." After about two hours in the hot sun on the unpaved, sandy roads of the village, my mother was in despair. "Why are they so dirty?" she moaned. "I wish the sea were in Transylvania," she added, a remark that intrigued me. She then explained to me that the peasants in Transylvania were clean and able to husband their resources, unlike the Romanians. "Why?" I asked. "Different cultures," my mother said, shrugging, preparing me for the knowledge that cultural diversity is not a level playing field but one mined with envy and contempt and emulation.

Just as she started for the station to tell my father that we'd have to take the train to the next town, she saw the farmhouse on the hill. It didn't matter that all the rooms were rented and there would be no vacancy till the next day; the force of her conviction about the place moved our hosts, a Turkish couple, to let her talk them into making sleeping arrangements for the three of us in a vestibule. And how could the woman resist my mother's eloquence when it spoke of the perfection, the beauty, the cleanliness, the elegance of her own home, of the happy contrast it made with the others? That comparison, I think, is what tipped the scales in favor of letting us lodge there. A spark of recognition arced between the two women, and they smiled knowingly: *you too are of a foreign tribe.*

The truth was that our Turkish host's feelings had already been bruised by her Romanian lodgers, who addressed her as "you Turk," whereas my parents, and afterward the Armenian family, properly called her Mrs. Amdí. The other Romanians had also burned cigarette holes in her handmade quilt, she later told my mother when that special feeling between them lasted longer than a momentary illumination. As for me, I was in heaven. No chickens were allowed in the front yard, but there were plenty of animals in the back. Our host rode to his fields in his wagon at dawn and we saw nothing of him till dusk, at which time he frequently called me over to tell me stories of how he'd met his wife; he liked telling them to me mostly because they were fantastical and I believed every word, to his wife's great embarrassment. I remember him saying that she was still wearing the veil when she'd seen him at the market, and, overcome by his great beauty (here he winked at me), she'd started following him everywhere. He didn't want anything to do with her, but one evening he drank from a well and laid eyes on her and was a lost man, only realizing in retrospect that he'd seen her by the well a little while before and that she had undoubtedly put a spell on the water to catch him. His taller, extremely slender wife would punch his arm and laugh and beg me not to believe him, but I wanted this great romantic story right out of the *Arabian Nights* to be true.

Inadvertently, how inadvertently I can't begin to say, I entered Mr. Amdí's narrative repertory. That summer my father was reading a collection of plays by his good friend's brother, Mihail Sebastian, a renowned contemporary playwright whose works nonetheless remained out of print since they had little to do with social realism. The author had been killed in 1945 by Romanian Nazis in a so-called street accident as he was walking toward the University of Bucharest to give a lecture. I had nagged my father to let me read the book of plays. He thought they were a bit difficult for someone my age, but he acquiesced, acting on his principle that a child's mind would cope with what was comprehensible, and what was not would prompt it to re-read as it got older. He warned me, however, not to take the book out of our room to read on the verandah because the book was irreplaceable and in my hands something untoward would happen to it.

I was in the middle of a play when my parents, irritated by my making noise while they were trying to take their siesta, sent me outside. Naturally, I managed to sneak the book out with me. I finished the play, and, before beginning another, laid the volume carefully down and went to make my afternoon visits to the barn and the henhouse. Often events conveniently shape themselves around Aristotelian principles: the puppy who was one of my chief joys on that vacation found the book on the seat and quietly tore it to pieces, strewing the leaves far and wide across the immaculate front yard. The howl I let out upon returning woke everyone up and drove them out of doors in various states of undress. My parents found me hitting my head against the flagstones, which they took as an act of contrition, but which I recall as sheer desolation at Delphic prophecies come true. Mr. Amdí, childless and at a loss how to console this crazed small person, offered to bring out the ax and cut the puppy's head off to punish him for having made me so unhappy. At that I began to howl even more till my father, whose quick temper on other occasions had landed his hand on my behind, put a stop to it by generously letting me off with, "I hope the next time you'll listen to me."

Being a child, I had no consciousness of the impression this event had left on witnesses; I was of course concerned only with its imprint on me. But a great storyteller like Mr. Amdí recognized a good pattern when he saw one, and though our summer visits to his farm were cut off by my father's death, we continued inhabiting each other's memories. After my wedding, my mother arranged to return to Romania for the first and, as it happened, the last time. I see her pilgrimage back to the city of her youth and to reunions with her many friends and the few relatives still there as a compensation for having in a sense lost me. She even went to the sea coast and decided to visit the Amdís one late afternoon. By now they had acquired electricity and indoor plumbing, and their house looked as distinctive and as pretty as before, but their fields lay fallow since they had been collectivized for some years and Mr. Amdí found no profit or pleasure in working them. The summer guests and the two hosts were chatting on the verandah when my mother arrived, conferring instant authenticity to yet another seemingly fantastic narrative of Mr. Amdí's, about a little girl insane with grief over an old torn book, who would not let him kill the culprit, which got to grow into a fine dog. My mother laughed about her propitious arrival and their greeting. She went tentatively, not sure that they'd recognize her, having seen her for only brief periods during two summers a very long time ago, but there was Mr. Amdí, jumping to his feet to hug her and drag her over to show the summer guests the mother of the very child he'd been talking about.

On our vacations to the sea coast the rainy day that inevitably came was by tradition devoted to a trip to Constanţa, the port city, Ovid's point of exile. There we always went to visit the mosque and climb the spiral staircase of the minaret, and we walked along streets whose shop signs bore Turkish names, looking for philo pies and baklava, which we then carried to the seaside promenade and ate, often close to Ovid's monument, in sight of the old casino gleaming on the water and within touch of the spray raised by furious waves crashing against the large rocks of the dike. The food from the privately owned little shops was always very tasty, but never equal to what I had tasted much closer to home.

At the corner of our street and the perpendicular avenue that led to my school a Turk whose name we never learned opened a shop only a bit bigger than the watch-repair shop of my friend Simon's father, which consisted of a counter underneath a stairwell. It nestled in a protuberance of a large apartment house; to me the shop and the swallows' nest built in the right angle between the outer wall and the first-floor balcony of that same building became somehow inextricably connected, although as it turned out the nest long outlasted the business. I place the shop's existence after my father's disappearance, for I cannot recall him in connection with it. The Turk, as the owner was soon to be known to the whole neighborhood, set up his business in that tiny space and in a short while people were crowding the pavement surrounding it, hoping for a taste of his philo pies and desserts. He used to make a philo-meat pie so savory that to this day my mouth waters at the thought of it. Not my mother nor any other indisputably talented cook was ever able to duplicate it. His meat pie was one of the foods, all equally unobtainable, I craved in my pregnancy, as if the life shaping within me were already testing the limits of access, already preparing for impossibilities. I see as if before me the huge metal trays with golden philo coming out of the oven, and his expert cutting and folding into triangles for the eager hands reaching through the window—that was his counter, the windowsill; the place wasn't big enough to contain trade inside. His *sarailee*, cigar-shaped philo steeped in rosewater syrup and filled with crushed nuts and honey, dripped with sweetness and fragrance; those were my favorites. My mother always chose the *cataifs*, haystacks of stuff that looked like angel-hair pasta, topped with dollops of whipped cream.

I remember my mother's delight that a place with good, affordable food where she could stop on the way home from work and not—for once—have to cook had materialized out of her wishes. Word spread, and soon people we'd never seen, from other parts of the city, began to line up in front of the Turk's, as it was called without the benefit of advertisement or a marquee. He seemed never to run out of his magical pies and desserts, and the crowds before his shop seemed more convivial than most gatherings I remember from my childhood. Of course it couldn't last. The shop was too good, too cheap, too efficient; it showed up the government-run stores;

and most of all it was free enterprise. I can't imagine the man, laboring from daybreak till dark in that incredibly tiny space, doing it to get rich; he didn't charge enough, for one, given the price of meat alone. He loved to see people eat. His dark eyes sparkled as his customers held up the square of brown paper containing their pie and moaned, ecstasy on their faces, "Mmmm."

One day, like Yugoslavia on the pull-down map of Europe in our grade school, the shop vanished. We found on our daily walk the window of the shop papered over and the door bricked up. As with the white blot like a movable Antarctic on the face of Europe, which none of us children ever dared overtly notice through all the boredom of our primary schooling, everyone in the neighborhood knew better than to ask what had happened. The general silence no doubt contributed to my imaginings: I had horrific visions of the poor man forever trapped inside. I'd often heard on the radio the folk ballad of the master builder—we were big on folkways until Ceaușescu began to bulldoze villages—in which the good wife, unlike the slatterns, brings the master builder's meal while he's at work and thus gets chosen to be cemented into the foundation as a charm against the structure's crumbling. At the sight of the shut-up shop, I began to cry uncontrollably, and my poor mother, who was almost as inconsolable as I for less fantastic reasons, kept telling me not to worry, we'd find the pies and desserts elsewhere. But of course we never did, and I was too caught up in my vision to let her know why I was crying, taking it for granted, as children do, that their parents know their fears and arbitrarily respond in ways that are beside the point.

On that corner, which I passed almost every day of my seven school years in Romania, I would stop to watch the swallows feed their young each spring. I watched their elegant, sleek arrow shapes almost disappear down the gullets of their voracious yellow-beaked nestlings. Always as I stood on the pavement looking up, I recollected reading that when sparrows take over a swallows' nest, the pair alert their tribe, and swallows for miles around swarm around the nest with clay globules in their beaks, depositing them at the opening until the intruder is walled in forever. We too, Armenians, Greeks, Jews, Turks, wanderers brought by triumphant empires or diasporas and abandoned on this hostile shore—people whose dearly bought *savoir faire* oiled the wheels of commerce and kept cottage industries alive, who could not give away much but, in Shaw's words, gave you value for your money—found ourselves deprived of the very rootlessness that had made us Other, immured inside the boundaries of a country that would let us neither out nor in.

My mother was an exceptional cook. In a cardboard box in our base-ment, among guidebooks to several European countries, there's a rusty burner, no bigger than two inches in diameter, atop three curved legs blackened by fire that give it the appearance of a large spider. My mother, who refused to part with it through her myriad moves, used to joke that it belonged in the family museum. She had bought it in Paris in a hardware shop that also sold the small, solid, white blocks of alcohol used to light a fire inside the spider's circu-lar body. A lid that looked like a miniature frying pan covered the opening so the flames wouldn't leap out and escape onto the table. Despite that minimal nod to safety, the little burner tipped over many times, and I watched, awestruck, as my mother deftly put out the flames; twice I had seen her avert incendiary disasters. Once was in our kitchen in Bucharest, when the oil in the frying pan went up with such a sudden whoosh and flash of orange that I, who was about five at the time, ran out of the kitchen, yelling, "Fire! Save yourselves," to my father's amusement. He then reproached me for having left my parents to perish while I ran away, and I, who took everything my father said literally, felt guilty a long time for my cow-ardice.

Earlier in my life, during my father's absence, my mother had wanted to give me an extra-special treat for the new year. The Com-munist government had melded Christmas and New Year's so as to erase religious overtones from the holidays, and my mother, who

disliked Christmas almost as much as Easter, felt more at ease celebrating the birth of a new year than the birth of someone who, she'd
say, had done nothing but bring hatred on the Jews. We had a small
pine tree, which we decorated with ornaments that seemed magical
to me. We had tiny pastel-colored candles attached to metal clips
that we put on the branches as the final touch. My mother then lit
each candle and told me to turn off the lights. The tree glowed
beautifully for a moment, then began to burn with a fast, bright
flame. My mother shouted, "Turn the light on," ran to the bedroom, grabbed a blanket, and embraced the tree, wrestling it to the
floor amid a muffled clatter of jarred and breaking ornaments. The
fire was out almost as quickly as it had begun, with only a tiny dark
spot on the parquet as a reminder of what might have happened. In
my life I've been lucky not to have been tested as my mother was; I
somehow apprehended at that early age that she had a presence of
mind few people matched. On occasion, I got to witness contrasting
behavior: one spring day Loulou Herczog was chopping something
on a cutting board that for some inexplicable reason she had placed
on the balcony rail. Her cleaver fell from the eighth floor, acquiring
lethal velocity in its descent, and her best thought was to look down
and yell, "Don't anybody take that! It's mine!"

Over the alcohol burner, in various one-star hotels around Paris,
always in secrecy since cooking in the room was forbidden, my
mother made miraculous meals. She made gefilte fish and stuffed
veal breast, chicken in myriad sauces and shapes, and once, to feast
my getting over an illness during our stay in Paris, she even managed
to bake a small round cake, using a recipe that required building an
aluminum and paper shelter around the minuscule boiling pan she
had bought along with the burner. When anyone knocked at the
door, she'd blow out the flames, wrap the pan, its contents, and the
burner in an old thick towel, and shove it in the bottom of the
wardrobe. Most of the time she cooked with the large French windows open, regardless of the cold, so the fragrance rising enchant-
ingly above the pan would not permeate the hallway. Once a hotel
proprietor did catch her at it. She stormed into the room unexpectedly and "confiscated" the burner, lecturing my mother about the
dangers of fire and threatening to evict us. I was at school at the time

and missed the excitement. "What are we going to do?" I asked, knowing that the money we were being given would not suffice if we had to buy food ready-made or go out to eat.

"I'll have to buy another burner," my mother said, with a matter-of-fact shrug.

"But what about the landlady?" I asked. "If she wants to play cops and robbers with me, she'll lose."

My mother was right. To prevent the woman from surprising us, she began propping a chair underneath the door handle every time she cooked. She found elaborate hiding places for the cooking utensils and the burner, and she'd wrap scraps in newspaper, carry them out in her purse, and throw them into the first trash can. It was a risky procedure; we arrived in Paris at the height of terrorism against decolonizing Algeria, just when *plastiques*, disguised as small parcels like those my mother carried in her purse, were being abandoned in trash cans outside important buildings, like the offices of *Le Figaro*. One night we heard an explosion and, immediately following it, the wail of sirens. The next day we learned that a bomb had gone off a block and a half from our hotel, in a place with the lovely name of Rue de la Montagne Sainte Geneviève. Sometimes police would stop people in the street and ask them to open up their purses and briefcases. The first time it happened, my mother instantly fished for her papers, pressing them on the officer, who smiled and told her he was only interested in looking inside her purse. My mother, whose French was excellent, felt embarrassed at seeming so provincial. She told me, "Old habits die hard." In Romania, not having one's identity card to present whenever stopped by the police usually meant a night in jail.

In Paris, being surrounded by a bounty such as I had never seen but that my mother said was not as lavish as that available in Bucharest before the war—shops filled with baked goods, fish and shellfish with whose names and shapes I was unfamiliar displayed on grape leaves, chickens turning on spits in front of butcher shops, the dizzying array of vegetables, fruit, cheese, dry meats spread out as if on the magic tablecloth of Grimm's tale in Place Maubert three times a week, only to disappear without a trace four hours later—would have been constant torture, like Tantalus' punishment, without my mother's determination to keep cooking. Not that she always wanted to cook, although her triumphs over the restricted means of producing a meal gave her great satisfaction; sometimes we could buy a half a chicken with french fries, wrapped in butcher-shop paper, and savor its succulence. "What I couldn't do in a normal kitchen," she would sigh. She arranged for me to eat lunch at school. The subsidized program made the cost nominal, and the meal consisted of three well-prepared courses.

She herself began eating her midday meal at a soup kitchen for refugees. We had both gone to one, run by a man reputed to be a concentration-camp survivor, now wealthy and Westernized, in the Jewish quarter around Rue des Rosiers. No sooner did we arrive than my mother ran into people she had known in Transylvania before the war and hadn't seen for almost twenty years. The reunion was tearful. They stood in the aisle between tables, looking at one another with expressions of wonder on their faces, clasping their own hands and one another's in surprise. Just then the owner showed up and began to scream, in Yiddish-accented French, that they were impeding traffic and that he was not running a social club but a soup kitchen where people ought to eat and get out and be grateful for his generosity. Everyone was stunned into silence, including the groups at the long tables, except my mother, who turned to him and said in a low, firm voice, "Charity requires knowing how to give." She grabbed my arm and made for the door, fully expecting her friends to follow, but they waved a hasty good-bye and took their places, somewhat shamefaced, in the food line. I don't remember seeing them again.

Through the émigré network, my mother discovered another charity canteen, run by a group of White Russian ladies who tried to create a pleasant ambiance as well as provide cheap and filling food. I liked going there every Thursday, when school was out. But for my mother it became harder and harder to go every day. The good ladies treated people with respect, thus salving the wounds of men and women whose skills and education had become irrelevant and who'd been stripped of any class privilege, earned or otherwise, but they had no imagination. Every blessed day they served the same meal. In the six months that my mother ate there, they varied only once from the menu of white bread, crusty and delicious, and beef stew. It was tasty fare, but after a while the mere smell of it would take my mother's appetite away. Since on Saturdays I got out of school early, without lunch, and the canteen closed on weekends, for those two days my mother and I would deliberate between seeing a movie or eating three meals. Often we opted for the movies, where we could escape the drab hotel room and the stares of owners who disliked us because we never ordered breakfast and rationed the pay-per-use showers we took. In the darkness of the theater we could shelter against the seemingly constant drizzle of the Paris spring, could dream about being elsewhere than in a place where no one wanted us, not even on a temporary visa. On those weekends of perhaps two meals a day, my mother's culinary skills and the movies made life a bit more bearable.

Because of my mother's genius, I took excellent cooking for granted, as part of ordinary life, and until some time into my adulthood I never let myself be honest enough about my dependence on good food. Even now I like to think myself above matter that so quickly disperses itself into blood and excreta. But the truth is that hunger makes me grouchy and bad food makes me grouchier. A good meal may not warm the seat of the soul, as the anorexic Woolf claimed, but it does wonders for my mood. I grew up in a family with splendid cooks—my father's mother, my mother, her aunts, the one cousin who kept me overnight most often, my mother's friends. During the three years of blessedness—for me—following my father's release from jail, when he was only loosely or illegally employed, even he became a cook. He managed to convince me—I took his jokes as gospel—he had taught my mother to cook. She used to tell me that she'd had infallible proof of his attachment in the days of their courtship: she had told him she'd done little cooking, for a short while, and had probably forgotten it all; yet, she used to say with a laugh, he didn't back out of marrying her. I suppose it's to him that I owe my dependency.

I remember my first and closest childhood friend, Teddy, listening to his mother describe mine to an acquaintance. His mother, who was a snob, went on and on about my mother's literary accomplishments, which at the time were plastered all over Bucharest on posters advertising a successful comedy she had translated. When she'd almost finished, Teddy added, "And such a cook!" The poor kid used to smell his way to the kitchen when he came over, and he was enraptured if my mother gave him something to taste. Once she was making pork and beans, a simple enough dish, but more like a cassoulet the way she made it, though the pork was mostly rinds. Teddy looked so pathetically unappeased after inhaling the spoonful or two my mother had dished out for him that she took a fair portion and gave it to his mother for his dinner. Later, she asked if Teddy had enjoyed it. Mitzy, his mother, told her that she'd eaten it herself before dinnertime because she didn't want her husband to begin comparing her cooking with my mother's.

In retrospect I understand why Mitzy insinuated herself into my mother's life. At the time, my mother was a famous person. But I never understood why my mother, with her unfailing insight into people's characters, would let her. Mitzy was the only woman I knew during my childhood who used her sexuality to manipulate men. Other women did the same, I could see it even as a child, but they were not part of my universe. Despite her miserable failings as mother and homemaker, or perhaps in some perverse way because of them, I remember her as one of the liveliest, most spontaneously funny people in my early life. Yet she behaved in beastly ways. Once, when she had offered to feed me before school—space shortages in elementary schools meant that half of us were on the afternoon shift—she became incensed when I spat out a piece of uncooked potato in the watery stew she had served Teddy and me. She threw me out, and I remember sitting for some hours on the steps in front of our apartment, waiting for my mother to come home.

After my mother's fall from grace, when the government blacklisted her for having applied to leave the country, she desperately sought employment, and whenever she found a temporary position the employers desperately desired her to stay on. Some even took risks for her, keeping her longer than the position allowed or finding her other temporary spots in the same office. But invariably the regime caught up, and orders came that she be fired. Mitzy's husband, who had been a good friend of my father's from their student days, proposed to help my mother since my father, now dead, had helped him in his time of need. He offered her a job selling vegetables at a state-owned store on the outskirts of the city. My mother thought it over and calculated that her transportation costs wouldn't make the job worth it. Mitzy then told her, "You're obviously not hungry enough." That was the last time my mother visited with her. Our living in the same apartment house made the silent treatment impracticable, but other than surface greetings there was no more intercourse between them.

What was it about Mitzy, who more often than not smelled unwashed, whose house was exemplary for its filth, who fed her child macaroni and fried onions for months so that she and her husband could go to the mountains on weekends, that made men wild about her and made even me prefer her to my own mother when I was very ill? I remember asking for her, and since at the time my mother's star was high Mitzy would come to stay by my bedside and always, no matter how wretched I felt, would make me laugh. When I was so ill, what I read in my mother's soft brown eyes was terror; what I felt in the touch of her knotty, capable fingers was desperation. It made me afraid, and I needed Mitzy, Mitzy who couldn't give a damn about her own child, let alone me, to make light of my disease. And now as I think back, I realize perhaps my mother needed Mitzy for the same reason.

When the Herczogs came to live in the "extra" bedroom of our apartment, I thought Loulou, whom I had met a year or two before in Sibiu, a medieval Carpathian town of great charm, was just like Mitzy. They did have certain traits in common—their restless calculations about seducing men for one—but Loulou, for all her superficiality, was not a soul betrayer. Why would they want to leave their beautiful mountain town with the little zoo and the carp farm to come live in our cramped apartment? I wanted to know. My father laughed, replying, "Loulou exhausted her possibilities in Sibiu," and I could see my mother's admonishing look stop him from enlightening me further. Later, I would learn that Loulou and her affairs had become notorious in the small town, whose mores were shaped by a more devout population than Bucharest's. And besides, Loulou, crazy for fashion and high society, could not find her scope in little Sibiu, despite its labyrinthine streets and Gothic nooks and crannies.

Shortly after the Herczogs' arrival I overheard neighbor women say to my mother, "You know how she is. You and Herczog go to work every day, Loulou and Paul are alone at home" (they forgot my presence), "who knows what might happen?" "If Paul wants to sleep with her, he doesn't need my giving him the opportunity," my mother said, but I was to learn that her equanimity had been hard won, she being a jealous woman. Years later, not taking credit for having raised me to think myself worthy of being loved, she said to me, "I'm happy to see you so secure. It would have bothered me to see my husband go out with attractive young women while I stayed home to work." At that time, I knew she was telling me only about herself, since my unthinking trust and her reasoned faith in our respective husbands had proved right. Our bitterest fights would stem from her fear of being displaced in my life and, later, in her granddaughter's love.

When I was five, Loulou began making a habit of bursting into our room and demanding of my father, "Look, look at me," while he, amused, would barely lift his eyes from whatever we were reading. "I put on this dress to bring out the blue in my eyes." She'd twirl around.

"Did you ever see the eyes of a white goose?" he'd begin. "That washed-out vague color, that's your eyes. You want to see true blue, look at Herczog's eyes," and it struck me at once that Herczog's eyes were indeed a remarkable violet-blue.

"You, you Greek," Loulou would shriek and disappear, leaving behind a trail of expensive perfume.

"That woman knows nothing about the subtleties of wearing cologne," my father would mutter. "Now your mother," he'd say, and stop, making me ache for the exquisite scent of her hair and face, which in order to smell we had to be in her arms. For wasn't much of my father's companionship with me built on our longing for her?

Since I slept on the daybed in our living-dining room, now separated from the Herczogs' "apartment" by a wall, a door, and an armoire arranged so as to provide a corridor of privacy from the common vestibule to their room, I would be awakened in the night

by shouts and knocks from the room adjacent to mine. I would hear
Loulou and Gjury yell at each other, could surmise that they were
throwing things at each other, and often would hear sounds of slaps
and punches. On the rare occasions when I remembered my wakefulness in the sea of childhood sleep where I had my own storms and
monsters to withstand, I would ask my mother in the morning, "But
why does she say to him, 'You never sleep with me anymore?' They
only have one bed in their room." "Oh," my mother would say,
"people say any crazy thing in the middle of the night."

After my father's death the fights got louder, and often now one
or the other of the Herczogs would shout, "Miiiimiiii," waking my
mother to arbitrate between them. They'd then breathlessly reiterate
their grievances against each other and try to get her to decide who
was right. "My grandmother taught me never to judge between husband and wife," my mother would demur, then, turning to Herczog,
would say gently, using his first name—an uncommon occurrence—
"Gjury, you and I have to get up early. Why don't you two stop this
nonsense and get some rest?" For some reason, this seemed to calm
the two, and they retreated into silence. The scene would recur,
almost without variations, every few months until our departure. It
did not disturb me much—the field of battle did not include me, and
children have a great capacity for overlooking actions that do not
touch them. Perhaps the better adjusted, the happier of us maintain
this equanimity of indifference to others' squabbles, violence, suffering as long as we're not directly implicated.

Years later, they too came to America, to Massachusetts first,
where we had our reunion with them, then to Long Island. Having
known me since childhood, they maintained a sporadic curiosity
about my doings. I remember my one and only visit, an overnight
stay, with them at the time when a number of people in my department were working hard to prevent me from being considered for
tenure. A then friend offered to let me in on a private showing by
Granada Distribution Company of Ken Russell's BBC biographies
of Coleridge and Wordsworth. He thought it an opportunity for me
to write about my field in conjunction with another medium, on
films that at the time were not available to American audiences. The
trip led to my third article, and the articles, together with a manu-

script that had received two favorable readings at a university press, would earn me tenure. Since my husband and I had little money, my mother took it upon herself to call the Herczogs and ask them if they'd let me stay with them. They were delighted—in their small one-bedroom apartment, with three of us to one bathroom, we would be reliving in some small part our shared past. Besides, they wanted to know what had become of me in the flesh.

The first thing that astounded me was Loulou's domesticity. She served Gjury and me a lovely veal stew—the same woman who in my childhood would manage to burn soup. She said to me as if he weren't present, "He has high blood pressure, you know. He's got to have low-cholesterol foods."

"She's afraid I'll croak and leave her without means of support," he said, laughing, then turned on the *MacNeil-Lehrer Report* and was lost to us.

"This is how we dine together," she said, pointing at him, then brought out a bottle of sour-cherry liqueur. "Want some? I made it myself. We go to pick the cherries from an orchard in New Jersey. All you hear among the trees is Romanian and Hungarian." Suddenly, a Woolfian vision of birds singing in East European languages rose before my eyes, and I laughed out loud. "You have the same laugh as when you were little," the Herczogs said almost simultaneously. As my palate burned pleasantly with the fire of alcohol and the sweet sting of the cherries, the thought of all these people migrating to New Jersey to pick sour cherries to make the liqueur that would momentarily transport them home made me feel very tired.

"You're too skinny," Herczog had appraised me as soon as I took off my coat. Of the vase that I had presented to them, purchased at a gallery in Detroit and quite expensive for me, he said, "Ah, a single-stem vase. Good, you're letting me save money when I bring her flowers." The next day, when he drove me to the commuter train station, he paid for my ticket, dismissing my protests, and was terribly solicitous about my not getting lost in Manhattan.

"Herczog," I had to remind him, "I've been traveling through big cities alone since I was little."

"Well," he said, "I owe it to your father the one time I see you to look after you."

At their apartment the night before, some irritated remark of his had prompted Loulou to ask, "How much insurance am I going to get when you die?" Launched into their bickering, they almost forgot me, and I sank into not exactly the warmth but certainly the familiarity of a past that, so often unconfirmed by anyone but my mother, had begun to seem more and more hallucinatory.

"*La forme d'une ville, hélas*"—Baudelaire lamented the violation of his still-medieval Paris by Napoleon III's ripping wide boulevards. A Paris without those pulsating strobes of avenues radiating from L'Etoile seems unthinkable to us now. For the constitution of a city is neither the chronological accretion of marketplaces, street after street, monuments, parks, fountains, way stations, nor the orderly and miserably failed incarnation of an urban planner's dreams. For those of us in love with a city or the idea of a city, its constitution is forever subject to remembrance, the superimposition of the seen upon the lost, the imposition of the imaginary upon the real. A city, as Calvino knew, is often invisible, consisting of layers on layers of knowledge about what used to be at specific epochs, about its fossilized remnants or its petrification from the mutability of the living to venerated history—or, in the experience of those for whom history was the latest official narration, the obliteration without trace except for memory—and that discouraged—of what was.

It's easy for me in some ways. Bucharest will remain unchanged in my mind, the squalor of its basement one-room apartments housing families of seven side by side with lovingly tended parks where as a very young child I fell in love with the grave monkey faces of pansies and hunted for snails under bushes after the rain, singing them the verses that were supposed to coax them out of their shells with promises of muddy water. I vividly remember the dark, dirty floors and shelves of empty or near-empty food stores—in which one could, however, always buy toothpicks and mustard—located not far from the art-deco or Victorian restaurants and pastry shops—lit up by chandeliers, reflected in walls of beveled mirrors, whose light was absorbed into the plush velvet of banquettes and chairs—where into the early 1960s they still managed to serve coffee and sweets of a quality and profusion I haven't encountered anywhere but in Salzburg.

In the brief time when my personal history took shape concomitantly with that of Bucharest, there already were bewildering duplications: the adults would give us directions in prewar street names, and we would stare at them with blank looks until they translated into Communist commemorative nomenclature. Sometimes the names themselves even began with the same initial, Boulevard Brăteanu now Bălcescu—like the last names of Jews christianizing but keeping the trace of origin in the first letter, so that I would hear my parents ask, in regard to an acquaintance, "And what was his maiden name?" entangling me further in the gender confusion of an archaically inflected language. A song popular when I was growing up celebrated the opening of yet another little park in Bucharest; these corner parks sprang up on lots where buildings had stood before the bombing raids during the war, but also on the gaps left by the always surprising collapse of houses and apartment blocks during earthquakes. Bucharest is situated directly on a fault line that runs down from the young Carpathian mountains through the vast fertile plain on which the city was built, and my childhood was punctuated with periodic notices of lamps swinging or floorboards groaning and people asking each other for the rest of the day, "Did you feel it?" These were so much a part of mundane occurrences that I never had a moment's unease about the tremors, which we children treated as a mild amusement. The grown-ups seemed unaffected as well, their minds on the more pressing daily task of being able to find and buy food.

Yet the Bucharest that I remember is no more, violently rearranged by the earthquake of 1976 that killed more than 6,000 people, whose bodies, those that were recovered from the rubble, were placed along the banks of the river Dîmbovița, which cuts the city and carries its rat-brown pollution to the Danube, which in turn takes it all the way to the Black Sea. And what those natural forces left intact of the charming late nineteenth-century structures, Ceauşescu took care to demolish with intentional anti-aesthetic precision. I hear that the boulevards gape wider now, their sides decorated by socialist-prescription housing and office buildings whose architectural style resembles nothing so much as Mussolini's Euro-Brutto gigantism.

Still, since I've not revisited the city, what rises in my mind when I think of Bucharest are the vistas from our two balconies. In one, to the east, the highest point on the horizon was the old fire tower from whose circular walkway a century before the night watchmen looked for signs of conflagration. The other, to the west, was constricted and crowded on the left by the bell tower of the abandoned Italian church where the pigeons and bats roosted, and on the right by the wing of our building that provided an infinite variety of glimpses of tenants in their lit windows like distant TV screens; that vista opened nonetheless into full frontal sunsets sinking, with socialist symbolism, behind what had been the royal palace. Across the boulevard sutured with streetcar tracks lay a sports field of selected access, paved with crushed brick. Often I would watch the privileged members of the security police, tiny as ants, play volleyball. One afternoon, after a summer storm, when the sun struck against the sheen of wetness with an effulgence painful to the eye, my father, who was color blind, looked across with me and exclaimed, "How beautifully the grass shines after the rain!" while I, who wasn't sure whether he was joking, said, "But it's red, Tata, bright red." He hugged me, laughing, I think, that I could distinguish the colors he could not.

Every New Year's upon the stroke of midnight fireworks would burst from behind the palace and light up first the Royal Square, then more and more of the city as they rose, drawing shadows like stage curtains behind them as they fell. We still made a habit of watching them, my mother and I, after my father's death, but soon the government began building a new apartment house right on the sports field, and our view could go no farther than the other side of the boulevard, coming to rest on the pastel blue, pink, and yellow panels of the new balconies. In the now pencil-thin opening between the gracious nineteenth-century building and the splashy new one, which I preferred, we could see another new apartment house being built to the left of the Royal Palace. It was supposed to be the *dernier cri* of modernist architecture, though hitting Bucharest, to be sure, with a delay of at least a half a century. My mother's friend Milka was going to live there, so we watched with interested fascination the progress of the occasionally visible bulldozers and cranes. As the tower grew, we could see it beginning to form an acute angle instead of being parallel with the buildings across from ours on the boulevard. At first we thought the angle was due to our skewed perspective, to distance, to the differing levels of the Royal Palace square, which sloped downward from the slight elevation where we lived. Soon after, we realized that we had been among the first to notice that the pride of Communist architecture had been mistakenly built on a tilt. After Milka moved in, she would come over and tell us of the latest mishaps in construction. She had us rolling on the floor with tales of how the hot and cold plumbing had been switched so that people disinfected their toilets when they flushed but had to shower with cold water, how the elevators for the forty floors would only go down one day and only go up the next, so a tenant was wise to be the first to use them.

Yet modernity was not without its uses. The main floor of the apartment building with garish balconies now fronting us became the first supermarket in Romania. It had carts on wheels, which all of us children loved to push. Commands about going to the store were more readily obeyed after the opening of the supermarket. My mother even sometimes found pieces of frozen meat that proved quite palatable when grilled. Otherwise, the store exhibited the same bounty as the others—stacks of presumed canned salmon, herring, sardines in tomato sauce, all tasting exactly the same regardless of the picture of the fish on the label and all unbearably predictable to the palate after the first hundred times; shelves and shelves, now accessible to customers rather than protected behind counters by vendors' ill tempers, all empty of almost everything save mustard and toothpicks; Western supermarket-style open freezers with nothing inside except the frosty metal grills; cheese and cold-cut windows where one still had to stand in line to be waited on, be given a ticket, then stand in line at the cashier's and pay, then return and stand in line to pick up the item, often the wrong one. It was in the supermarket line that my mother's wallet was lifted for the first time, causing her no end of trouble with the police in re-establishing her identity.

I remember the supermarket in the days after the initial excitement of its opening had given way to lassitude on the part of people forever engaged in the food quest: its large empty aisles, its cool quietness. Now that I think of it, it resembled the Language & Literature floor of the Detroit Main Public Library on a weekday. Then, one afternoon, we children saw mobs forming in front of its doors. Those of us whose parents were home ran all the way to give them news that something was being sold. We then watched people leave, their arms loaded with oversized cans, their pockets bulging with what turned out to be cellophane-wrapped rolls of sugar candy. All of us got to taste these available marvels since the supply seemed endless and no one left the store empty-handed. They were Cuban products, the candy and the canned fruit in syrup, obviously rejects from the Soviet-bloc market that no one, neither we nor the other famished people behind the Iron Curtain, would eat. Few things apart from the candy thrown to us by the embassy Americans had tasted so vile. Garbage bins reeked of fermenting fruit from opened cans that everyone threw out. For days the sidewalks bore the same pastel colors as the balconies of the new building that housed the supermarket—pink, lemon, pale green, baby blue, as children used the candy rounds as colored chalk, fittingly, since that was precisely what they tasted like. I'm reminded of that gagging consistency of powder suspended but not dissolved in an artificially flavored medium on the unhappy occasions when I'm forced to swallow barium.

Bucharest for me remains a not entirely connected series of routes. I don't remember ever seeing a map of the city, so my navigation of it depended on mysterious signals and seasonal cues. I first learned the walk from our apartment building to my mother's office when I started kindergarten. I had gone to the same day-care center two years earlier and suffered with the intensity of first experiences the bouts of keen loneliness and boredom that would often recur in my schooling. But now my father was home from jail and from unemployment, and he actively championed my independence by insisting that I learn to walk with my friend Teddy to and from kindergarten. My mother was not pleased by this arrangement: the avenue where the kindergarten was located had heavy streetcar traffic. So as to secure some peace of mind for the duration of my fifteen-minute walk, my mother had me stop at the gatehouse of her office, housed in the magnificent mansion of a former exploiter of the people and now guarded by a kindly old man whose duty was to keep anyone without proper identification from walking beyond the forged-iron fence up the gravel driveway to the marble steps and through the immense paneled doors. I would come up to his window at the little gatehouse, say hello, and bow to him (the latter my own addition to the courtesy I was instructed to exhibit); he would then call my mother and announce that her little girl had passed by (in other words, I had negotiated the avenue safely); ten minutes later my mother would call home to find out if I'd arrived. It astonishes me to this day that she had both of us keep up this routine for an entire year; I myself have sometimes forgotten to pick up my child when school discharge times have changed.

Yet despite this system of checks, my mother would not escape the occasional hair-turning parental panic. One day, as I was walking home with two friends and snow had just fallen, we decided that we would not take the shoveled path but climb instead and walk atop the mounds of snow at the edge of the street. While I made it to my mother's office in due time, the search for mounds to conquer and the inevitable slipping and sliding and starting over again delayed us considerably, so that when my mother called home, I hadn't arrived. Phone calls between my parents continued until my mother's fears moved my father to begin looking for me, and I looked up much surprised to see him loom before me with a displeased face. My father did not make it a habit to correct me, although he'd get mad at me easily enough. His gusts of anger came and passed, unlike my mother's smoldering resentments that burned subterraneously only to surface with the velocity and unexpectedness of volcanic eruptions. I remember only two times when he made it a point to teach me proper behavior, one so indelibly impressed on me that I follow it to this day, forgetting my own growing privileges of age, the other nothing more than a funny memory of childhood. On the first occasion, we were in a streetcar, seated side by side. My father suddenly sprang up to give his seat to a very old man, who at first smilingly protested, then accepted the seat with visible relief. My father apologized profusely, then, after we got off, relieved himself of his guilt about not having noticed the old man sooner by explaining to me how one must be polite and kind to elders, whether or not one respects their opinions. He went over a whole list of what I had to do: greet people as I entered and left the elevators, always greet people I recognized from the building, always respond to a greeting, whether or not I knew the person. Years later, I was telling friends about the boorish manners of academic colleagues who would not respond to greetings and added, "My mother taught me better manners," to which my mother immediately protested, "I didn't teach you to greet men first. That is their obligation." My mother firmly believed that women should hold on to all their privileges until they had full rights with men.

The other time my father corrected me makes me laugh out loud. He took me along, as he often did, on his tutoring rounds. We finished the afternoon at the house of his friends, whose daughter he tutored in math. After the lesson, the girl's mother brought our spoonfuls of preserves on small china plates, accompanied by the traditional glass of ice water. Without knowing it, she happened to serve us the preserves that I adored, black cherry, whose sweetness was undercut by a sharp bitterness that lingered on the tongue. I tried to scrape every bit of that wondrous blend of tastes from the little plate, but was jarred by my father's knee knocking rather violently against my leg. "Are you all right?" I asked in all innocence, looking at his leg under the table, thinking he had been seized by a spasm. I felt another knock. "Daddy, is your leg all right?" I asked again, looking earnestly into my father's now somewhat roseate face. In the street, my father remonstrated with me for almost licking my plate clean and explained that his knee jerks were meant as a warning. "Ah," I exclaimed, wide-eyed. He never again undertook the subtle approach to reforming my manners, and I'm not sure that even now I can resist scraping the plate when I really like what's on it.

That time I was late, however, my father's displeasure had less to do with my snow adventures than with his own fear that my mother's apprehensions might for once be proven right. I had had no idea that the usual fifteen-minute walk had been lengthened to over an hour by our mountaineering. Later that evening, I overheard my parents rather animatedly discussing this episode, with my father making light of it while my mother tried to impress upon him that years had been shaved off her life in the half-hour of my disappearance. Nevertheless I continued to walk to kindergarten, laden with strict injunctions about not straying from the straight and smooth, as it were.

The route took me past my cousin's house, then the horrid sight of the day-care center where my mother had deposited me for a month during my father's jail term, then a fence where morning glories grew every spring and summer. Each day we would pluck a few and suck the nectar gathered in the tips of their funnel shapes. When we walked back in the afternoon, they'd be rolled inward, closed tight against the heat. Farther, just before my mother's office, was a large shady yard with a huge walnut tree. We would pick up the fallen leaves and smear the dark juice on the sidewalk, pretending to draw with it. In autumn, we would gather the nuts discarded by the side of the street, still encased in their green cocoons, crack them open, and stare at the undeveloped, brainlike insides. As I got older, I would walk to my mother's office not merely to bow to the gatekeeper. I would be allowed inside, into the hall of mirrors, sometimes up the elevator that with its pretty sculpted doors and diminutive size seemed so much like a toy it always amazed me when it actually moved.

My mother worked in a small office down a long corridor; she told me the series of offices reserved for the translation department had formerly been the servants' quarters. But under the aegis of the new government the house had become magic. My mother worked with magic. I would go to her office and see a film pass through her editing machine, which, long before any of us had seen a television set, looked like a miniature movie screen where figures moved sporadically and made little squeaks like panicked mice. My mother, headphones on, would stop the motion with a flick of her wrist and use a waxy yellow marker to make an X every so often on the film strip that passed through her fingers and over her lap and wound itself up neatly on the other side of the machine. Her office was filled with round metal cans containing that fascinating world that on rare occasions I was allowed to see projected on a regular screen.

There were two projection rooms: one for the use of the translators and editors; the other, the plush private projection room built into the house by the former owner, now reserved for viewings by the censorship committee of the Communist Party. My mother knew she was taking a chance by letting me into the fancy room when she was required to do simultaneous translating for the censorship committee, the members of which, she stated with contempt, spoke no foreign languages and barely their own. Entirely misreading the situation, I was immensely impressed by my mother's authority on these occasions: she sat at a booth in the last of three rows of rocking armchairs, her hands and the script illuminated by a high-intensity bulb, matching the script before her with the action on the screen without missing a beat, even when she had to turn the pages. She had a beautiful but soft voice, and once, when the committee got loud and she was commanded to read louder, she said, "If you were silent more loudly, you'd be able to hear me." Her boss almost ripped the sleeve off her dress in his attempt to forestall her from saying more, but it had been enough. I had no idea she had run any kind of danger talking back to the censorship committee until afterward, when I heard her boss tell her, "Do you want to land us both in jail? Isn't it enough that you're always arguing with them about making cuts as if this were your father's business or you made the movie yourself?" All I noticed was the room grow silent in response to my mother's comment. Because she herself seemed so unawed at these moments, I did not hesitate to exclaim out loud during a screening of the Hollywood *Ulysses*, "But it's not like the book!" My mother worried about being reprimanded for allowing me to see the film, but the committee members laughed. It surprises me to think that even among the constipated members of a repressive regime there was more tolerance of children than there is in the United States, where it would be unthinkable for youngsters to attend rushes or board meetings, let alone to speak.

Made up of walks to and from streetcars and trolleys, the city segments itself in my memory like slices of a Droste chocolate apple, held together by gold foil and falling neatly into equal, discrete pieces when rapped sharply on the hard surface of involuntary recollection. Under my father's continued campaign for my independence, at the age of five I learned how to get to my grandmother's house. She lived with my aunt and uncle, so a visit to her was a visit to all three, and it was always they who invited me, never she. I recognized the nameless streetcar stop where I needed to get off, then crossed the street and walked along a lengthy boulevard less urban than streets in our neighborhood. Here were houses with sizable yards stretching in front, always fenced in some fashion, whether by pickets or forged iron or stone walls. I would peek through the gates and dream of having a yard like that for my own, even though few of those houses were inhabited by single families. Most had an array of unrelated people, and I would often overhear the same kinds of shouts about someone taking too long in the bathroom or someone not cleaning up in the kitchen that I heard on our own shared balcony, where four doors opened—our kitchen and our neighbors' kitchen doors; the door of the "maid's room," now occupied by a working man who, though he could afford no better, was happy for his privacy; and the kitchen of the other apartment on our floor, in which three families shared common facilities, with predictable frictions. The children in these yards I dreamed of even had an occasional dog. Yet neither the yards nor the dogs seemed to make them happier. I saw them fighting and spitting at each other in the same way that my friends and I carried on.

In this less citified part of Bucharest, there was an imposing municipal administration building landscaped with paths of asphalt interrupted and softened by large, cement-based, elevated beds of flowers. The old women who were my grandmother's cronies would gather and sit, especially if a military brass band was playing, on the cement edges of these beds as the shadow of the apartment house where my grandmother lived began to fall over them and cool the stones on a summer evening. That's where I first heard the women, dressed in black from head to foot even in summer, cluck at the low flight of the swallows and predict rain. I asked them how they knew, and they answered the way my grandmother did, with the circular logic I associated with old-age female mysteries: "Because the swallows are flying low." More often than not, they were right, which impelled me to seek elsewhere for answers. It was my father who finally told me that the wings of insects become heavy with rising humidity and that the lower barometric pressure no longer holds them aloft, so the swallows who eat the insects have to fly low to catch them. Whereas my grandmother would say anything to quiet my questionings, sometimes providing me with extraordinarily comic visions, my father would make sense of the world for me. I adored the dessert called in English "floating islands," in Romanian "bird's milk." I asked my grandmother how she managed to create those clouds of soft meringue that stayed afloat on a sea of liquid pudding the color of sunshine. She told me she got up at dawn and milked the birds, and suddenly before me rose the image of my black-clad grandmother perched atop a telephone pole, coaxing milk from the underbelly of a swallow. I laughed, and my grandmother seemed pleased, thinking I had gotten the joke, not having an inkling about my literal imagination. But she never told me how she really made anything.

On my way to my grandmother's there were vacant lots where stray animals wily enough to escape the periodic round-ups sometimes roamed. I had an intense desire for a dog, so every stray became to my mind a candidate for adoption, although my mother made it very clear we would not keep a dog in the eighth-floor apartment of a building with undependable elevators. My uncle, who was a physician and like my mother disliked the idea of my premature independence, came when he could to wait for me at the streetcar stop. We ambled companionably, both taken with the wisteria whose name neither of us knew, the purple clusters delicious to the eye as ripe grapes. Years later, when I saw those drooping blooms hanging from a Monet painting placed over a doorway in the Marmottan museum, I felt a vacuum in the pit of my stomach as if someone had thrown a hard punch into my solar plexus, so intense was my momentary longing for place and for my uncle's company. On one of our walks I told him of my taming wild dogs, and he told me about rabies, a warning that had as little effect on me at the time as his warnings a few years later, when we took vacations together in the mountains, not to drink the milk offered me by the old woman who rented us the room, milk that I had watched spurt from the udder of her black-and-white cow and that was still at cow temperature, rich with flavor.

His stories about diseases from strays and raw milk remained abstract enough to let me disobey him until my cousin, bitten by a dog, underwent a series of abdominally administered antirabies shots. My mother's entire family held up my cousin as a model of bravery. I understood the drift—I was terrified of injections, and tales of my outlandish behavior to avoid being punctured had made the rounds. Once, when my mother and my uncle took me to a hospital to get some blood tests, I raised bloody hell with my screams. Apparently my yells had dire effects on the heart patients in a ward nearby, who, like me, thought child murder was about to happen. When the nurse slipped the tourniquet over my arm and tied it, I knew that they were preparing to amputate it. I couldn't believe that my mother and my uncle, the two people I most trusted in the world to pay attention to my fears, would stand by while the ghouls in white were readying to remove a perfectly good limb. Nothing anyone said would calm me. They all practically had to sit on me to get the blood. Afterward, I was somewhat shamefaced, but not enough not to expostulate with a doctor who held up his own daughter as a good kid who never cried at shots, "But she's three years older than I," to my uncle's visible satisfaction. For years, whenever I passed the high stone walls of the hospital, I would look up uneasily at the second-floor window of the lab.

So my cousin Shoshana, the same child who made a habit of taking bites out of me sooner or later whenever we were together, became a hero because she endured her rabies shots with great fortitude. She didn't tell any of the grown-ups, however, what she told me one afternoon as she pulled up her skirt and lowered her pants so I could marvel at the pock mark of the needle on her belly. She had been sent to the corner store to buy one egg. A little dog was tied up outside the store. My cousin kicked it because its shrill barking annoyed her, and the dog bit her. On the way home, she was so unconcerned about the bite that she experimented with the surface tension of the egg, squeezing it until it gave way. Since she knew that her mother would not take the loss of the precious egg lightly, she decided to divert attention to the dog bite. She of course didn't tell anyone but me that she'd provoked the animal. By the time they rushed down to the corner to find the dog, it was gone. Stubborn to the last, she chose to have the shots rather than revise her story. Ultimately, this streak of obstinacy led her to make, from my point of view, a demeaning choice in marriage and led to the irrevocable breach in our relations. We later stopped communicating altogether, for trivial reasons, as families tend to do.

But what I remember most vividly, like an indelible film scene, from my childhood with Shoshana is the helpless little girl, terror in her slanted green eyes, as the chauffeur-driven car left the driveway, dragging her behind it, her kneecaps bouncing along the cobblestones. Do I retain this recollection because I was, to a lesser extent than she to be sure, traumatized by the scene? Or is it some measure of revenge against my remembrance of her plotting with her friend to halve rose hips with razor blades and dump them down the back of my shirt so as to induce unbearable itchiness? Is it an image in which I take some small satisfaction? And can I trust the accuracy of such self-interested selections?

I remember the June day. I know it was June because the white mulberry tree on the west side of the driveway at her house was in fruit, luscious plump berries of a dirty white tinged, like a nipple, with a hint of purple when ripe. All of us children were out, snatching at the lower branches and stuffing our mouths with mulberries. My cousin and the other children in the villa that their families shared made it a habit to hitch rides on the back bumper of the car kept in the garage of the carriage house. The car belonged to no one at the house—it was put in storage there until the chauffeur was summoned to bring it to one or another of the Communist leaders who wanted to go somewhere. The chauffeur knew nothing of the games we children played in one way or another with cars, fascinated as we were by their existence and unavailability, by their gleaming black carapace and the glimpse of gray plush inside. Instead of jumping off with the other kids when the man turned out of the driveway, Shoshana slid down and in her panic kept clinging to the bumper with both hands. No one had the presence of mind to shout at the chauffeur to stop or to her to let go. Instead, a crowd of horror-struck people lined the street and screamed, until the chauffeur, puzzled, stopped, and my cousin dropped off, her knees skinned clean, her shins covered with torn pieces of flesh and rivulets of blood. Neither of us covered ourselves with glory at the time, but we were very young, after all. She kept screaming in regular, piercing bursts of sound like an alarm, and I, after seeing her into the house where her nanny carried her and made her sit on the kitchen table prior to cleaning her wounds, ran away home, unable to stand the sound of her voice and the sight of opened flesh.

I knew I had left her in good hands. As my mother often noted, Shoshana's mother was lucky to have found a woman for hire who fell in love with her charge and proved a more attentive mother than the biological one. "Why couldn't I have been so lucky?" she would exclaim to my father, after recounting the various abuses my caretakers had practiced on me. "You know what they say about dumb luck," my father would reply. "Since the requisite is fulfilled in your cousin's case, the conclusion necessarily follows." Anna, my cousin's nanny and *bonne à tout faire*, had a much older son and had indeed fallen in love with my cousin, the daughter she never had. After Shoshana and her parents had left for Israel, Anna would haunt the rest of the family, lapping up the crumbs of news that my cousin's mother, scattered as she was, sent at long and sporadic intervals and never directly to Anna. "I have to see the pictures that Mrs. Marcus got," she lamented to my mother. "I want to see Shoshana with tits." Her description made my mother laugh but shocked me, since I was beginning to reach a similar anatomical moment and I heard men in the street make remarks about my body in the same coarse way, profoundly wounding the sense of inviolability that had helped me negotiate the city on my own since my father had championed my emancipation.

Between the street that led to my kindergarten, on which my mother's office and my cousin's house were located, and our own there must have been a side street that we never took. It was probably out of the way. I remember it because I lost myself one day, when I was still young enough to believe absolutely in the inexplicable, such as the power granted me one time to press my index finger into the granite step where I sat waiting for my mother and find a small dent in the stone beneath my finger. I was daydreaming as I was walking; the lilacs, which I worshipped with a full pagan heart, were in bloom; and when I looked up I saw that I was on a block I didn't recognize. It had paving stones made of little pebbles, not asphalt, and soft, bright-green moss grew between them. The only other place I had seen such moss was on our vacations in the Carpathians, so I bent down to touch it, a bit fearful of having lost my bearings and yet enchanted that an unknown world lay before me so close to familiar ground. After I managed to find my way again, I told everyone I knew about the street. I even talked my mother into trying to find it with me, but I was never able to get back to it, and to this day I wonder whether I might have slipped for the briefest moment into an alternate universe or more likely into a hallucination induced by the strong perfume of the lilacs. For Bucharest in my mind also lives in odors: the gasoline fumes of freshly polished parquet floors that I inhaled like an addict, the cauldrons of tar by the curb, the fried-onion smell permeating the hallways of our apartment building and making my mother wrinkle her nose, the scent of boulevards lined with linden trees in bloom late in May, so sweet as to sicken the senses like honey lapped from a jar spoonful after spoonful.

EIGHT: *Contingencies*

I think my mother lived in expectation of my death. Having lost her own mother before she was old enough to comprehend loss, having heard of the deaths of her father and her beloved aunt during the war years when travel for Jews was restricted, then having seen a whole town—shopkeepers, teachers, lawyers, her doctor, the restaurant owner, the rag man, the young women with whom she had coffee, her favorite pupils—swallowed up by the wagons and then the gates of the death camp, and watching her husband give the slip to the three doctors attending him, my mother had no faith in the benignity of the universe or the endurance of the human organism. Of Auschwitz she had told me many stories and seemed not to spare me from what I might make of them at a young age, but two she saved till I was well into my twenties. Only in contemplating the uniqueness of her accounts did I begin to understand why my mother only most reluctantly participated in any survey or study of survivors. Men, and often not the best of them, have come to own Holocaust literature, memorials, museums. Even from this, the greatest extremity, they have carved out copyrights and patents, so that the memories we are left with are for the most part dominated and ordered by the very standards—ethical and aesthetic—of the version of Western culture that betrayed Jewry, taking them to the brink of genocide.

I remember my mother attending an "event" sponsored by the people involved in putting together the Holocaust Memorial in

Detroit. We went to a meeting in a northwestern suburb, a location to which my mother always referred as the ghetto, to hear about the progress made toward the memorial and see the kind of videotapes they were collecting of survivors' testimonies. It turned out to be a disgraceful evening of hollow talk and self-aggrandizing. The single video shown, narrated by a man present that night, was, however, very moving. After the show, people in the audience were invited to speak, and the women were systematically silenced, not only by male fellow sufferers but by wealthy younger men who took over because they were donating the money. To cap the evening, the rabbi invited everyone to have coffee and cake made and served by the women survivors. On our way home, my mother said, "You saw them. It's as if nothing at all happened to them. They're unchanged!"

I tried to appease her bitterness partly because I felt guilty for having talked her into participating in the Holocaust Project. "But the video was moving, and that's what will be preserved."

My mother was silent for a moment. Then she said, "Did you hear his voice? When he talked about how the children, torn from their families, screamed and screamed? Did you notice the annoyance in his voice?"

I hadn't thought about it, but she was right. The man had sounded more annoyed than pained by those remembered screams. "It's probably his tone," I said.

"No," my mother said. "That's how they were on the trains too. Shut the children up, they'd tell the mothers. Well, the Nazis shut them up for them. That's why I could never live in Israel—the cumulative effect of all those people unchanged even by hell . . ." her voice trailed off. I shuddered at my mother's harshness, yet undeniably something horrible had happened that evening. As it turned out, it was a prelude for a coup, a takeover of the Holocaust Project from the history professor who had started it by a rabbi, who became more and more proprietary about it, to the point where he owned the whole thing. The history professor was ousted, and my mother along with him as the unruly supplement to a narrative whose contours had already been determined.

In addition to no longer having a Jewish last name and never having made herself part of the Jewish community by joining a synagogue, my mother, who had gotten along famously with the woman assigned to audiotape her, serenely announced to the new interviewer sent by the Project that since in the audiotape she'd spoken about Nazi crimes, in the videotape she wanted to talk about Jewish collaboration with the Germans in the precamp ghettos of Transylvania and in the camps themselves. The young woman who was to videotape her ran out of the apartment and never called again. Not only was her testimony silenced, my mother was not invited to the opening ceremonies for the Memorial, which she heard about on the local news along with everyone else in the Detroit metro area. I've not yet had the heart to visit the Memorial, and it's only through one of my students' research that I know my mother's audiotape made it into the archives.

These, then, were my mother's two stories, and in setting them down I myself must decide how to order them, what chronology along the page to give them. I too am committing the theft, the supplanting, of memory, for what defense have the dead against our misrepresentation when we take it upon ourselves to speak for them, in languages most would not recognize, according to rules of *bienséance* that make sure to exclude the raw scream, the excess of sorrow that will not respect containment? My mother told of two undetected pregnancies in the one barracks in which about a thousand women, including her, were forced to live. One of the pregnant women proved not to have been entirely undetected except initially, in the triage performed as the bewildered victims descended from the cattle cars that brought them there. Mengele's riding crop, his elegant phallus, pointed the woman in the direction of the slave compounds instead of the crematoria. But someone else, with a woman's instinct, understood why the deportee hunched so, and she kept watch. When the prisoner went into labor, Ilse Koch was there, in full SS regalia, looking, my mother said, with her halo of wispy blond hair and her perfect features, like an angel. Koch ordered the prisoner's legs tied together and stayed, her arms crossed, smiling, until the woman and the child, struggling to sever themselves into life, became inextricably tangled up in each other, until they both ceased to move.

The second woman managed to evade the guards' eyes. As her

pregnancy advanced, women in the barracks took turns supporting and camouflaging her weight as they dragged her out for predawn prisoner counts. The night she went into labor, the women divided their efforts between uttering loud laments and stifling her groans so the guards wouldn't hear. When she gave birth to a fighting, healthy baby boy, many tore pieces out of their own rags to fashion coverings for the baby and bandages for the mother, who had been hemorrhaging so heavily that she lost consciousness before she knew she'd given birth. The women had been warned and had also witnessed the penalty for harboring anyone or anything against the regulations: they would be locked up in the barracks, to which fire would be set. It didn't take them long to decide that they couldn't hide the child indefinitely, so he would surely perish, and that they wouldn't risk a thousand lives to try keeping him. Someone sneaked the baby out and left him by the latrines. Infuriated by this breach of nature against the machinery that was Auschwitz and by the impossibility of searching every woman among the tens of thousands for signs of recent birth, the camp commanders had all the women file out and spend three hours on their knees in the frozen mud of the early dawn. My mother often said the weather was so harsh in Auschwitz that some prisoners maintained the Nazis controlled it. The women who fainted in this interval were carried away to the gas chambers. Among them was the woman whose fellow sufferers told her she'd had a stillborn and who went to her death never knowing that she had given life, that a new life had braved, however briefly, against all odds, Auschwitz itself.

Occasionally I would ask my mother to tell me whether she had taken any part in what had happened, but she would mostly shrug and say, "I did what everybody else was doing," "I did what I had to do," as if she needed to speak of what had happened only from the protection of the collective "we." Only by chance, impossible coincidences through which we met up, sometimes a continent away, with women who had shared that year with my mother did I gather any sense of her tested and proved mettle, of the chances she took in snatching coats for her friends from under the Nazis' noses, in doing washing twice daily in ice-cold latrines for her fiancé's sister when the woman's digestive tract, weakened by hunger, lost continence. The only story my mother told about herself was one in which a misguided Nazi overseer of her barracks put her in charge of food distribution because she could speak fluent German. My mother protested, to no avail. By the end of the day, she was hoarse from begging starved women not to cheat each other of the ladleful of slop she was dishing out, and she had to go around gathering spoonfuls from her friends since she hadn't left enough for herself. The German laughed at her, telling her that all the other food distributors had gotten plump from the surplus they kept for themselves, and promptly dismissed her, whose anarchic spirit was happy at not having to collude with any system, and emphatically not the one sustaining the concentration camps.

Is it any wonder that my mother, even in my fortieth year, would panic if she misplaced me? She would go through intricate daily calculations of where I was and how long it would take me to be elsewhere, and she would wait to hear from me within what she thought was a reasonable time. If she didn't, she'd call anyone who might have last seen me. Nothing made me more resentful than her attempt, I always thought, at controlling my life. But since she rarely told me not to do what I wanted or go where I wanted, I now realize that she merely had to know that I was there or in transit, that I made it to my next destination, that even though I traversed a treacherous and malignant world she had not lost me through one more day.

I remember a time in my late pregnancy when my mother began to interfere with my eating. She would look at me fixedly and hold her breath, then the words would come out, almost without her will: "Don't eat so much."

I would pause, stunned, between bites. I would tell her that I hadn't gained all that much weight.

"I know," she'd say. "I don't care about that. Just space it out more," she'd say, then stop, holding her breath again.

This new attitude drove me crazy. My mother hadn't kept me from eating since my pudgy preadolescence. Cultural differences in diets are a subject unto themselves: Romanians believe that you can eat as much bread as you want when you're on a diet, provided it's toasted. In my American phase, I would laugh at this custom and say, ha, the calories evaporate when you dry the bread. But in a culture in which bread was a staple, not merely camouflage for the protein within, eating toast was different from eating the aromatic, rich whole-wheat bread whose shiny crust resembled the skin of a newly shelled chestnut, or the blond crisp sweetness of white bread. Eating toast was like licking bones once the flesh had been removed. The soul of the bread went up in pungent smoke, and the dieter had the leavings. How much of it could one bring oneself to eat? The other peculiarity of Romanian dieting was the prohibition against drinking anything, particularly water, during meals. I found this equally hilarious in my assimilated period, though now it makes a sort of sense. If I didn't drink, the dehydration I felt made me not want to go on with the meal. As a dramatic ten-year-old, I would kneel in front of the intermittently dripping kitchen faucet, glass in hand, begging my mother to let me have a drop, just one drop. She would ignore me. I would then sink slowly to the floor and pretend to expire. She would commend me: "Very good performance. Now please clear the table so I can wash the dishes."

Under her regimen and the liquefying effect of hormones coursing through my body, my waist dissolved from its barrel dimensions, and by the end of my eleventh year I was slim again, although in my own eyes never sufficiently slim. My mother resumed her habit of scouting out and preparing delicacies for me, and I spurred her on with my absolute devotion to good food, an idolatry I inherited from my father.

That was why I was shocked and outraged when she tried to stop me from eating during the brief time in my life I felt justified in feeding myself as much as I desired. After I came home with the baby, my mother confessed that she knew of a friend's wife who had died because she'd eaten a big meal, gone into labor, begun to regurgitate, and suffocated in her own vomit. My mother, of course, felt she must anticipate every contingency for my sake, all the time knowing that mere living leaves us forever unprepared.

My mother also lived in expectation of her own premature

death. She didn't tell me till her fears were allayed that she had been horrified at the thought of leaving me unprotected in the world before I had a chance to finish my schooling and earn a living. Her impoverished youth, after her father's partner absconded to America with the firm's funds and the family finances took a dive into negative numbers, as did so many in the 1929 crash, weighed more heavily on her mind when she thought of my future than did her extraordinary career successes in spite of the economic abandonment and every other adversity she'd suffered. To add to her anxieties, my father's sister, who envied yet reproved my mother for having applied to the government to leave Romania, yelled at her in the street, "How could you think of leaving? Suppose you die among strangers! What will become of the child?"

My mother looked at her levelly and said, "What will become of her if I die here?" which silenced my aunt, whose maternal instincts were at best sporadic and who was not hypocritical enough to make vain promises about taking me in.

Yet my mother was haunted by that remark and ruined a number of good years of her life because of it, something for which she never could forgive my aunt, not even when the latter, sick with an illness that proved terminal, wrote asking for a reconciliation. It's true that, as usual, my aunt's timing was rotten; the letter arrived during the last great crisis of my mother's life, and neither she nor I found the time to write back; by the time we might have thought of it we had already received news of her death. So, worried about dying among strangers, my mother walked the streets of Paris and imagined what would happen to me if a car lost control, jumped the curb, and ran over her. The three-inch headlines in *Paris-Soir* about the white slave trade and the sinister disappearance of young girls certainly didn't ease her mind. From a society in which, at least in the news, nothing untoward ever happened, no fires, no accidents, no violence whatever, she had entered the maelstrom of the West, in which everything is reported but the normal and the everyday.

Thus it happened that when my stepfather-to-be came to Paris to see us, as we thought, and after a couple of mysterious absences proposed to my mother, not for the first time, she gave in despite all

her misgivings. She saw herself going to America, the unknown continent where, she knew from all her years of translating American
movies, people shoot each other with alarming frequency, and saw
me alone, a tiny lost speck on that great continent, and decided that
the affection my stepfather-to-be showed me would outlast the
fragility of her life. It did not outlast a month of their marriage.

After life—as we call such passages of time for convenience's sake—
with my stepfather, I could no longer believe what people told me.
Curiously, I, who am the best audience for fiction because I never
anticipate plot, who was outsmarted by my three-year-old daughter
when it came to guessing what was coming in a film—"Something
awful's going to happen! Can't you hear the music?"—can no longer
hear a story of real life without detecting in it the faint traces of fiction's scaffolds. I blame myself. Like the dunce Rodolphe, who left
his passionate lover Emma because she could not express her sentiments in an original way, having at her command only the camou-
flages of amorous discourse that cracked and ran like makeup after
heated exertion, I too feel betrayed that the stories people tell me so
conveniently follow expected narrative lines, the very paths that in a
novel lead me by the nose through the most eroded terrain. How
could it be true, I say to myself at startling moments, just as I'm
touched to tears, for instance, when it sounds so much like such-
and-such a scene in *Bleak House* or *The Color Purple*? As if writers
lived in pure invention, as if the shape of narrative belonged to them,
not to the people they heard tell stories, as if I suddenly fell into academic idolatry and put up a fence between language and what really happens.

I remember my stepfather, a great storyteller in his own way, as
never being able to capture my whole attention; so much of his tales
were devoted to his own ideal self. Besides, he'd inevitably break

down and weep over the incidents that exalted his heroism or his sensibility. I wasn't as shocked to see a man weep, though a shock it was, as I was vaguely bothered by his affection for himself. I was happy in my mind to remain loyal to my father and his manner of storytelling, which lit up like uncanny phosphorescence the small twilight made by my night lamp around my bed, so that even now dark recesses of my memory glow with magic stories about his pet monkey; or the time he fed fried chicken shit to his exceedingly annoying little brother; or Mucius Scevola, who held his hand over the flame to show his enemies no torture would make him betray his comrades; or the homely little girl saved by the aesthetically reluctant bear; or the Olympian wars.

Whereas my father's stories made room for the world, albeit in a funnier and more intense rendition, my stepfather's stamped him large on every cranny of the habitable globe. He had been everywhere—London, Paris, India, Africa, South America—and everywhere he colonized everything, including always the most ravishing women. My mother, who had an unfailing memory for language, remembered whole phrases of his talk and caught him many times in the nets of his own making, without, however, confronting him with the naked truth of his invented life. She merely observed and let disappointment bite deeper. Years later, she recounted to me a walk they took in Paris. She and I had just gotten there, and my then-future stepfather came to visit from Germany, where shady friends had secured him a work permit. The two of them stood on the quay side of the Tuileries, and she looked up and instantly recognized the gardens from the way they had been described in books—a remarkable feat of reconstitution, I think to this day, but then she lived so thoroughly in language and in brute reality that she had no postmodernist suspicions. He contradicted her. She retreated—after all, he'd been to Paris every other weekend on his private plane before the war. So as to lord it over her indisputably, the man who was to become my stepfather, who could never leave well enough alone, went up to a passerby to ask him where they were. The Parisian pointed to the gardens and said, "Les Tuileries." My stepfather then launched into an extravagant story about how streets were being restored much of the time of his sojourns in Paris and how he'd not seen the Tuileries from the Seine side before. Reflecting on the moment some ten years later, my mother mused, "If I live to be a hundred with memory intact and never come back to Paris until then, I'll recognize the Tuileries."

Once in a while during the time that we lived with him, when she saw that I too had caught on, she'd say, "But he believes it to be true when he tells it. Look how he sobs over the great love of his life who never was." "I don't care," I'd say, and promise myself the habit of truthfulness, too young to understand that it's easy to give up something when you've not felt the iron grip of its pleasure. Those interminable stories, to which my mother and I listened with various degrees of patience and more or less successful attempts not to point out glaring inconsistencies from the last time around, those and food were my stepfather's greatest compulsions. Like the continents in his imaginary travels, food was the terra incognita that required absorption into his system in order to exist. He consumed vast quantities in record time. He pretended great discernment in culinary matters, but his chief concern remained the amount. He fought my mother and me for food as if we had suddenly all shrunk to prepubescent size and were eating without adult supervision. To pacify his endless orality, my mother produced ever vaster quantities, of which ever greater portions went to him. He'd look at a soufflé and keep making inroads until he had eaten at least two thirds of it. When my mother became sufficiently embittered, she'd say, "He wants to get his money's worth. I pay half and he pays half, but he wants more than half so as to be sure your share comes out of mine." Money too became a point of endless battles, but those he fought, I suspect, out of family habit, without the passion he reserved for his tall tales and for his meals. As we watched him practically inhale half a pan of cake still hot from the oven or hide his head in the refrigerator to eat raw the red stripes of meat from a pound of sliced bacon, we marveled at his robust constitution. I inherited a nervous allergic stomach from my father, and my mother had been through periods of prolonged starvation, so we knew how quickly we'd become ill if we ate like that.

For some years before his death, we had stopped talking with him except when we met by accident. In hindsight I see him engulfing food to satisfy who knows what craving that made him cry so often over the better self he stowed away in his stories. I see him smoking one cigarette after another and rolling the smoke in his mouth as if it had become good to eat. I see him getting the news that he had stomach cancer and being so panic-stricken when the very part he catered to most had betrayed him that he dropped on the spot of a massive coronary and saved himself a lingering, hideous death. Even to this day I, who weep easily, cannot shed a tear over his passing, cannot regret the vindication I felt when my mother obtained her divorce from him on my eighteenth birthday.

What I'm about to record next will no doubt shadow the preceding narrative, although it's only in retrospect that I'm able to name the barter of my teenage body twice attempted and once made by my stepfather. At the time it seemed to weigh more lightly on my mind than did my mother's daily unhappiness. Putting it as bluntly as I have makes his acts against me seem more sinister than the thousand others committed against most young girls all over the world. Yet what he did was so subtle, so matter of fact, so seamless that otherwise it hardly appears as the violence it was. Why, then, so many years later, do I still taste the rise of acrid water at the back of my mouth?

It was the beginning of our first summer in America. My stepfather, the sentimentalist, had bragged about my intellectual prowess to his teachers in a course for foreign students he and my mother had been taking at Detroit's International Institute. The teachers, well-to-do ladies who volunteered their time, were immensely impressed with my stepfather's love of me, especially when he let tears well up in his eyes and discreetly cleared away a sob with his smoker's cough. Innocent of American conventions, he harped so much on my brains that the ladies were convinced I must be a horror to behold. The first time they saw me, at a dinner-dance the Institute gave in honor of the graduating class, they all exclaimed, over and over, to my great delight, "But she's pretty!" It took me a while to register the contradicting conjunction.

I was wearing my Paris dress, not the one my mother and I had really liked because, the boutique owner told my mother, I was too chubby (just as on my return visits to Paris my hair was too thick for a barrette I fancied or my calves were too muscular for patent-leather

boots) but another in my size, one that my mother liked more than
I, which I accepted since she had sacrificed her own desire for a
leather purse, for sandals, for white gloves, to buy me the only piece
of clothing not from *Prix Unique* we were to purchase in our six
months in Paris. At the party I was standing next to the ladies to
whom my mother had introduced me when I felt I was being looked
over. What happened next is the stuff of romance novels, but life
rarely arranges itself more than momentarily into neat generic plots.
The young man gazing at me was a Euro-Indian with very dark skin
and eyes, and hair so black it had a blue sheen to it. He towered
above me when he came to ask me to dance, and my mother, pleased
with his obvious admiration, turned to me and said, "This is Carlos,
from Peru," and returned to her conversation. As we danced, I discovered very quickly, through our differently incomplete English,
that Carlos and I would probably never have meaningful discussions.
But the pleasure I felt in looking at his lovely mouth, only slightly
lighter than his skin, and in holding his hand, whose edges were
yellow-gold, was in no way diminished. Carlos became my object of
desire, the most beautiful and possibly the most empty-headed man
I've known.

For a short time that warm spring we would meet and sit on the
lawn of the Institute of Art or, when the outside air hung over us like
damp hot wool, on a bench of the air-conditioned, newly opened
wing of the Detroit Public Library, saying nothing. We would gaze
into each other's eyes. He would hold my hand or move his fingers
gently, slowly up the inner side of my arm, and pangs of pleasure
would shoot through me. I was not yet fifteen, but I felt with my
whole body that this man, who hadn't yet kissed me, so patient in
pursuing his own ends, would make a wonderful lover. My stepfather, who just a week before had had a violent and protracted fight
with my mother over my summer-school tuition, which, he insisted,
would cut into his few diversions such as hot dogs and beer, decided to take on a fatherly role. With my mother's consent, he sat me
down for a talk about what young men of eighteen want from fourteen-year-old girls and told me not to see Carlos anymore. Thinking
back to the battles I had with my mother over every love interest in
my life, I am amazed at my fairly untroubled acquiescence. I wasn't

yet in love with Carlos. My best friend at the time, a French girl three years older than I, had just stopped seeing a young man she'd met at an International Institute picnic. She told me, "We went to the movies and all this open-mouth kissing, I was afraid I'd end up falling in love with him," but she didn't say "fall in love" exactly— she'd used a slightly derogatory expression, *amouracher*, meaning something like puppy love, that had stuck like an irritant in my mind. I had also just found out the week before that abortions were illegal in the United States. Since I had stopped believing most of what my stepfather said, I didn't give weight to his reminiscences of what he'd wanted from girls when he'd been eighteen. But I knew damn well what I was after and I had a vivid sense of risk, so the next time Carlos called, I told him, somewhat tremulously, that my parents had forbidden me to see him. Over the years, as I recalled the ease with which I had detached myself from Carlos, I couldn't hide as comfortably in righteous condemnation of abandoning lovers. It's easy, when only the senses are engaged and either live in deferred desire or are surfeited, to let go. Not once did I ask myself whether Carlos felt more than a brief disappointment. I met up with Carlos again on the site of our old haunts, around Wayne State's campus, when I began my freshman year. He was always surrounded by women and to me invariably polite and distant. Then, after a while, I no longer ran into him. The papers had carried a small item about political unrest in Peru, and I knew his father held an important government post there.

I might, however, have had the opportunity to take up with him again a year before his disappearance, had his pride or my embarrassment or my mother's good sense allowed it. Three years after my Carlos summer, my stepfather became intent upon getting a minor in Spanish, not because he was good at languages or because he had any interest in Spanish but because my mother was learning it with her usual rapidity and would soon begin to teach it. He decided that his old International Institute classmates who spoke Spanish would help him out and struck upon the bold notion of renewing their acquaintance. Among them was Carlos. My stepfather told my mother, with a leer in my direction that made me jump up and leave the room, "I think he'd be interested." My mother said, "If he was a danger to her when she was fourteen, he'd be that much more of a danger now that she's seventeen." I don't know whether my mother's reasoning carried the day or whether, far more likely, my stepfather went ahead with his schemes and was rebuffed, but the Spanish speakers and he never got together, and he never got his minor in Spanish.

The other time my stepfather tried to exchange me for favors seems even more bizarre in a late twentieth-century account, although it follows a pattern so classic that I think of it as my Dora episode. What is more nebulous here than in Freud's narrative is my stepfather's motive. He wanted to ingratiate himself with a man who taught math part time at Wayne State University, but I can only speculate about the reason. Had my stepfather been interested in sex, the exchange in which I was involved would be easier to fathom. Did this man, who though a Romanian immigrant had found a job as a math instructor at the university, impress my stepfather with his connections? I know that my stepfather, competing with my father's shadow, would have dearly loved to call himself professor and write to his relatives and friends of his ascension to the exalted sphere of university teaching. As it was, he was spending the summer taking equivalence courses in the School of Education while my mother and I journeyed to Minnesota, glorying in being free of him. When we returned from her summer fellowship at a small Catholic college in Winona, we found my stepfather with a number of new friends, one of whom was this man. Dick (the unfortunate nickname my stepfather chose to mask the incontrovertible Jewishness of his given name, Avram) prepared us for meeting him by describing him in his usual hyperboles as an extraordinarily cultured, fine, sensitive being, a Victorians' Shelley at the very least.

When we went to the instructor's apartment, kept by his sister— who was better employed and knew how to drive but nevertheless shouldered all the duties of the household—we met a sickly pale, insignificant-looking man in his thirties. At sixteen I believed in the stereotype of the genius as pale and wan, so I looked forward to hearing the wit and wisdom so enthusiastically described by my stepfather. I soon found his conversation so boring that I took up an art book from the table and began perusing it, as if I were a child excused from adult doings. Imagine my surprise at his asking me, despite this obvious rudeness, whether I wanted to visit the Art Institute with him the next afternoon. My silence trapped me; my stepfather answered for me: I was spoken for.

The next day I dutifully made my appearance in the Kresge court of the Art Institute. I still believed that I was in only for a tedious afternoon, but as Bruno led me to his favorite paintings, all nudes, and began whispering Torvald-like endearments in my ear, it struck me that this horrible, vapid being grabbing my elbow thought of our encounter as a date. I couldn't get out of the Institute fast enough. I feigned illness. He in turn had to feign concern. He wanted to walk me back to the hotel my stepfather had chosen as his summer quarters. I found myself suddenly revived by the hot afternoon air and ran down the marble stairs, away from his dirty little insinuations and from the Thinker's distorted body, back to the horrible dive of a hotel where, to save myself from my stepfather's smiling innuendos, I pleaded a migraine, which wasn't long in coming when so eagerly summoned. Had I read the Dora case, I might perhaps have devised other, more explicitly hysterical symptoms, but I was not to discover Freud for yet another year.

I think more often of that hotel, where my mother and I joined my stepfather for a couple of weeks before returning to Harrisville—the hamlet where we were living—than I would otherwise, were it not for a quirk of location. I used to give a glance, once in a while, as I drove by, to the gap it has now become between two buildings on the west side of Woodward close to campus. I still wonder how all those rooms, lobby, elevator, and stairs fit into that now-empty space that looks to be no more than a decent interruption, breathing room between the structures still standing. The people inhabiting it at the time that my stepfather made it his summer residence are still around, I think, or perhaps it's only people like them, similarly marked by the mysterious mishaps of coiling strands of DNA unraveling in the dark space of the womb. Some look benign in their various afflictions, others positively evil, but apart from occasional outbursts they move gently through the world, in a parade of seeming self-containment that reminds me of the embracing and unintrusive vision of Fellini's camera.

At sixteen, enamored of bodily perfection, I was terrified of them until I saw that I traveled more safely among them than either on the mean streets around the hotel or inside our own room. Twice a day, at 6:30 in the morning and at 4:00 in the afternoon, the dim long corridors of the hotel were pierced by a shriek. I still hear it as I look out my office window and see them filing into their chartered buses in front of the building rising into my view with large letters on it, ASSOCIATION FOR RETARDED CITIZENS. And I remember that exceedingly sunny afternoon and the close room, and my saving headache, and that skewer of a scream, "Medicaaaaation! Medicaaaaation!" which, like the probe we used to scramble a frog's brains before dissecting it, helped my own brain shut down.

My stepfather and his accomplice did not give up at once. Aware of my pleasure in carnivals and amusement parks, he arranged a moonlight trip to Bob-Lo, a pleasure island on the Detroit River, without letting me know that Bruno was to be of the party. On the way there, I stuck to my mother's side every moment; set free on the island, I went in quest of shooting booths where, in my fury at the parading ducks with Bruno heads, I managed to win a couple of the oversized stuffed animals they still give at fairs as marksmanship trophies. I successfully eluded Bruno, bodily at least, and the rest of the group till it was time to take the boat back. By then my stepfather had had time to refine his tactics, and I found myself alone with Bruno on deck while everyone else went in to dance. I stared sullenly at the moon. He tried to converse, at first on neutral topics; then inevitably he started again, with Russian literature and its sweet depiction of first love, to which I replied that my favorite scene in Russian literature was the description of Raskolnikov's murder. Bruno's head, with its wispy hair and skin even sallower by moonlight, distinctly reminded me of the old woman, and the handle on the fireman's hatchet on the near wall took on obsessive sensual qualities, especially since he would listen to no warning but went on and on in his monotonous voice like the buzz of a mosquito, circling around a recumbent body, talking of first love, then closer, of a young girl's opening to love, closer, until it lights to draw blood—except that just before that moment I heard the strains of a polka from inside and rushed away, saying I must dance it, with him in my wake, not quite able to catch up. It was a piece of deliberate cruelty. His health was frail. He couldn't finish a polka without breaking into sweat and coughing, a consequence of having had TB as a child. I would have liked him to die of it then and there.

Years later, when I was able to talk to my mother as one adult to another, I asked her if she remembered Bruno asking me to the Art Institute and coming to Bob-Lo with us. She still had some contact with his family, and once she even visited; Bruno was now married to a woman older than himself, who seemed delighted to take care of him. My mother remembered him asking me to go to the Art Institute, but she'd forgotten all about Bob-Lo. Then for the first time I gave her details. "My God," she gasped, "Dick even dreamed for a moment I'd let you tie yourself to that half-corpse?"

I reminded her that I had been sixteen and found the man abhorrent, so I hadn't been in any kind of danger. "Why did you go along with Dick when he accepted an invitation in my name while I was standing there thinking of a polite way to get out of it?" I asked.

"We're so different," my mother sighed. "I always went out with much older men because men my age seemed so immature. I thought you were flattered by his attentions. I wouldn't have dreamed he'd get out of line." Then she asked, "Do you remember meeting a Greek man at Wayne and telling him you weren't interested in going out with him?"

"Yes," I said.

"You were seventeen, and you said he was too old for you. He was twenty-eight," she said, laughing.

"He *was* too old," I protested, but she and I could find no accord on this point. By her twenties my mother in her full-blown beauty and accomplishments had already survived Auschwitz and the deaths of two lovers, and no man would ever presume to school her. I, standing on the shaky ground of an uncertain and sometimes inimical culture into which I wanted desperately to fit, aware of my odd looks and of an intellect always suspect for too much or too little, would feel oppressed by men who wanted against my will to teach me, mostly that they knew more than I.

Yet in telling these tales on my stepfather, I'm compelled to ask myself, am I different from him? They're not the incandescent, airy, generous creations of my father's subtle mind. They're grudge stories, inventions that shape the truth to my remembrance or convenience, which are so often synonymous. Having only skimmed the surface of griefs inescapable for others (after all, I only stayed at that hotel two weeks, I only stood at the edge of the market in girls), what right have I to make them centerpieces of my youth? Where, for instance, did the Palmer Hotel tenants find their next shelter once it was demolished? What halls, if any, now reverberate with the call to medication? As for the girls bartered for various favors, there's no need to go farther than each day's news.

Once, after I read a poem in which I related a conversation I'd overheard between my mother and Ritzi about Auschwitz, my mother corrected my facts. It was she, not her friend, whose wooden shoe split on the march in the snow. It was her sole that blistered with blood, then broke, exposing raw flesh to the vise of the opening and closing crack in the shoe at every step. It was her friend who, weary beyond care, had asked the soldier to kill her; when my mother overheard the answer—"I won't waste bullets on you. You can lie down and freeze"—she decided not to ask for anything. Besides, she told me, she would have never asked to die, not even there. "I guess I have an optimistic nature," she said, shrugging.

I said, irritably, "But does it work as a poem?"

"It doesn't matter," my mother said. "There are enough people who want it all to be fiction. No need to distort the truth."

But how can I write without distorting the truth, even if I reproduce accurately, without regard for rhetorical effects, what I remember, now that so many of them are no longer able to tell their own stories? Will I turn into a Dick and smear myself all over the narrative, leaving a trail of self-pitying tears that discloses my presence like a snail track? Is silence the only path to truth?

TEN: *Growing Boys*

In bombed, drought-ravaged Romania, the postwar baby "boom" could more properly have been termed a baby fizz, manifesting itself in a sparse generation of only children. Among the three hundred or so families that lived in our building fewer than two dozen people were children. Of those, the five closest to me in age were male, and since as only children we needed each other for practically any game, we grew up gregarious, yet always divided between our street and our home behavior, between the savage society of children left to their own devices and the highly regulated manners and speech that we used in our contact with adults. Sometimes one of us would slip, as I did at my very proper great-aunt's house when I expressed admiration for snapshots from abroad with a Gypsy word then much in use among us children as the summation of all that was "cool." At times, one of us would be whisked from play and taken along to social duties. The face of the prisoner of civilized life, mirrored by those of the tribal cohort left diminished, bore the image of melancholy resignation and occasionally showed a small sign of rebellion such as rolled eyes or a tongue stuck out while the adults weren't looking. Other times, one of us would arrive for play in fancy dress or with eyes dancing with joy, and we knew that a family outing was in store, something fun entailing cake from which the rest of us were barred, and the child this time would leave us in triumph, happy to disengage from the daily round of games and fights and insults, especially since the playmates left behind were so visibly envious.

It never troubled my parents that I hung around with a gang of boys, although many people on the street and especially in our building made it their business to tell my mother after my father's death how improper it was. The general displeasure escalated in the summer when I took to wearing a pair of short overalls sent to me by the great-aunts in Detroit. Since my mother always made me wear my hair short, I became almost indistinguishable from my friends, who were also in short pants at that period in our childhood. The overalls freed me for climbing, since even my buddies were prone to make idiotic remarks about my underpants showing. I could swing on the swing as high as I wanted without incurring the muttered comments of passersby who appointed themselves arbiters of decorum. Yet I discovered that summer that the cross-dressing itself had become a fiercer bone of contention than my wild adventures with the gang. I loved the freedom of those overalls, which by the end of summer had gotten too short in the crotch, with a passion that mixed defiance and a new shame, for not even the expected and utterly banal remarks about my underpants had made me so conscious of my body. It was a feeling of profound disquiet from which I still, however, was young enough to find respite as I returned to my usual worn skirts for play and to freedom from the close scrutiny to which I'd been subjected all summer long: "Is it a girl or a boy? What a disgrace—you can't even tell!"

Yet we were bound to grow, together and apart, my playmates and I. In the riot times of summer, when most of our parents were working and we were on our own all the long day, we engaged in ferocious street contests and games. On a rainy day, we'd go to someone's house to play a board game, usually chess. I remember the summer when we all, more consciously than ever before, stood on the brink of that horrible divide, adolescence. The younger two among us, especially the one boy whose ethereal, white-blond Jewish mother was reputed to have affairs and whose dark, evil-looking German father was said to beat her, began uttering obscenities and constructing pornographic scenarios about people we knew. Our own parents were off-limits in this new discourse, but no one else was sacred. I mostly listened. My own body had betrayed me into womanhood sooner than I'd expected and certainly sooner than I wanted, and what I knew seemed so much more precise than these kids' imaginings that I felt a mixture of contempt and pity for them. They spoke unreservedly before me, and I still don't know whether they were attempting to draw me out or see how discomfited I might become, or whether they continued to think of me as one of the gang. But my playmates' early, anatomically inexact fantasies gave me a new insight into the male psyche, something other than what I already knew about boys fighting, competing, staving off the boredom of the long summer days, and in adulthood I find little about men's pornographic imagination that surprises me—often wounds me, as my friends' confusion about semen release and urine wounded me—but rarely shocks.

Our long-established, near-sibling familiarity led us to imprudent acts, which were all too readily misperceived by other people in the provincial little neighborhood where we lived. Once, all of us crowded onto a bench in the courtyard to watch a chess match between the finalists in one of our unending championships. There wasn't enough room for all of us and the chessboard, so I seated myself on Simon's bony knees. I can't remember which adult came by—his mother, mine—but under that gaze of wonder and disapproval we suddenly felt embarrassed about something we'd been doing for years, piling on top of each other to fit on streetcar seats and park benches. Later, my mother tried to explain to me that she herself had no worries about my virtue, but that other people might find it strange to see me on a boy's lap. After that, I started noticing IT, that look, more and more often.

A youngish man in our building had developed a comradely relationship with our gang. He would emerge, on his way to wherever, and we would feign an attack on him. He'd spar with us for a bit, we'd yell, "Gangster," at him, then he'd proclaim, "Enough, you win," and make his exit. One time only Cornel and I were in the courtyard when the Gangster happened by, and as we rushed him he kept Cornel away with one hand and said to me, "No, no, it's not right," leaving us both, mouths gaping, to stare at his retreating back. After that, to the surprise of the others, I no longer joined them in their Gangster attacks.

Since all of us but Simon would be sent by our parents on

errands that involved standing in line for a long time, I devised a system whereby whoever was hanging about would be obligated to accompany the errand runner. As I grew to look more and more like a girl, I found it advantageous to have one of my friends along, not only for the company. Men began making remarks about my body in my hearing, and occasionally a young man would follow me, verbalizing his desires several steps behind me while I fought tears of frustration and pent-up violence. My friends, who looked so much younger than I and behaved toward me as toward a comrade, served to give me the proper generational context for these predatory males, who were beginning to make the familiar streets unpleasant and who in cities of the West would make them unsafe.

But no context helped against the courtyard bully, Attila, named so by his culturally naive Hungarian mother. He was an older boy who, for the most part, had shown no interest in us except to torment us in the rare moments when he wasn't engaged in mischief with kids his own age or swallowed up in his family drama, which I would sometimes witness from our kitchen balcony. The window of his apartment, directly opposite but four floors lower, appeared when lit as the stage of a nineteenth-century domestic theater. Thus I knew that his stepfather beat him, frequently and hard, with a belt. One time, when he became particularly angry, he hit Attila's mother too, then smashed a chair and hit Attila with a chair leg he'd wrenched off, a technique of "using the environment," as my self-defense teacher calls it, that my father had told me his own mother was prone to in moments of fury. In the winter of my eleventh year, Attila looked at me as if for the first time. He began to join our games and invent disputes that required picking a fight with me. Since he was much larger than I, I would often lose and come home bloodied. My mother started to get tired of the spectacle and of my complaints against Attila. "Have nothing to do with him," she counseled. "Whenever you see him, go in the other direction." But I was embarrassed to tell her that Attila picked fights with me because, as he had declared to all, he had decided he liked me.

One time I went to meet my friends in fancy dress. I was about to go to a party of my mother's friends, and I wore a hat my mother had fashioned from the plaid fabric of a dress I had loathed in early childhood and from some lovely lavender wool and navy ribbons. We were in the street, fascinated by a new vendor who had brought a cart drawn not by a horse that looked about to die, like most horses in the city, but by an adorable and healthy little donkey. We stood around petting the animal, and Attila came and, as usual, taunted me. I decided to heed my mother's advice and ignore him. He began escalating the insults. I continued to ignore him. Exasperated by the lack of attention and by our joint interest in the donkey, he punched me hard in the face and started pulling off my hat. I heard the seams between the fabric and the wool give way and knew what pains my mother had taken with those stitches, and that she'd think it was my fault for having stayed in Attila's presence, and I went blind with rage. I kicked and bit and punched and shoved until I stopped, exhausted and battered from return kicks and punches, and saw Attila put his hand to his cheek, now gashed, look incredulously at the blood on his hand, and start to cry. I was glad he ran away because at the sight of his tears I softened, but that public display of childish pain so humiliated him that he never bothered us again.

I was to become all too familiar with Attila-like assertions of dominance as expressions of erotic interest. As I left Romania and my childhood friends, I entered the fully gendered world of Western adolescence, which seemed in many ways a harder exile than the strictly geographic. I acutely remember the sexual anxieties attendant on my solo train rides, first between Brussels and Verviers, then between Verviers and Düsseldorf. One time, a large group of boys going from Brussels to their boarding school in Liège boarded the train and chose, instead of one of the empty compartments, the one I sat in. They crowded in on me, five or six on a seat meant for three, taking turns at sitting beside me, pressing their bodies against me, until I took my briefcase and stuck it between me and whoever sat next to me, which they seemed to appreciate as clever. Then they began talking of their sexual conquests in the pornographic language I had grown accustomed to with my friends, and, though this verbal assault by strangers was altogether more offensive, they almost made me laugh. A less prepossessing bunch of gawky, acne-ridden boys I'd hardly seen. In Verviers, when I told one of my fellow inmates at boarding school about the train encounter, she looked disdainful and said, "I would have made myself at ease. All they wanted was a little fun." And I was left to wonder whether there was something deficient in my personality that made me shrink into myself when so approached.

Practically each weekend that I traveled from Verviers to Germany, I was subjected to searches by the German customs officials, who took delight in lifting my change of underwear from my small suitcase and holding it aloft, asking me questions that I refused to understand until they switched to French. The return trip was easier. The Belgian customs guards didn't always find it amusing to behave like twelve-year-olds. But one night, as I sat alone staring into the night flashing by the train window, a sinister, short, dark man entered the compartment. I forced myself to read. Out of the corner of my eye I saw him reflected in the window and saw that he kept his gaze on me. Flustered, I stood up to open the window a bit. I hung with my whole weight to the handles without effect. He stood up and in very broken French offered to help. After that, there was no stopping him. He poured out the story of his life. He was a delightful, comical Italian imported by the Germans for some dirty work that they no longer did themselves, and he was going to Brussels to visit cousins. Of course he carried wine, among other things he was hoping they would take to Naples to his mother since they'd be going back before he would. This time the customs officials hardly looked at me, so eager were they to show this dubious foreigner their thoroughness. Of course they confiscated the bottle of wine. He laughed, his very dark eyes narrowing, and held up three fingers to me. "Three hours' work that wine cost," he said. "Fine stuff. I wanted them to enjoy how well I'm doing. But," he added wistfully, "these Northerners, they got everything, but they don't know how to live. No joking, no dancing. This beer, it just makes them stupid and heavy, not like red wine." I nodded, agreeing with all my heart, having found in that compartment at that unpropitious moment in his unlikely company the camaraderie with the other sex, neither boringly free of the pleasurable sparks of difference nor mired in self-consciousness, that I had lost and would so very rarely find again in the West.

For years now, I've been able to recognize the constriction of

breath, the painful tightness in the lungs that characterized my physical reaction to Attila's attentions and returned when my panties
were held up on display by the border guards and when those repellent boys violated my privacy and space. It comes upon me now and
again when I am forced into a social situation with academic colleagues who crowd me in much the same way, only on an intellectual plane, at conferences, professional lunches, meetings where my
presence is merely a spur for obscene displays meant to leave me outside, behind. And on occasion, I go back to my boarding-school-
mate's diagnosis and ask, why can't I make myself at ease? Why can't
I let them enjoy their little fun? Is it perhaps because I associate these
moments so strongly with my childhood friends' erotic scenarios,
where to piss on a woman was the same as to make love to her? And
knowing that I'd heard from my mother and her women friends all
sorts of stories of how they had foiled attempted assaults and rapes—
in the office storeroom, in the dark of the screening room as they
translated for the censorship committee, on the trains back from
concentration camps, even on our building's elevators—how did my
mother dare leave me, first in the care of men and then to my own
wits?

Surely, she must have thought childhood was an unbreachable
shield, and so for lucky me it was. For three years my father attend-
ed to my most intimate needs. We were inseparable for the better
part of the day, often, as I so clearly recall, walking long distances in
companionable silence, but also taking naps together, and going
swimming, and spreading oil and vinegar—my father's idea of sun-
tan lotion—on each other's backs so that we smelled deliciously of
green salad. Then, in the fateful summer of my father's death, I
began taking vacations in the mountains with my uncle, and continued to do so every summer till I left the country. We never had
money for separate rooms, and the rented rooms had only double
beds, so my uncle and I slept in one bed. He was so fearful of
wounding my innocence that he would wake early, on his only two
weeks off in the year, to go outside in the chill mountain morning
and perform his ablutions by the pump in the courtyard. My mother's
unsuspicious mind was met in kind by the men who raised me, for
whom I was, as I should have been, a child, not a woman in small.

Yet both would confide in me about dangerous topics like politics and religion, my uncle about the wretched medical training beginning to be practiced at the universities, so that I felt mature and capable.

My uncle, notoriously inept with money, would let me take charge of our daily expenses during vacations except for his momentary bending of the rules, such as the time when he bought an extravagant amount of salmon caviar, my favorite food, rare and expensive in Bucharest but plentiful, expensive, and unappreciated by the locals in the mountain town, while I climbed mountains with friends of my father's who had "borrowed" me for the day; or the time when he took me for dinner at the still elegant casino in the next town, the ex-royal summer residence, in recompense for what he had taken to be my disappointment. We had gone to Sinaia, where the express from Bucharest made a stop, to meet my mother's cousins, bound for Belgium, and say good-bye to them for the last time, or so I then thought. My uncle was gleeful—a telephone summons from Bucharest not to fail to meet them at the train surely meant a great big gift, no less than the bicycle I coveted, he conjectured, and told me so. I remained skeptical. These cousins had never been kind to me and had certainly never given me gifts before. Sure enough, my cool judgment proved right, and my poor uncle, crushed at the thought that he had raised my expectations, ushered me into the posh dining room of the casino and said, "This time, money is no object. Don't look at prices. Order what you want."

I remember the give and resilience of the breaded calf brains, the pleasure I felt at the good food, the slight anxiety that my uncle would spend all the money we had left on this meal, and my sorrow over his own disappointment with his order—stuffed zucchini—into which, he mourned, they had put chopped onions along with the meat. "But that stands to reason," I said to him, speaking from my culinary experience as witness at my mother's kitchen counter. "But I asked the waiter, and he lied," my uncle said, filling my heart with sadness for his continued faith in human nature despite the blows it constantly suffered, because my uncle, who but for this quirk was a most competent and progressive physician, was thoroughly convinced that onions and garlic were the bane of humankind and should be avoided by everyone at all costs.

What follies of extravagant compensation would my uncle have been driven to had he not been urgently called back to Bucharest that summer, the first of our vacations together? We had left my father ailing, else he would have been with us. When the notice came that my uncle was to be at the post office to receive a long-distance call, I began to fret. "Don't worry," he told me. "Perhaps your father's feeling better, and we need to meet him at the train," an idea that made me jump for joy, although I knew that my authority with money and plans would be much diminished on my father's arrival. He did not let me lead him by the nose as my uncle did.

At the post office I waited while my uncle took the call. I watched his hunched back recede as he went toward the designated booth and thought how funny it was that someone who looked so unimposing had people practically genuflecting before him. A few times I'd accompanied him on house calls and had seen old women try to bend over his hand, to his embarrassed protestations. Once, when I needed the attention of a lung specialist for a post-measles complication, he took my mother and me to a renowned pulmonary specialist in Bucharest. We sat together in the waiting room until the doctor, ushering a patient out, saw him, exploded into greetings and apologies for not noticing him sooner, and insisted on taking us immediately in, telling the two other patients waiting, "You have no idea who this man is." Neither had I, so I pulled on my mother's hand, demanding an explanation. "Later," she said, and she meant much later, because she must have thought the information too hard for me to absorb at the age of four.

My uncle subverted the racial laws imposed by Romania's fascist government wherever and whenever he could, with a nonchalance about his own safety that to some extent guaranteed his being above suspicion. Nobody could be that naive, to expose himself that way, the fascists thought. My uncle, with perfectly feigned innocence, would ask, "Oh, is Dr. So-and-So Jewish? What makes you think so?" and would go about his business, protecting all the staff directly responsible to him. He feigned incompetence and delayed firing his Jewish colleagues or nurses on some pretext of missing evidence or official forms until the fascist government toppled. Every Easter, my grandmother would cook a turkey, a rare delicacy to come by in those days, sent without fail by one of my uncle's wartime protégés, until the man emigrated to Israel.

But what I liked even better were the little gifts his poor patients, whom he always forgot to charge, would press into his hands or drop off at the apartment. One day when I was visiting I saw a little plate with greenish fruit on it. "What are these?" I asked.

"Fresh figs," my aunt said. "That's how they pay him now," she added, and I, who had never seen fresh figs before, mistook the contempt in her voice for admiration. "Have one," she said. "They're not very good."

I gingerly bit into the small pear shape, my teeth meeting with a toughness I hadn't counted on; then it gave, and I ripped open the skin and held the fig before me, marveling at the deep pink, seed-dotted flesh, at the grassy sweet taste that invaded my mouth. "They're wonderful," I declared, thinking that my uncle must be the best doctor in the world to merit the fruit of paradise, the fruit that I had only eaten on grand occasions in winter, all squashed and dry and strung ignominiously on a straw rope, come all the way from Greece.

At the post office of the small mountain town, when my uncle finally came out the pleated door of the booth, the violence of the news was writ large on his face. I never saw and hope never again to see someone so changed. Every inch of skin, from his bald pate to his neck, was the color of a fresh bruise. I knew instantly my father had died and I went wild with grief, while he tried bravely to pass on the "official" lie that he had gone to recuperate in Herculane. That afternoon my uncle made arrangements for me to stay on with my friend Alexander and his aunts and cousins, who by chance were vacationing in the same town. When he got to Bucharest, he told my mother, "The child knows. You might as well tell her," but my mother could not bear the double burden of her loss and mine. She traveled on the weekend to see me, convincing me with her frantic caresses and bouts of weeping of what I already knew, and passing on to me the virus, lethal for my father, that was to lay her low and incubate within me in the next days.

I remember a night of white dreams and a subdued morning, when Alexander's aunt drew the shades in the room where I lay and forbade the children to come in. I remember them sneaking in, going right up to my bedside, and rummaging through the nightstand, showing me a bar of soap and saying, "Blowing bubbles. Mum's the word," and leaving me not entirely sure whether I had dreamed them or they had been there, within touch of my contagious, fever-racked body. I remember being carried into a car and passing out, then waking up at home with my mother's face coming in and out of my darkness and lighting it briefly with a pale, fear-stricken beauty that seemed painted. A week later, my pediatrician took hold of my feet as I lay on my back, pressed against them so my knees came to my stomach, and instructed, "Push as hard as you can," whereupon my legs threw him against the bookcase on the wall opposite the foot of the bed. A couple of books crashed on his bald head, which made me laugh uncontrollably. "She's out of all danger," he announced, and my mother breathed in as if for all that time her head had been held under water.

While we were still in Bucharest, about a year after the Attila episode, my friends and I had another intruder in our midst, a boy from the country who'd come to live with relatives in our apartment building so as to complete his middle schooling in town. Although the same age as the oldest among us, he was the shortest. An outsider, he was impervious to our hierarchies and rules, which we found both outrageous and amusing. He began to talk sex as soon as he started hanging out with us, and at school he initiated a system of rating the girls according to bodily attributes. "He's anti-Semitic," we all agreed after a chance remark he'd made, but how could I point out to my friends that, like a Circe devoid of humor, he was turning them all into pigs?

Nelu was the most natural, unadulterated, unself-conscious pig I'd met at that age. When he discovered that Simon had a minor crush on the prettiest and most popular girl in our class, he took some pains to follow Georgia home and spy on her movements. He came back triumphant and told Simon, "You don't want her. I took a look at her mother, and she's all wrinkled, so that's just what she'll look like in twenty years." I was shocked, first because our wildest sex dreams never took in this span of time, second because Georgia's mother was an elegant, tall, slim woman who smoked cigarettes through an ivory cigarette holder and had seemed to me the epitome of sophistication. And I was frightened when my friends believed his genetic insights and bought his vision of Georgia's mother. At the time I didn't have Oscar Wilde's wonderful line, with which I could have demolished his constructions. Inevitably, the moment came when he fought with one or another of us. "I won't fight with you," he told me one evening when I was most anxious to punch his lights out. "All I have to do is hit you in the tits."

"Just you try it," I said, adopting the boxing stance my father had taught me.

"And besides," the coward delivered his *coup de grâce*, "you'll grow to be a fat cow like your mother."

I looked at my friends, who stood by staring at the ground and saying nothing, punched Nelu, who for all his talk was no good at defending himself, as hard as I could, turned on my heel, and left. In a certain way, that evening I turned my back on the playground forever.

Neither my mother nor the Herczogs were home when I came in. I took the darkened apartment as a stroke of luck; I needed time to recover, to begin to accept the idea that for a dirty-minded little hick all my mother was reduced to was a warning of what I'd become, a danger sign to keep off desire. I ran to the bathroom and gazed at my face in the mirror, as I had been doing for the last year. The charming gap between my upper front incisors, inherited from my mother, had closed up as my smaller, sharp adult teeth came in. The middle of my nose had begun to grow away from my face, my forehead to acquire two hollows over my eyes, my hair to turn from the auburn waves that matched my mother's to unruly dark curls like those I remembered my father fighting to keep away from his forehead each morning. I had lost the beauty of my mother's perfectly symmetrical features and was looking at an afterimage of my father's face. And I could sense that my body, already taller than my mother's, would never grow into that sensuous voluptuousness that had enveloped and warmed me in my lost moments, would never have the lovely, round strength of her flesh. About me the relatives will not sigh to my daughter as they do to me, "Ah, your mother, there was a beauty. People used to jostle one another on the street to catch a better glimpse of her." No one will write me, as a renowned painter, friend, and sometime colleague of my mother's wrote her in her seventieth year, "You didn't know it, but in the fifties at the *Contemporary Review*, when you walked into the press room in the morning, we men would melt in our seats. If you smiled, the day began for us." And yet my mother walked through life as if she had been an ordinary person, and she ended up in a country in which her body, not her moral weight or tenderness or explosive laughter, would be the thing that to most people mattered most.

*Mimi and her father,
Aaron, studio photo, 1932.*

*Mimi, age nineteen, and
acquaintances on a
Bucharest street, c. 1938.*

Mimi at twenty-five, on a balcony in Oradea,
shortly before being rounded up for deportation
to Auschwitz, 1944.

*Paula Tudorescu,
actress and friend, with
Paul and Mimi at the
spa Herculane, 1947.*

*Mimi and Paul at New Year's, 1948,
in a restaurant at Herculane.*

*Me and my father on a park bench
in Bucharest, 1950.*

My father, playing chess, c. 1955.

Anca and Paul at home, 1955.

Me with my uncle, Alexandru Lazarescu, in a Bucharest park, c. 1957.

Mimi and me (in Chinese costume) on our
balcony in Bucharest, summer 1958.

Eating chestnuts on the street in Brussels,
fall 1962.

Anca and Mimi in Amsterdam, January 1963, a week before departure for the United States.

On board the Rotterdam, en route to America, February 1963.

Mimi on board the Rotterdam, February 1963.

Me in our backyard in Harrisville, Michigan, October 1963.

At thirteen I was too young to understand Paris, although from the first I had it etched in my mind according to the circulatory system of the metro, coursing beneath the streets like the well-regulated flow from a healthy heart. The West, shimmering before me like the mythical promise of a Holy Grail, endlessly assuaging my desires, was to be everything that Romania was not, and more. What was it, after all, that was so chimerical about my expectations? I only wanted tolerance, plenty, perfect freedom, safe solitude—abstractions that I wedded to images of shining edifices, clean, windswept boulevards, horse-drawn carriages with purple leather seats, and of course gorgeous people clothed in rich and tasteful fabrics. I wanted to obliterate from my consciousness the Marxism that I had almost literally suckled at my mother's breast, as she and my father engaged in intense discussions about the direction the country should take in those early, heady days when it had seemed to them possible that what they constructed out of words might somehow become reality; and as they then took measure, almost daily, of yet another betrayal of their hopes. I no longer wanted to remember what's involved in production, in surplus value, no longer wanted to think about exploitation, those gems of "the Human Soul" and the "countless gold of the akeing heart." From the moment our apartment began to be divested of furniture, linen, pots and pans, and the precious radio by processions of rapacious strangers, neighbors, and even friends, I burned to be gone. For the first time I started getting bad grades in school. Then I stopped going altogether, with my mother's consent, since once the authorities knew that a child's family had been granted a passport, the child was ritually expelled from the pre-Communist Party world of the school in a ceremony mirroring the obligatory renunciation of citizenship that the adults were forced to perform.

Not that I cared any longer about having the red kerchief, mark of the Pioneer, ripped from my neck as if I were being stripped of military honors. That humiliation, presented by some of the teachers and by the Pioneer director of each school as the worst disgrace to befall any child or adolescent, had lost its sting for me and many of my classmates by the time we reached middle school. Initially, the red kerchief had been conferred as a sign of scholastic distinction; only the top students were allowed to wear it, and those of us who had received it even wore it outside school, to our parents' silent annoyance. Soon, however, more and more kerchiefs were given at more and more ceremonies, until all the students had them, since the point was not to honor the meritorious but to induct young cadres into the Party. Meetings about the role of youth in the Communist state followed fast upon the indiscriminate kerchief giving, and those of us who had been most proud of our red scarves started forgetting them at home. We would be sent back to fetch them, a punishment that got us out of either the unendurable meetings or the largely boring classes. *Realpolitik* began unfolding before our young eyes, making cynics of us rather too soon.

My mother's loss of occupation and its cause, her application for a passport, could not be kept secret from the school administration, since my mother was a public figure. Consequently, I was banned from "future Communist leadership" but only covertly, since the regime did not openly acknowledge the doctrine of children suffering for their parents' sins. I remember the end of the sixth grade, the last I completed in Romania, and the plots and counterplots surrounding the selection of the student who was to get the first prize. No wonder whole societies go to wrack and ruin when overworked people are forced to expend their energy on ideological face saving, and it takes all their courage to fight symbolic battles.

All the students, though in classes divided by gender for this course alone, had to take locksmithing so as to balance our effete academic training with something that required the labor of our hands. Our locksmithing teacher was a handsome young man with whom half the girls were desperately in love. He was a representative of the best type created by the regime in which my parents had believed: the child of poor, working-class parents, he had been given the opportunity to go to university and teach school, albeit a nonacademic subject. An untrained but passionate lover of classical music, he transferred some of his ardor for music onto the Bucharest symphony harpist, daughter of a Jewish family, whom he was seen escorting about town. His romance with the harpist only made him more desirable in the eyes of several of my classmates, who were more preoccupied with swooning over the teacher than filing the truncated metal oblongs that were to become the faces of our locks. Not that any of us brought any lock to completion, but some, including me, tried hard. Unlike some of the other girls, I wasn't yet worried about breaking nails or getting the dark powder from the filings into the pores of my hands and ruining their beauty. I was entranced with the idea of producing a tangible, useful object.

Why, then, did my doting uncle talk one of his ophthalmologist friends into writing me an excuse citing my strabismus as reason to avoid the girls-only home ec course? How did I seduce both him and my mother to the point where they perjured themselves to let me avoid something so harmless? For one thing, I think, my mother told my uncle about the home ec teacher, an older, illiberal woman bitter about her loss of status under communism, which upheld the honor of locksmithing but not embroidery as labor. For another, my poor mother would invariably rescue me from my aversion to needlepoint by using her precious spare time to finish my handwork. She would take the little napkin on which cross-stitch flowers were assigned to appear on her visit to her aunt's house, so she'd use chat time to work on it.

My great-aunt looked at me through her horn-rimmed spectacles, then turned to my mother and said, as if I weren't there, "What's wrong with her? Why do you do her work?" This was one of the two aunts by marriage who, during my mother's lonely adolescence, had rarely bothered to take her out on a Sunday from her boarding school when her father was away on business. My mother looked up from the napkin. "Two reasons," she said. "One, I always envied the girls who had mothers to help them finish their hand-work, and two, she'll have a profession and a family. When in heaven's name will she have time to embroider? What good has it done me?" My great-aunt shot my mother a look of pained reproach. Her own skills with the needle were legendary, and her failure to guide her niece through a motherless youth had given her pangs in later years, especially when my mother came back like a ghost from the dead at the end of the war. And then my great-aunt had had to work for a living only for a short time and never had children, so she could ply her needle with a leisure unknown by most women of my mother's generation.

Thus, from my own mother, who could put her hand to anything, from changing fuses to upholstering chairs to sewing fashions of her own design to copying any knitting pattern after just looking at it, as well as from the regime, I got the sense that needlework was a waste of time. Later, when as an adult I asked her to show me how to sew, she said, "I will not. If you learn, you'll feel obligated to do it. If you don't, you'll manage without and save yourself a lot of time." So at thirteen, freed from cross-stitches and stocking mend-ing, I threw all my bodily creative impulses into making locks.

My teacher must have been impressed with my seriousness. He winked at me one June day as the year was coming to a close, say-ing, "Another first prize this year, right, Vlasopolos?"

"I don't think so," I mumbled. My Romanian teacher, our class sponsor, had intimated to me that because of "external" reasons I would not get the prize that year.

"How so?" my shop teacher exclaimed, and proceeded to spread open the grade ledger, an immense folder the size of an artist's folio that teachers carried from class to class and that contained each child's grades for every subject. "What's this?" he said, frowning; when some of us approached his desk, he waved us away. Then he signaled to me to stay near him during recess. "Look at this," he said, taking an immense risk in opening the ledger to a student. "Doesn't this look a little fishy?" He pointed with the tip of the file to the line of grades under the name of the student who had come in second or third to my first place all through our elementary and middle-school years. My rival's grades in art, at which he did not excel, had been average, I knew. I could see that the 7s had been scratched out with a razor blade, the standard procedure for erasing ink so as not to rub and put a hole through the thin paper, and 10s had been substituted for them, thus raising his average above mine. I looked at my teacher's handsome, open face, and I shrugged, trying to be noncommittal—after all, he could be setting me up—but my eyes filled with tears. "Not to worry," he said cheerfully. "Where's Mihai when he's supposed to be cutting out his lock face? Out playing soccer." I didn't understand what he was telling me and didn't have time to think about it since he ordered me out for what was left of recess. All I knew was that there had been a conspiracy on the part of my teachers and principals to keep me from getting the honor I had earned.

At the awards ceremony that concluded the school year, I was so shocked to hear my name called for the first prize that I walked up the stage somnambulistically and barely responded when my Romanian teacher, who had a motherly affection for me, gave me a great big kiss in addition to the traditional handshake. Reflected in my mother and my uncle's faces was the same astonishment. My mother was struck speechless for some time, her prepared consolations and admonishments about the unfairness of the world out of place for once. On the way out, the locksmithing teacher caught up with us. "A good worker, your daughter," he said to my mother, who, making sudden sense of the ledger episode I had confusedly related to her, held out her knotty, strong, small hand and shook my teacher's large, callused one for what seemed like a long time, without saying a word.

So I luxuriated in skipping school, a prelude to our imminent departure for the West. The leave-taking was tinged with just a touch of bittersweetness since I would abandon not my childhood friends, whose parents had all applied for passports and with whom I firmly believed I'd be reunited, but my first love, a schoolmate, the first in a series of boys and men utterly unsuited to me whom I found attractive. In a psychic defense against melancholy that I now recognize in others about to leave, I began to break away long before our actual flight, so that by the time we reached the airport and were told that we could do no more than wave to friends and relatives left behind since they might slip us state secrets, or worse, something of value to take with us, I felt relieved. No long embraces, no close-ups of tearful faces, just frantic moving arms, a sea of waves like wings lifting me, bearing me up toward my reincarnation. I smiled from ear to ear while my mother held in her sorrow for fear of making me sad. That evening, as we emerged from the Paris metro and trudged up to the hotel designated for us by the Jewish relief agency that would loan us money for it, I looked at the Latin Quarter, saw nothing but ancient buildings black with soot, and cried, "This is Paris? It's so old and dirty," while my mother burst out laughing at my change of mood, her own mood altered by the myriad connections her mind had begun to make between the scene unfolding before us and the books, films, pictures, postcards she'd grown up on. The next day was her forty-fourth birthday, and we had not a centime between us to buy a single flower. Contrary to the news we'd received from earlier émigrés, the West was not eager to open its arms to us and make amends for our deprivations.

Yet old sooty Paris seduced me as I've not let myself be seduced otherwise, and my feeling for it will always retain an ambivalence made up of regret for lost purity and nostalgia for the novelty, the surprise of the awakening. Six months later, the taxi that took us to the train station for our departure for Brussels and thence to America passed from the Porte de Saint Cloud by a number of monuments and vistas that had ineluctably become part of my mental landscape and that I saluted with a greater twinge of sadness than, I confess, I had felt on leaving the city of my birth.

It seems to me now as if I never learned French, as if it was always there in my head and only needed honing now and then, first under my father's tutelage, from the primer with the drunk wrapped around a streetlight, then after his death with my aristocratic tutor, whose sons, now in jail, had been my father's pupils when as a starving university student he had supplemented the rare packages from home with lessons for upper-middle class children. My French tutor's story, at least, has a happy ending, or so I like to think. Her sons did get out of jail; since they had been baptized and raised in the religion of their father, they for the first time acknowledged their maternal Jewishness and so were allowed to obtain exit visas for themselves and their families to Israel. After a while, they managed to get their mother to join them there. I know she loved her sons and was happy to be reunited with them. What did they do in Israel, they who all their lives had deliberately shunned anything hinting of the Semitic? I remember my tutor's exceedingly elegant daughter-in-law, visiting somebody in our building shortly after it had become known that my mother and I were to leave. "How old are you now, dear?" she asked, then mused, "Ah, thirteen. Just the age I was when I first saw Paris."

As my mother and I huddled under blankets and coats for warmth in our Paris hotel that shut off the heat the first of April no matter what the weather, I was haunted by those words. Even during the Communist regime her family had shored up enough to keep comfortable, to buy clothes mailed to lucky and enterprising recipients by relatives in the West so that they all looked far better than the rest of us, and I thought of her at thirteen, riding in carriages, wearing beautiful feathered hats and green, always green clothes to bring out the green in her Asiatic eyes, staying in a lovely small hotel somewhere near the Opéra, in a room with a private bath no doubt, ordering breakfast brought on trays like the ones I saw on the floor outside other guests' rooms even in our poor one-star hotel, with crumbs of croissants and cups holding empty half-eggshells and steel pots with a trail of dried cocoa from the spout. It would be convenient enough, now when between long intervals we travel to France, to eat breakfast at a café, but even though I tend to shun extravagance not merely out of economy but out of a superstitious fear that the gods will sniff out my small good fortune, in France I always have breakfast brought to the room. The demons of deprivation I am exorcising are insignificant enough, small demons of snobbery and bourgeois satisfaction. How unlike my mother's demons, devouring fears that even in America sent her out frantic to the store every time she heard about coming winter storms, every time the freezer stock, neatly wrapped, labeled, and dated, fell below a good two weeks' supply of food not just for her but for my husband, my child, and me.

For that was Paris too, the endless good food, tomatoes shining out of the dreary February fog like bouquets of red balloons; the chicken carcasses, plump and so symmetrical they looked like cartoon chickens, browning on spits in front of butcher shops; the salads of enchanting colors—grated carrots, celery root, *ratatouille provençale*, green beans—winking from the crowded windows of the *charcuteries*. It was the unobtainable luxury of a Nuts candy bar, bought for me by an acquaintance and long-time resident, half of which I saved in the pocket of my coat to bring back to my mother, sick with the flu in our hotel room, because I wanted her to taste this marvel and I knew that we could never spend any of our five-francs-a-day allowance on one-franc candy bars. Paris taught me denial, the small daily heroism of not even uttering my desires, holding in even a too enthusiastic expression of admiration for anything that had a price on it, for inevitably I would see a look of preoccupation on my mother's face and notice her silence as she calculated by what sacrifices she might contrive to buy me pleasure, and the sadness that almost always concluded her calculations.

But the Louvre was free on Sunday, and for the price of a skipped meal we could go to the movies. There I learned not only why movies, which had always been part and parcel of my daily life, were a greater opium than religion but also what it meant to lose one's personhood. People lose many things at the movies, and I could say that I lost my innocence, only not in the general sense of that phrase. I discovered that practically every time my mother and I went to the movies, a man would seat himself on the other side of me and drape a coat on the armrest we shared. Sometime in the course of the film, I would begin to feel his hand fingering my thigh. I was so stunned when this first happened that I thought I must be mistaken, but the sensation persisted. From then on, whenever it happened, I would violently push the coat and hand away. Occasionally I would hear a murmur of excuse and see the fellow slither away. Other times he'd protest loudly, "What's the matter? What got into you?" at which point my mother would threaten to call the usher and the man would change seats in a huff, as if persecuted by hysterical females. I wonder to this day whether my experience was an anomaly, something brought on by my being only with my mother and by our being so perceptibly foreign, or whether this was common filmgoer practice in Paris in the sixties, whether it still is. And of course, I wasn't innocent of desire—after all, on the streets everywhere there were lovers kissing so long that their mouths and bodies seemed to melt into each other, and on the screen there were Alain Delon, with his gorgeous blue eyes, and the close-up kisses and glimpses of bodies that none of us had seen in Romania suddenly giving my sexual reveries an objective correlative. But who were these men who thought that because I was in the theater and I was young and there was an empty seat next to me they could play out their fantasies on my thigh? What had that to do with *my* desire, with my dreams of the boy I had left behind in Bucharest, of a stranger who looked very much like Alain Delon, dreams to whose rhythms I walked along the Left Bank and often crossed the bridge to the Ile de la Cité, where Notre Dame de Paris, sooted over in those days like negligée lace, like boudoir sin, rose, always surprising one's consciousness, above the Seine?

Amid our poverty, somehow, my mother would find the odd 25-centime piece and slip it to me to buy a rolled-up sheet of paper filled with corn for the pigeons in the park of Notre Dame. I would walk down from Place Maubert, trying each time to take a different street to the Seine, once the street with the arts-and-crafts supplies shop whose odor of fresh notebook glue and inks I would breathe in longingly, once Rue du Chat qui Pèche, which was so narrow that only pedestrians could pass. Did my mother let me buy corn for the pigeons in memory of the balcony-feeding birds for which my father saved all the tablecloth crumbs? Did she react against the outrage of a cousin by marriage, who came from Brussels to greet us when we first arrived and chided me about spending money to feed the pigeons when we had so little but didn't, as my mother liked to recollect, think to take out her billfold and give me a five-franc note? Did she simply think it was the cheapest way to procure me harmless joy?

I know that had my father been with us, he would have disapproved, despite his having made me adore pigeons. He had grown up poor and resented spending for ephemeral things; it took him a long time to understand how important fresh flowers were to my mother. Once, during one of their interminable walks through Bucharest, which became the only way they could talk with some certainty of not being overheard or tapped, my mother noticed a brooch in the window of a jewelry shop and stopped to comment that it was surprisingly tasteful among the garish stuff surrounding it. Some blocks farther, my father pretended he'd forgotten to call someone, ran off, and reappeared a few minutes later with the brooch. So he didn't mind the money, in this case a much greater sum than the price of flowers, offered by Gypsies persistently and loudly at every busy street corner. But just as he had not bought my mother flowers in their early years together, he forbade me my ephemeral enchantment, balloons. Only street vendors sold them, mostly in parks, where children whined until their parents gave in and bought them a balloon. Whining had no effect on my father, but I had my mother and my uncle to run to if I wanted one and would bring balloons home from my walks with my uncle, to my father's mutterings about how I exploited my poor uncle and how the stupid things would burst or deflate anyway.

My mother would laugh, and on those rare days when she thought she had a bit of money to burn, she'd abscond with me for "a whirlwind," as she called it, meaning a little adventure with caution thrown to the winds, on which she'd buy me chocolate pastry and balloons and whatever other little thing was available and affordable. After he came out of jail, my father made practically no money for nine months. Afterward, he was in such demand as a tutor that he not only made money but had to turn people down almost daily. In the interim he once had a talk with my mother; I don't know whether I overheard it or she told me about it many years later, but our little whirlwinds stopped for that period. My father felt he could not compete in the same way for my affection. He didn't see that, as the parent who stayed home, he'd become the necessary and unglamorous anchor, my mother the exciting visitor.

The closest we came to such whirlwinds in Paris was when my stepfather-to-be came for a weekend from Düsseldorf, where he sold contraband jewelry. He would give my mother a wad of bills right at the station and say, "You're so much better with money than I. You keep it"; then he'd gradually extract it all from her during the weekend, mostly to spend on food, most of which he ate, so that by the time he left there'd be nothing, not even the memory of pleasure. "But didn't I give you all my money?" he would later remonstrate in one of his countless fights with my mother. At first, she'd say nothing. "You gave it to me and then made me pay for everything you wanted, which by some coincidence always equaled or exceeded what you gave me," she'd tell him much later, when the leitmotif would appear, but these corrections to his imagined scripts were indications that my mother had already given up on their togetherness.

The enchantment of Paris stole upon me retrospectively. I didn't know any better, after all. Paris for me was the West, or at least representatively so. It took distance and time for me to measure and savor its uniqueness, and, I admit, to forget how intensely I hated it during our six-month stay. I have American friends and acquaintances who, in reply to my nasty remarks about the meanness of the Parisians, say, without an *arrière pensée*, "But they couldn't have been nicer or friendlier to us." Even my husband, on his first trip to Paris for our belated honeymoon, forewarned by all my stories, found his fears completely without basis—everyone could not have been nicer to him. And in my resentful heart I judge my friends and husband harshly, knowing as they seem not to that the French, for all their cultural elitism, still preserve the Europeans' American mystique, still see every American as a millionaire in ordinary tourist drag.

I read in the paper, on Bastille Day, 1993, as it happened, that the French passed a law making it impossible for foreigners to marry French people and stay in France, bring their families to France, or stay beyond the strictest time limits, and making it easier for the police to round up delinquents for deportation. That, alas, is also the France I knew, where after an old woman made a purchase of one slice of ham at the local deli, I heard the customers whisper behind her back, "Elle n'est pas de chez nous" (she's not from these parts), "chez nous" being defined as the length of the block. It was the place where I felt, in my cheeks burning with shame, my difference, not as a Jew-Greek but as a member of the more encompassing category of dirty foreigner. At the time my mother and I lived in Paris, the French Right was obsessed by the influx of the *pieds noirs* from Algeria, and before I opened my mouth, I with my olive skin and frizzy hair sent salesgirls into palpable aversion at the bakery where my mother sent me for bread.

I was to meet the French Left not in the petty-bourgeois establishments of the neighborhood but among my high school teachers; they treated me with undisguised contempt as a deserter who had come out to spread ugly rumors about the ideal society. As soon as he set eyes on me, my teacher of Russian announced that I was only one among a number of refugee Romanian students of his, "none brilliant, few even adequate." How could I begin to point out that not only were we studying Russian through the medium of a language not our own, French, but that our aversion to Russian had deeper roots? Would he have understood that back there, where I grew up, at first only the reactionaries hated the Russians? As my mother would remind me, the Russians had been the ones to break open the labor-camp gates that the Nazi guards had locked behind them as they fled. How could my father, repeatedly threatened and sometimes battered by the Romanian Iron Guard, not look to the Russians as liberators when they marched through Bucharest flushing out German and homegrown fascists? But it turned out that they didn't simply march through: they set up headquarters; they sent representatives to all the labor syndicates.

As the nationalization of industries and land proceeded after the election of the Communist government, the Soviets became more and more entrenched and the Stalinist presence more pronounced; among other signs, such as the huge posters of Stalin everywhere, Russian had become overnight the only foreign language in schools. Russian institutes proliferated, and Marxist-Leninist study groups became compulsory for high school and college students, as well as for non-Party members in the workforce. By the time I started studying Russian, instead of thinking of it as Pushkin's language, and Tolstoy's, we reacted to it as the language of the people who took their yearly tribute of the grain in Romania, leaving us in want. I thought of it as the language of the men my mother would never call anything but brutes and barbarians because they exercised *droits de seigneur* upon all the desirable young women at the Film Distrib-

ution Enterprise where she worked, and these young women would
then come to her office in tears to ask her for the name of an abor-
tionist and a loan for the procedure. Could my teacher in Paris
understand what separated the failed emigrant students whom he
taught Russian and the subject matter we had learned only to forget?

My teacher of German, who carried *L'Humanité*, the PC paper,
under his arm every morning, one day divided us into teams in order
to play a game of cultural literacy. He would ask the questions and
award points to the team who answered first. I distinguished myself
for the first time in the course that I loathed most. Without realizing he was making me an example at a time when my most ardent
desire was to pass through life transparently, or at least as a skilled
chameleon, he pointed his index finger at me and told the class that
I was representative of a true communist education, which was clearly superior to theirs. In his class I learned the duplicity and rage of
the oppressed; tongue-tied by self-consciousness and fear, I said
nothing but harbored utter contempt for this man who mistook the
knowledge I had gleaned mostly from my parents and their friends
as the cultivation of a communist. In this postmodern moment, I
find it amusing that what that petty Western communist valued
about his political *beau idéal* was a knowledge of the canon, particularly that of German derivation.

My experiences with schoolmates and teachers, my Paris world,
made it hard for me to muster anything like my mother's only occasionally dented enthusiasm for the French, whom she had met in
two of the slave-labor camps during the war and whom she regarded as a revolutionary, anarchic people, ready at the drop of a hat to
oppose injustice despite the risks. In retrospect, I recognize the ker-
nel of truth in her perceptions; nowhere else did I find classmates,
colleagues, neighbors, even friends so quick to mobilize and demon-
strate against unfairness. I remember the entire school suddenly
emptying the sacred lunchroom to run into the courtyard and chant
"Down with the Head of Studies" until the principal came down, listened to the charges that a student had been unfairly dismissed from
lunch, and gave the crowd some satisfaction. I was exhilarated. I
knew from experience that in Romania it was impossible even for

middle-school students to vote for any but the candidate selected by the Pioneer Director.

But what I didn't know, despite my joy in freely participating in one spontaneous demonstration at the Lycée Claude-Bernard in Boulogne-Billancourt, was that the mass of students in the West, as close as Belgium and as far away as Detroit, would not be so easily moved, would, in fact, hardly be moved at all except in cases where self-interest played a large part. Inevitably, as time passed, my disenchantment with Paris dissipated in the flow of ruder awakenings in other cities and other countries of the West, leaving behind contradictory feelings twisted and braided like the silt at the bottom of a dry river bed, and as impossible to extricate from one another and hold up between one's fingers for discernment in the light of reason. And, inevitably for someone obsessed with harmony and order, I began to yearn in other cities for the inescapable, beautiful rationality of the metro where no one who can read can get lost, for the public-access promenades along the Seine, for the breathtaking contrasts between the medieval streets of the Latin Quarter harrowed by church bells every half hour and the extraordinary spans of squares like Place de la Concorde or wide avenues like glacier paths radiating from the Arc de Triomphe.

After Bucharest and Paris there were the cities I knew fleetingly, Brussels, Düsseldorf, Frankfurt, Amsterdam. When I arrived in Brussels in the middle of my first Western summer, I no longer had the inviolate gaze of wonder that explained all oddities as "the way things are in the West." The Romanian expression "in strangeness," used to describe territory that lay outside the ever-changing boundaries of the country but also to define the corresponding state of mind, "among strangers, amid an alien culture," no doubt contributed to my own attribution of individual quirks and peculiarities to the customs of the wide world I was entering. But having resided in Paris for six months gave me a point of Western comparison, and I knew at first glance that Brussels would fall short.

Unlike Paris, Brussels was not a city to inspire violent emotions in the temporary sojourner. It had its own staid, calmer charm, except for the incomprehensible divisions among its two-tongued population. The riots that periodically broke out struck us as not only senseless but quaint—this was what they fought about, which language should prevail, at a time when we were made acutely aware of the worthlessness of our own language outside Romania's borders? Of course, it was easy for us to adopt this false naiveté, we with our cardboard IDs issued by the United Nations labeling us stateless, conferring on us a world-weary, urbane detachment from national passions and at the same time the vertigo of rootlessness. We felt envy too that this was what the Belgians had—food, leisure, freedom, housing, clothes—to fight about, although the absence of necessities, as we well knew, did not forge national unity either.

I began missing Paris, its more spectacular parks, crustier bread, more succulent shrimp, more imaginative window displays, more French French, and the spontaneous, genuine wit of even its lowliest citizens. But Brussels became my threshold to vital comfort. Cheaper by far than Paris, it offered a pair of stylish shoes my mother was able to buy for me, my first grown-up shoes, navy, with tiny stiletto heels and straps across the ankles. I wore them for some years, on grand occasions. They always put me in a cheerful mood since they invariably evoked the same image I had conjured when I first tried them on—of playing soccer in them and puncturing the ball with a swift kick of those extravagantly pointed tips. For, despite the pointed toes and sharp heels, the shoes fit wonderfully. For the first time in some years, I had properly sized shoes.

In Romania, shoe half sizes were considered a capitalist frivolity, and the Communist economists phased them out soon after the takeover. My feet, which had yet to grow to adult size, perversely settled at 6 1/2 for at least two years before we left the country. Children's shoes, relatively comfortable, went up only to size 5, so that except for blessed summertimes when I wore American-made sandals, with plenty of adjustable straps, that my mother's aunts from Detroit sent her, or times when I could put on cloth sneakers, which we were not allowed to wear to school, walking became for me more or less painful. My mother would take me shopping for shoes. One of the great comforts of a communist economy was that the proverbial "you've seen one, you've seen them all" unfailingly applied to all stores, so one didn't need to comparison-shop. The nearest shoe store had the three styles featured at all other shoe stores throughout the country. I would settle on one and beg my mother for the size 6, which fit me snugly, but which, my mother knew, would constrict my feet unbearably soon after I had left the store. So she would talk me into a size 7, hoping for the growth spurt that would accommodate feet to shoes, a spurt that wouldn't come for another three years.

Then my mother would instruct me to pack cotton wads inside my socks to protect the backs of my heels from constant rubbing by the slipping shoes, only the cotton would move sideways and I would end up with welts that marked the shoes' contour around my ankles and with blisters, which sometimes broke so my socks stuck to the exposed flesh. My mother would give me her precious, pre-war heel-plate inserts, which she now wore for temporary relief from similar chronic problems, in the hope that they would elevate my wounds above the rub line. I would alternate wearing and not wearing them, waiting for each set of blisters to heal in turn. I still have scar tissue on the backs of my heels due to my feet's willful, unregimented growth. I remember when my mother and her friends got together they often discussed footwear, and they all tsked in sympathy at the sorry and seemingly irremediable state of my feet, which my mother would have me display. They would then plunge into a veritable sea of nostalgia for "before the war," when Bucharest was reputed to have the best shoemakers in Europe. "Women would come from Paris to have their shoes made to order here," my mother's friends would sigh, a story confirmed for me by a Parisian acquaintance some years later.

In addition to the shoes, Brussels also afforded us cheaper food at the cafeteria, called in French by the English phrase "self-service"—accent on the last syllable—of the large Common-Market department store newly opened next to the central railroad station. Thus in Brussels my mother said good-bye to the excitement of cooking illegally in rented rooms. I was to become intimately acquainted with that railroad station, as later with the Düsseldorf station, since for the first time in my life I would be separated from my mother, who would join my stepfather in Germany where there was legal work to be had while we all waited for the U.S. quotas to open up for the next year. My mother's marriage took place sometime in August 1962, at the Brussels City Hall. I was not present. I forget what excuse my mother invented to keep me away, thinking that the ceremony might give me pain. At the time, I still liked my stepfather a great deal, and the exclusion surprised me. After my mother's death, underneath a pile of carefully sorted health insurance bills, I found a wedding picture of her, with her cousin from Brussels and a few Romanian friends, and with the figure of my stepfather carefully clipped, so that my mother stands smiling, incredibly youthful at forty-four, alone, on the steps of the City Hall, with a group of smiling people behind her and a hole to her left to be filled by whatever background might lie behind the picture, anything but the image of her temporary husband.

At the Brussels railroad station one needed to buy a platform ticket in order to pass from the huge entrance lobby, with the familiar ticket counters behind glass, on to the actual platforms. This system was designed to cut down on indigents hopping on trains without paying at least a nominal fee before being caught and made to get off. Although it was new to me, my mother told me that the system was common practice in many countries. She then told me a story that to her typified German enslavement to regulations and that later I saw replicated in Mel Brooks's *Blazing Saddles* as an example of the bad guys' stupidity. Somewhere on the way from Auschwitz to the first slave-labor camp, my mother watched the SS contingent, which had already conquered and laid waste the little central European town they were passing through, stop and dutifully buy platform tickets in order to board the army trains that were to take them to their next onslaught. Trying not to seem sad for my sake, my mother often walked me only as far as the ticket gate, our financial state making it senseless for her to spend money merely to stand on the platform to wave me off to boarding school in Verviers.

Our separations were made more poignant by our common discovery, three months into her marriage, that my mother had made a huge miscalculation in thinking that by marrying she was providing some security for me in the event of her death. We found out what my mother had dimly suspected but not particularly wanted to face, and what all her friends and relatives insisted that she close her eyes to, namely, that Dick was a graying adolescent, emotionally incapable of taking care of himself, let alone of accepting the responsibilities of parenthood. I remember with special vividness the streetcars in Brussels because both incidents that rent the fabric of our hope in my stepfather occurred, curiously enough, on those public conveyances. The first seemed fairly minor. My stepfather made a feeble joke in Romanian about the rather extravagant hat worn by a woman nearby, and my mother and I laughed, knowing that he expected it. Dick threw a tantrum on the very streetcar, mercifully in Romanian so people could see his anger but not hear the preposterous reasons for it. Vainly we tried to pacify him, reminding him of the joke he'd just made. He insisted that we had looked at him, then at each other, and had laughed *at* him.

The notion of a conspiracy by us against him was utterly ludicrous at that period of our life together; for the next year and a half, before the marriage dissolved in all but name, my mother wasted her energy mediating between the two teenagers she lived with, explaining him to me and undoubtedly me to him. His more and more frequent and increasingly violent tantrums, she tried to reassure me, were due to his uncertainty in going into the unknown, a new continent, where his skills would be devalued and his expectations disappointed. And when we got to America, the same explanations continued, strengthened by the reality of disappointments that my mother had envisaged. I said nothing, making everything harder by my sullen silence, but in my mind I would ask, "What about you? Why don't you take your anxieties out on us? We're all going to— are in—a new country."

When in November, three months after they married, my stepfather, the most profligate of men, refused on the principle of economy to get a streetcar transfer so we could catch a second streetcar that evening despite my pleas of fatigue, I knew he would never be a father to me. All through adolescence I was plagued with cramps of acute intensity that announced the beginning of my menses. On the streetcar that evening, I turned pale, which for me means greenish, and started sweating profusely. I looked as ill as I felt. I begged my stepfather to buy a transfer ticket so I wouldn't have to walk the mile and a half back to our rooms. Outside the streetcar, when my mother took him aside to tell him what I was too embarrassed to say myself, instead of generously offering to catch the second streetcar, transfer be damned, he started shouting so loudly that people cracked open their wooden shutters to look out onto the otherwise dead street. He told my mother that she had spoiled me and that he would put an end to it. My mother said nothing. We walked back in silence. When we got back to the boarding house, she whispered to me, "Don't worry." I don't know what happened between them, but the next morning my stepfather apologized, with what was to

become his unbearably predictable abjectness following his outbursts, eyes moist, throat closing up in admiration and tenderness
for his own goodness. I must admit I fell for it the first fifteen times
or so. By the end of our life together, he had pushed my mother and
me into the indivisible alliance against him that he had projected on
us aboard that Brussels streetcar, an alliance that brought the two of
us into an unnaturally intense intimacy and forced me prematurely
to take on a protective role vis-à-vis my mother.

When I was little and we went to the mountains for our vacation,
renting rooms from villagers, I was told that domesticated ducks will
not hatch their eggs; a hen must be fooled into thinking the duck
eggs are hers and incubating them in order for the farmers to have
more ducks. At a house on the outskirts of the little mountain town
where I was staying with my aunt and uncle, I saw one such hen take
her ducklings into the yard and then follow them, squeezing
through the slats of the wooden fence, emitting pathetic clucks, as
the ducklings headed for the mountain spring flowing through the
ravine across the road. She ran up and down the shore as the fuzzy
gold balls bounced on the frothing, shallow water and would occasionally be carried away a few feet by the current. She watched, held
captive on land by an instinct stronger than the maternal, as they
made their way back. She knew she could do nothing but wait and
exhort in chicken talk, which they understood but did not speak,
until they got hungry and were ready to be led back to the yard. The
bond between immigrant parents and their children resembles that
of hens and ducklings. The innumerable conventions of child-rais-
ing in one society change so drastically in a new culture that the parents are left behind to fret, unable to come to their children's rescue
and depending on the children's good will to be temporarily reunited
with them.

Since my mother and I lived out a domestic gothic with Dick for
the first three years of our life in the United States, we were dis-
tracted from working out the more familiar patterns of adolescent
separation or even the novel ones of immigrant children's puzzling
and abrupt departures from the old ways. After my mother and I
moved away from the apartment the three of us had shared, I began
breaking away with a vengeance, which my mother resisted with

equal vigor. She would imagine nonexistent dangers but not even suspect the chances I knew I was taking. She would mock my attempts at assimilation, not realizing how torn I was between being faithful to what I saw as a higher, more civilized mode of behavior and wanting to be, at least at moments, like everybody else—something I never managed, though I laid down my knife to switch hands and pick up the cut meat with my fork, and intoned words with a midwestern nasal twang that prolonged vowels into diphthongs. Inevitably, I picked up cues about American culture that my mother did not notice or, having noticed, rejected, such as the surface friendliness of empty chat, greetings, and smiles. "Why did that woman smile at me?" She'd turn to me, as if I were the guide through this new universe. "She's trying to be friendly," I'd say blandly, while my mother would launch into a critique of the superficiality of American notions of friendship, and I would fall silent or contradict her, either of which made us end up arguing. Her refusal to let things be made her the target of attacks and forced me to come to her defense. One time, a woman about her age cut in front of her in the supermarket line, and my mother remarked on it. The woman turned on her with the cliché, "Go back where you came from," whereupon I began questioning the woman about her origins and suggested that she too go back where she came from, since she was not an American Indian. Even on these occasions, I would bestow upon my mother the mixed blessing of knowing both that I was loyal and that I was better able to win in this new world.

Having had to struggle against oppressions unimaginable to many Americans, my mother over time deliberately abandoned the skill of small talk. She would be sitting in a plastic chair at a Bell Telephone office waiting, as so often she had to do, to return her phone and be issued another for yet a new apartment, when suddenly I would turn to find her in intense discussions, mostly with older black women, about politics and education. At my husband's family picnic, where the level of political discourse is minimal at best, she and a couple of the men would plunge into long, embittered assessments of labor-management relations, to the displeasure of the women, who wanted to steer the talk back to who had married and who had died. At these gatherings, one of my husband's uncles by marriage has fallen almost completely silent since my mother's death. He once took me aside and said, "I could talk with your mother."

Yet I often felt caught, as in a closing door, between what I knew was needed for the circumstances and my mother's utter disregard for social niceties. Not that her manners, especially as host, were not impeccable. It was just that she rarely talked about anything dispassionately. My irony would wound her, and it was only later, when she had had ample proof of my unfitness for assimilation, that she became the best audience for my jokes. For despite it all, she could laugh, dissolve in peals of laughter that made us the target of outraged gazes from genteel people, since inevitably my mother, the least snobbish of anyone I've even known, would comically deflate the pretensions of a place or people by mimicry of word or facial expression.

For my mother was far more than a fool hen raising a foreign brood; she gave me my intellectual formation. In one of her many prescient political moments, she saw the future and saved me from the degradation of a system in which a spark of spirit would set off alarms as if it were a conflagration—burn, baby, burn. After living in the United States, she would remark, "There, you couldn't allow yourself to say anything for fear they'd hear you. Here, you can say anything, shout it at crossroads, but nobody will listen." And to save me, she severed herself from her chief intimacy, her greatest love—a language whose rhetoric, nuances, brutalities, and subterfuges she inhabited fully. So it was that my acculturation became for her even more painful because she understood to what extent her own intellectual standing had been diminished when she had left her sphere of knowledge.

Sometime in my fifth year of living in English, it suddenly came to me, with the effect of a thunderbolt, that the language had become supple in my mind. The only similar experiences of illumination I've had were when I first began to swim and when I centered a lump of clay on a potting wheel. Suddenly, conscious effort has seeped away, body has taken over, everything feels right. My mother, who had devoted most of her life's work to finding the closest correspondences between languages, told me with great sadness, not long before her death, when she was thinking of writing a book,

"I've lived here for over twenty years, and English is still a foreign language to me." I tried to console her, pointing out how well she spoke and wrote it compared to most native speakers. "But," she insisted, "when I write Romanian, it sings under my pen. It's effort-less." I was happy then that I had not told her, long ago, about my having started even to dream in English.

After Brussels, there was Verviers, tucked away in the hills, almost not changed from the walled city it had once been, charming to pass through, subject of a traveler's reminiscence—for me, however, the site of a series of painful ignominies. In Verviers I learned about dialects, girlhood conspiracies, and my own thitherto untapped Ithacan wiles that surfaced in dire psychic need. There were two locations for my humiliation: one, the Lycée Royal, where I studied; the other, the boarding house of the Ecole Normale, to and from which we lycée girls were walked by a young woman employed to her visible unhappiness as our *surveillante*, an apt and untranslatable word meaning among other things an overseer.

At the Lycée Royal, in gym class, I managed to lose all self-possession when the teacher ordered me to climb down a gigantic wooden frame made up of sixteen smaller frames through which I was to twist my body in a diagonal movement from the ceiling to the floor. I easily climbed to the top, hung by my hands and the back of my knees through the top square, and became paralyzed by fear. The square frame swung gently, just centimeters from the wall, and I could see myself being squashed against the wall in my downward movement or slipping and ending up mangled on the cement floor. My teacher had no sympathy with my imaginings; she ordered me to perform the descent, each time more severely, while I swung unmoving from the top of the frame. I became gradually more imbecilic in my responses to her orders, until she had to let me forego the writhing exercise and allowed me to climb directly down. She then had all her students go through the exercise in order to convince me that anyone could do it, but to her and my classmates' open contempt, I abjectly fought against it till she desisted.

In music class, we were required to look at a score and sing it. I asked the teacher if I could name the notes rather than sing them because I had no voice, but what I said was, "Je ne peux pas chanter." This put my classmates in hysterics. "Who's not letting you?" they wanted to know. In the context, it became clear that the Flemish influence, which the Walloons in Verviers would have denied and historically have denied even to the death, had transformed the French verb that confers power and agency to a Germanic verb in thrall to higher authority. "I am able, I can," and "I cannot" became "I am allowed to" and "I mustn't." When I uttered a slang phrase of mild contempt I had learned from my French schoolmates, the surprised Belgians raised their eyebrows and laughed at my foreign quaintness behind my back until Gisela let me in on the cause of their snickerings. She was a German girl studying to be a teacher at the Normal School who, despite being three years older than I and having already had lovers, had begun looking out for me, no doubt recognizing the ostracism she herself had had to endure and had defeated with her unfailing good disposition and often her moral courage. I replied, not without studied arrogance, "It's a Parisian expression. I don't expect them to understand it," and she said nothing, but her eyes widened, and soon the mockery, at least on that account, died down.

Gisela's look when I mentioned Paris was replicated many years later when, after my husband and I returned from Paris, we visited his grandmother. She was a woman the size of a seven-year-old, wiry, fast, obsessed with getting bargains. We would run into her at the large open Eastern Market in Detroit on a Saturday, laden with more food than she could possibly consume, because it was so much cheaper than at the local market. Over years of living alone, she'd haunt every department-store sale and buy an assortment of things, dish towels, underwear, baby clothes, nylon stockings, which she would put away for future use or presents and which were found, still in boxes from stores that had ceased to exist, after her death.

Savvy peasant woman that she was, she hid her money in several banks and in various caches throughout her flat, betting on her children's expectations of hidden wealth rather than their affection against the time when she would need their care. But when Anthony and I came to visit her and she opened the little jewelry box and found the brooch we'd bought her, she held it up, her eyes wide as she looked beyond us into the distance of the mirage, and murmured, "Da Parigi." She who would literally push gifts back into the giver's hands and refuse, loudly protesting that she didn't need them, changed before our eyes, for a few moments, into an extraordinary apparition, a diminutive Madame Bovary loosed from the moorings of house and children and the endless sequence of mundane duties to sail on the seas of her own desires for luxury and worldliness. For even when all vestige of Europeanness falls from us women, Paris subverts our refuge in respectability, remains that call of what might have been, had we, like Ninotchka, got there in time.

It's curious that, although I remember the unexpected triumph of getting the highest mark ever given by the French teacher at the Lycée Royal, what I recall most distinctly from my passage through Verviers are the horrors of boarding-school life. Under the pretext of my incomprehensible foreignness and consequent lack of urbanity, my colleagues in misery treated me with brutal rudeness, ranging from commenting publicly on my "savage" table manners to throwing my precious new winter coat, for which I had carefully brought a wooden hanger, on the floor of the cloakroom after I had left it. One of them won a prize for a poem in a local magazine, and I, enamored of Baudelaire and Verlaine, asked if I might read it. Surrounded by her court, she looked at me in astonishment and said, "There's no point. You couldn't possibly understand it."

One time, when for some reason I no longer remember I was condemned to the limbo of staying over in the dorm for the weekend, the other girls who, like me, stayed behind the weekend exodus and were consumed with self-pity at being locked up for twelve continuous days, decided to amuse themselves. They concocted an elaborate plot that involved at least one of the boys, and this must have taken a great deal of deliberation, for surveillance was particularly heavy when it came to any exchanges between the boys and the girls, housed for propriety's sake in different and distant wings of the school. Sometime during the unbearable Sunday afternoon, a boy came knocking breathless at our dorm door to announce that the concierge had sent for me, that there was a long-distance call for me downstairs in his apartment—the only phone to which students had access. I rushed down the long stairway, torn between pleasure that my mother was calling me and fear that something might have happened. I knocked at the concierge's door. I knocked again, more loudly. The man appeared, displeased. I could see the table laden with Sunday dinner in the other room and his wife and baby waiting for him. I asked him about my phone call. There was none, of course. The boy had disappeared, and when the concierge, knowing that I could not have left the study room without the surveillante's consent, asked me for his name, presumably in order to report the joker, I could not tell him since I knew none of the boys except as a throng that made disgusting remarks every time we filed by them in the mess hall. The concierge slammed the door in my face. I walked slowly up the stairs to the horrid dorm—seventy plywood sleeping partitions, three toilets, and two bathtubs—and the proverbial "*esprit d'escalier*" struck me, not after the fact for once.

When I returned to the study room, the sky was already darkening. The girls who had raised my hopes and disappointed them more keenly than they probably suspected were waiting for me, faces red and puffed up with suppressed laughter. "How did it go?" they asked, although they had never evinced interest in anything about me excepting my savagery. "Great," I said. "My mother and I had a lovely chat. She might visit midweek to make it up to me for having missed the weekend," I added, full of cheer. Then, enervated by their meanness and my momentary parrying, I sat in my corner of the study room, letting the excoriating sting of Baudelaire's fragments "*Sur la pauvre Belgique*" soothe my diminished spirit. When the dorm filled again, I heard from my friend Gisela that the story of the fictitious phone call had made the rounds and that I was enjoying a measure of grudging respect from my would-be tormentors. It was a lesson I still fail to remember, brought home again and again, about how modesty and shyness are confused with stupidity while arrogance and cruelty are taken for signs of intellect.

Then one day, Gisela, my sole ally and guide through the hell of communal adolescent living, confided in me because she trusted me, as we stood before a huge window illuminated by a November dusk of particular splendor, that she was convinced Hitler had been a genius. True, he had gone too far too fast, but nobody could deny that he had been the genius of the century. I gazed into her blue eyes, iridescent in the dying light, and was struck dumb, but something in my expression must have said much, for although we remained cordial until my departure, we were friends no more. I wonder now if the look on my face as she told me an innermost secret that she had not dared tell the Belgians seemed to her as deep a betrayal as the abyss that her words opened for me. A dear friend once laughed at me when I told him I could not sleep with a Republican or a religious bigot. I could have provided him with a longer list, of course, but he was emphatic about one point: sex and politics have no relation; he hinted that I was shutting myself out of undreamed pleasures. Perhaps if I had recalled precisely the arrhythmia that forced me to steady myself against the windowsill during Gisela's confession, I'd have specified that I did not want to love someone who'd turn out to be a Republican or a religious bigot. Our argument is over now. One March morning, not two miles away from my own house in Detroit, the same friend died in his home, slaughtered by a homophobe.

Frankfurt was the third large city in the West that I saw before coming to America. I went there on a vacation from the Lycée Royal of Verviers to meet a childhood friend whose parents had been my parents' closest friends in Bucharest, the only two of my father's friends whom my mother could stomach. Alexander was always more glamorous to me than the boys with whom I grew up in the apartment building, despite his having lived with my mother and me in the same apartment for six weeks during the terrible blizzard of 1953 and my concomitant measles. Fortunately for our circumstances, he had already had the disease and was immune to it despite our sharing my mother's bed, while his parents slept on my daybed in the living/dining room. Their arrival, at my mother's insistence, at our apartment in early March after the snow had begun literally to bury Bucharest, when many inhabitants, our friends included, found their wood supply almost exhausted and their water pipes frozen, made a festival for us children of the worst snowstorm in recorded history. Alexander was passionately in love with our bathroom, and I got out of the day-care center that prematurely and indelibly soured me on human nature.

They lived in what had been a lovely but was now a dilapidated house not far from one of the greatest urban parks ever, Cișmigiu. Intended as a rather well-to-do but by no means lavish one-family dwelling, the house seemed to shelter innumerable families. The wing in which Alexander and his parents lived was composed of a vestibule, which had become his room, a large living room, which was the all-purpose room by day and his parents' bedroom by night, and an extremely old, decrepit bathroom and kitchen, access to which could be gained only by going outside or through the two rooms that constituted the apartment of his mother's sister and her family. I rather liked the bathroom, even though it was unheated in winter, but the passage through his mother's sister's apartment filled me with trepidation since I had to make polite noises about not meaning to disturb the people I was obviously disturbing, all three of whom had developed a biting sense of humor in order to cope with the situation, an irony I didn't understand and that frightened me. When I finally made it to the bathroom, the spots on the wall, the ancient tub with feet, and the gaps in the linoleum that showed the dark cement beneath filled my head with dread and wondrous imaginings. But I could see how, in the long run, not having hot water or heat might wear down one's sense of adventure, and the peeling walls and floor would hold allure only for so long. In retrospect, I understand why every time Alexander came to visit, he would propose that we play boats in our bathroom sink, and we would take my two little plastic boats from America and make others out of paper and float them in the filled sink for what seemed to me interminable periods, which I endured because I liked Alexander and he didn't fight with me the way my everyday friends did. Until we lived together, of course, but even then our endless bickerings and games of upmanship were bliss compared to the day care from which his mother's presence in the reconstituted household saved me.

After my father was jailed, my mother looked for someone to watch me when she went to work. Not having much choice, she settled on a young woman, who took up residence in our apartment. Eric, the man in the "extra" bedroom, was gone most of the day. Alone with me, the woman began tying me up with rope whenever I refused to do whatever she required in what she thought was a timely manner. She complained to my mother that I was spoiled, and I started hanging on to my mother when she had to leave for work. Since my behavior aroused my mother's suspicion—I had been used to near-strangers taking care of me from an early age—she backtracked from her walk to work one day and saw me being trussed up for not dressing in time. She fired the young woman on the spot and took me to work with her, which seemed to me a heavenly arrangement that need not have been disturbed. Soon after, however, she began to prepare me for the day-care center, where a niece of her colleague was going; I would have her as a friend right away. The day-care center was on the way to my mother's office, the block before it, in fact. It had a nice wrought-iron fence set in stone and a pretty yard, even in January. It was a mild January, so mild that the forsythias were fooled into blooming, and our early morning walks were delightfully fresh and novel. I particularly remember one morning when the hoar hung heavy on everything, giving distinctness to the smallest dormant bud and to each blade of grass. The scene put me in mind of the story of the dancing princesses, their descent in the garden made of jewels, silver, and gold, and I told my mother, to her great pleasure, that the world looked like a fairy tale that morning.

But she would leave me at the center and walk on to work, and my entrance through those gates became each day more and more like a return to hell. By a stroke of bad luck, I wasn't placed in the same group as the little girl whom I vaguely knew. I came mid-year, when the children had already formed their inflexible hierarchies and alliances. Since the center was primarily for working-class children, they immediately singled me out as not one of them by the way I talked. In the month that I was there—I only know it to have been a month from my mother's account, since for me it lasted an eternity—I learned class enmity, sex wars, mob violence, scapegoatism, and a host of other social systems and relations whose lessons I was too young to absorb without mortification and lasting disgust. There was a bookcase with doors that now housed a small store of toys in various states of well-being. One of the girls, Victoria, had already made herself the queen bee, and the boys each morning paid homage by attempting to kill each other for the honor of presenting her with her chosen toy, a large doll with brown corkscrew curls dressed in a satin gown. After this ritual, all the other children scrambled for what was left.

Before my father's return from jail and his boxing instructions, I was quite timid about fights. My friends from the apartment building, especially my best friend, would often hit me and make me cry, so the center children had no trouble intimidating me. Consequently, I ended up with the leftovers—a moth-eaten, dingy little stuffed bear, with which I began developing an intimate relationship, as children often do with beat-up toys, especially when they feel left out. One day, Victoria, who had seemed not to notice my existence, looked intently at me and my bear and said, seemingly to the air, "I want that bear." The boys rushed to answer her desires. I learned then that there were limits to the persecutions I would put up with. I think I won the fight for the bear because I caught my enemies, as well as my own self, by surprise. The boys did not anticipate such wild resistance and backed off. Led by Victoria, they taunted me all day about how ugly and undesirable the bear was, which of course made me hug it all the more. I lived to the next morning in utter terror that the attack would be repeated, but fortunately for me, Victoria's gang found other means of tormenting us outsiders, ways that for me at least were easier to endure.

My mother would tell people into my early adulthood that I had developed my dislike for macaroni and cheese at the day-care center because I was fed it almost every day. Even then, I edited my experiences for her, for I understood that she had no choice but to leave me there each morning, her eyes moist as she looked into my mournful face. What the children conspired to do, since one of the great disgraces at the center was to lose control of any bodily function, was to try to make each other vomit at mealtime, an enterprise in which they invariably succeeded with me. Each day one of the boys would eat his snot just as we were about to take a bite of the already unappetizing food. I had become so conditioned to having to run to the toilet to throw up my breakfast that by the end of the month the mere smell of the food would make me heave. I came home ravenous, in the hard times of the early fifties, when food was so difficult to come by, and my mother would often splash some sunflower oil into a saucer, in which I would dip slice after slice of black bread. Before she discovered my new aversion to macaroni and cheese and my day-care fasts, she attributed my unappeasable hunger to a growth spurt.

Yet even in the worst circumstances there are moments of joy. We were all taken out in the mild weather to plant shallots in the flower bed of the courtyard. A couple of weeks later, I was the first to spy the green tips spearing through the soggy winter ground, they too fooled into early sprouting by the strange warmth of the season. Since then, every spring I've felt the same irrational sense of triumph over adversity at the appearance of those seemingly tender shoots that I've seen pierce three-inch layers of solid ice. Wherever I live, if there's a bit of earth to which I have access, I plant bulbs for the promise hidden beneath their homely covering.

That winter made everyone improvident. People splurged through their provisions and used up more fuel to heat themselves, thinking we were bound for an early summer. Until the weekend in late February when my mother went to the Jilava prison to deliver a package for my father and found herself up to her knees in snow while she and the others were kept waiting by the jail gate. After that, it seemed as if the skies had forgotten how to stop dropping snow. In a week, Bucharest became impassable by any but military vehicles equipped with chains on their tires. In another two days, even the armored cars could no longer forge paths through the city. People dug seven-foot trenches through which they walked to work. Months later, when the hard-packed snows melted, bodies of people suspected of having been arrested appeared in various states of preservation. Our friends moved in with us in the nick of time, bringing their belongings and whatever foodstuffs they still had, tied to Alexander's sled. Since our building housed the leaders' cars in its underground garage, the methane gas that heated it was allowed to flow freely rather than being rationed, as it was elsewhere, so our pipes did not freeze. First people from the neighborhood, then people from all parts of the city came through the snow tunnels to our building to get water. Alexander was even more passionate about our bathroom than before.

We children, kept home by the closed schools and day-care centers, took to sledding down from the balconies of those of us who lived on the second floor, so high was the snow. On the days when even we couldn't make it out the door, we ran in warring gangs around the building hallways, raising echoes and hackles with our wild screams; but it was a period of misrule, and no one, not even Ion, could do much to stop us. My mother encouraged Alexander and me to eat condensed milk by the spoonful from the small cans her American aunts had sent her, since milk had become unobtainable and she worried about our calcium intake. I can still taste the cloying, nearly sickening sweetness on those spoons. She and Alexander's father, who were members of the "workforce" and got to their jobs only to spend the time digging trenches in the snow, each brought home a large loaf of dark bread that no one who did not go to work could procure elsewhere. The birds, desperate for food, attacked the slab of bacon hung out in the cold on the balcony. As for me, I had been saved: first I luxuriated in having Alexander's mommy at home to take care of us and his stimulating if not always pleasant company; then I sank into the hallucinations of high fever, which returned me briefly to the day-care center but from which I could awake; and after, I slid into the lassitude of convalescence, when nothing was expected of me. It was a wonderful and unforgettable spring.

So, in some measure Alexander gets mixed up in my mind with that festive time, when nothing was the same for a while. The two of us, who spent a good deal of each morning in earnest measurement of the slices of bread and cheese and bread and jam that we each got with our tea, jealously switching them back and forth several times in order to make sure that neither of us would be cheated out of a larger portion, grew shy, as if aware of the sibling closeness we had inflicted on each other, after things returned to normal and he and his family went home. When Alexander's parents received their official notice that they could leave the country, we were both on the brink of puberty, and Alexander looked more glamorous than ever to me, clothed as he had become with the strangeness and desirability of his impending habitation in the West.

My heart fluttered when I got off the train in Frankfurt, after not having seen him for the significant years that had changed us into inalterably gendered beings. He had indeed grown much taller than I, and quite manly looking, despite keeping his cherubic blond, blue-eyed looks. This was Frankfurt, then: his father taking my suitcase, towering over me, and smiling that salt-of-the-earth smile beneath his mustache; Alexander walking near me, making me feel acutely aware of the edges of my body; his mother coming out on the stairway to greet me, her prettiness even more refined by the West. Her mocking sense of humor was the same as I remembered when as a child I had taken her joke seriously and worried that she would force me to eat the portion of the jellied pig's feet cooling on the pantry floor into which I had accidentally stepped. Frankfurt was also a city of cacophony to me, negotiated by my friends, who spoke German and led me like a deaf-mute through the tangled traffic in and out of department stores almost choking under the weight of merchandise that seemed somber, solid, and terrifyingly well made.

It was also the city in which I first saw Charlie Chaplin, his extraordinary grace under the pressure of hunger in *The Gold Rush* making me rather weep than laugh. After the film, I experienced the double pleasure of being treated to ice cream by Alexander and discovering ice cream sundaes. I must confess to keeping a tender spot in my heart for men who introduce me to good ice cream. I wonder if it was predestination that made my future husband and me find the first evening showing of *Georgie Girl* sold out so that he would take me to the Italian ice cream parlor in his old neighborhood, where by all rights we should have held our wedding five years later, so unbroken a connection had we maintained with the place, its people, and its ice cream—now extended over thirty-some years.

The next time I laid eyes on Alexander we had trouble recognizing each other. Luckily, my mother was standing next to me, and he immediately fixed on her. He was standing in a line parallel to ours, waiting to put his message through the paging desk at the Frankfurt airport, when my mother and he called to each other, leaving me to wonder, did I grow so much taller? Did he shrink? For there we were, in our late thirties, each married and with children of our own, not quite unrecognizable but certainly past the bloom our teenage years had promised, and almost eye to eye.

We had made elaborate arrangements to meet at the airport, during a lengthy layover that my mother and I had between the flight out of Dubrovnik and the flight that was to take us to Nice, where my husband and daughter were waiting. When we got off the plane, we looked around for Alexander and his mother—his father having died some years before. Since we found no one by the gate, we went to the paging desk. It turned out that Alexander, accustomed to taking care of his mother and other female relatives, had started toward the paging desk with a sinking feeling that he was not going to find us, that having missed our agreed-upon meeting place we would be lost in the great hub of the airport. I was even more aware of his assumptions about female incompetence when he and his mother took us back to the airport after we had visited at her apartment, where she had spread in our honor a great feast made up of my favorite foods: salmon caviar and tarama salad, smoked fish and seafood, olives, crusty bread. There was a mix-up about the departure gates, and my mother, walking arm in arm with his, had disappeared from view while he and I went to get boarding passes. "They'll never find the right gate," he exclaimed, alarmed. I was amused, for his assumption only made him more kindly and more worried, not the least impatient or angry. I assured him that my mother had found her way on her own around half the globe, and he smiled and replied, ruefully, "Not my mother. She needs looking after." We overtook the two women on the way to the right gate, of course. Their leisurely pace, designed to accommodate their reminiscences and not the hectic rush of airport traffic, left us no time for long good-byes.

My last landing in Frankfurt, which avoided the city altogether, was on the way to Israel with my mother's ashes in order to fulfill the second part of her heterodox desires. Anticipating airport security checks, my husband and I talked to airline officials and obtained all sorts of approvals and proofs that the small rectangular shape we were carrying contained nothing more dangerous than what was left of my mother. But of course the people at the security checks could read no English and understood very little. In addition, I could see on their faces and could feel on mine, as they saw the Star of David seal on the chapel documents, old antagonisms turning us into masks of fury and contempt. Had my husband not been there, I would have probably been jailed. At last, when a higher official who could read the papers and understand our explanations was brought to the scene, he apologized, seeming genuinely embarrassed: "We don't see this sort of thing very often." "Not anymore," I wanted to say, but I didn't because I wanted us just to get out. With one part of my mind I could almost laugh at this bitter comedy about my mother, who in her twenties had just barely escaped being turned to ashes in German ovens, having her ashes indefinitely detained in Germany for fear that they might be explosive.

In order to come to America, we had to be sanitized. Not only did our relatives have to vouch for our future good behavior and, without exception, guarantee financial support so we wouldn't become burdens to the state, but both in Europe and upon our arrival we had to undergo extensive physicals lest we carry contaminants. Several times we passed the Marine-guarded entrance of the American embassy in Paris to be processed by M.D.s who barely spoke French. One of the doctors, who was of Greek origin and who expressed deep disapproval upon finding that despite our last name neither my mother nor I spoke Greek, nonetheless took time to walk me to a globe and point to Detroit, nestled among all that blue. I took a quick turn back to the map of Europe, and I could see at a glance that the Great Lakes were larger than many a sea.

I began to dream of a city of skyscrapers on the shores of a lake like the sea. There would be huge apartment buildings, neither the decorous old-regime ones on the boulevards of Paris and Bucharest nor the garish ones colored in nursery pastels built on Romanian vacant lots. Under the influence of a beautiful city, my taste in architecture was improving. These buildings would be black glass or soft gray cement. They would soar into the rainy night. I would be walking on the street alongside the lake, staring at the mobile circles made by raindrops on the water. There would be practically no traffic, though occasionally headlights would appear out of the dark, blind me momentarily, and metamorphose into the angry glare of brake reds. A boy my age but taller would be walking toward me. We would glance at each other, say nothing, and then go our ways—or he would sweep me up in his arms and kiss me, long and passionately, both of us knowing that fate had brought us together. In sleep and wakefulness I kept dreaming of the city by the lakeshore.

Years and many disappointments later, I went to Chicago for the first time and realized that somehow my soul and my weak sense of U.S. geography, the latter the product of a communist education, had gotten lost amid the lakes. I had dreamed Chicago instead of Detroit. I wonder if my immigrant experience would have been altered had I arrived in the city of my dreams. Surely other elements, the tall boy, for instance, would have failed to materialize, but it consoled me to know that I had not been utterly chimerical, that there was a city corresponding to my imaginings, though it happened not to be the city in which, on and off, I would spend my American life.

When the U.S. visas came we were in Belgium, and they came for my mother and me only. Panicked, my stepfather began making extravagant promises and abject apologies for past behavior, so that my mother wouldn't leave without him. My mother told him she would stay for the time during which the visas remained valid—two months. After that, she would expect him to join us in the United States. His visa came during the following month. "My bad luck always," she would lament almost daily for the last two years of the marriage and occasionally afterward, when something traumatic or an encounter with Romanian acquaintances made the memory of her ex-husband surface once more, for she remained convinced that he wouldn't have had the initiative to make the ocean crossing on his own. Thus the three of us left together for America.

By the early sixties the vast majority of immigrants to the States were taking planes, but I lobbied with great passion for a boat passage, and my mother found out that a medical dispensation would convince the Jewish charity that loaned us the money for the crossing to let us take a boat instead of an airplane. My stepfather for once came in handy: he had excessively high blood pressure. In medieval times he would have been classified as choleric. Together, he and my mother visited a cardiologist in a Düsseldorf hospital to obtain a professional opinion that flying would be bad for Dick's health. As they stood in the hallway chatting, the doctor noticed that his patients in the heart disease ward were also chatting softly. He ordered them to be silent. He returned to his conversation in the hallway, and the patients once more began to make soft background noises. "They're supposed to rest," he bellowed, then added, addressing himself to my mother, "If only I had a machine gun, I'd go in there and have quiet once for all." My mother had braved, and heavily bribed, the Romanian customs officials to let her hide my bear, the oldest and most beloved stuffed toy I owned, at the bottom of the 120-pound trunk that was to carry all our permitted earthly possessions into the West. In Germany she faced this man, yet another doctor with a final solution, to get the certificate that would provide me, though I didn't know it at the time, with the quintessential, if a bit dated, immigrant arrival in the New World.

I loved the ocean crossing. Europe was in the grip of a ferocious winter, even in temperate Holland where we embarked on the ship bearing the same name as the port, Rotterdam, and an equally dismal February would stretch before us in Detroit, but the mid-Atlantic rolled in springtime. The balmy sea breeze of the gulf stream gave us sunny or hazy mild days. Gulls followed the wake, eating the garbage discarded by the ship and resting on the mast at night. Dolphins frolicked alongside. We shed our coats and strolled out on deck in light jackets, letting the soft, salt-laden wind blow on our sallow winter faces. I loved the luxury of being waited on and fed every three hours, like a baby. I loved the ship's library, a large, quiet room where I chanced on a collection of *romans noirs*, with the arched black cat trademark on the cheap bindings. I began reading *Babbitt* in French and understood little of its untranslatable Americanisms.

In the library I met an unprepossessing young man who kept paper napkins about him into which to blow his nose, and a somewhat older French naval officer. They both showed some interest in me, the first chiding me for ruining my mind by reading mystery novels. He proposed to loan me his set of Gorky instead, and I laughed in his face, telling him that I'd had enough of Russian literature forever. In about three years, I would be writing my high school research paper on Dostoevsky, but certainly not because of this unkempt person, who'd picked up communist leanings in his sojourn in France the way others develop a taste for Camembert and who, despite knowing of my circumstances, insisted on trying to convert me to the very dogma I had so happily left behind. The French officer, uninterested in reading of any kind, asked me if I played chess. There were several sets out on chess tables in the library. The chess set we owned in Bucharest had been made of wood. The whites were unstained but polished, ranging in color from ivory to deep beige, and the black pieces were a light mahogany; respectively, they were rather like the people that call themselves white and black in my American city. The brown bishop lost his head at one point, and my father sought out a carpenter who could replace it. Private carpenters had so little access to the materials of their trade that the man had had to leave the wood in its natural state, so that the poor bishop sported an incongruous matte, cedar-gray head on his glossy body.

Ever since I was very little, I had been fascinated by chess. I would hover around the board or sit on the floor in silence as my father and one or another of his friends, always a man, stared motionless at the checkered board. To my father's irritated amusement, I would demand a matching piece—"I have three brown pieces. Let me have three white"—not understanding that I was asking for my father's loss. But it didn't matter what I wanted, because he always won. He had been a chess champion in his youth, and even now his invulnerability exasperated his friends. Once in a while, after a friend had left rather abruptly, refusing the proffered preserves, my mother would suggest to my father, "Why don't you let him win once?" while my father laughed at the outlandish notion of faking incompetence. Even when he taught me to play, in my fifth year, he would never condescend to let me win, despite my mother's pleas. "When she's good enough, she'll beat me, and that will be a true victory," he said, but of course I had no chance to become good enough in the time left us. Yet I did get so good that I won most of the games against my friends and schoolmates. All my chess partners were boys. My friends, accustomed to thinking of me as one of the gang, were no more irritated by my being a girl and beating them than by the simple fact of my winning, but my schoolmates had a harder time taking defeat from someone who looked like easy prey. As a result I enjoyed beating them all the more.

My French lieutenant, I realize retrospectively, wanted to use the medium of chess to flirt, but I, not fancying myself an object of desire to a man his age and intensely interested in the game, concentrated wholly on chess. I beat him. He was upset to a degree that almost frightened me. He demanded a rematch but was called away, not before exacting my promise, not once but three times, that we would play again. That night, our fifth on board (the Rotterdam was a slow boat), we must have crossed into currents from the icy coast of North America, because the balmy weather changed to a storm. The crew immediately equipped all stairwells and hallways with ropes on which people could steady themselves as the boat lurched and pitched. The next morning, the breakfast ranks were much thinned. Even my stepfather had no stomach for meals. I reveled in the storm and spent as much time as I could on deck, watching the prow alternately plunge, for a heart-arresting moment, into the gray waters right toward the bottom of the sea, then rise so high that the whole ship leaped heavenward, defying gravity. I would come back to the lounge half-wet, smelling of algae and salt. I would eagerly accept the bouillon and crackers or the tomato juice offered by waiters in white dinner jackets, who were able to anticipate the movements of the ship and miraculously maintain equilibrium when being buoyed toward the ceiling or sucked into the floor without spilling a drop on the crisp linen that covered their trays.

At one point on that first morning of the storm, the French officer spotted me and challenged me to the rematch. I accepted, somewhat reluctantly since the sensation of the storm was still new upon me and I would have preferred to return to the deck. We sat to play. This time I could see he was in earnest—the time between moves grew longer. I began to erect the impenetrable defenses that my adversaries found so unnerving that inevitably they would commit an error, at which point I would deliberately begin to break through their own weak defenses. Years later, when I played chess with my husband, I found the first male player who had the same basic strategy, and I was stymied. Our games took hours, days, with each of us so reluctant to dismantle any of our defenses that neither of us attacked. I would win ultimately, but it took much longer and gave me a clue about our uncanny compatibility. The man I was playing on the Rotterdam, however, fell for the offensive strategy. Just as I saw my opening and made my first threatening move, he stopped a waiter. "I have to take something," he said to me, "this up-and-down motion is terrible."

"Take the crackers," I advised, having read about seasickness and speaking without any feeling for his distress. "The bouillon, liquids in general, are no good."

He gave me a baleful look and drank a cup of soup. Then he moved, making yet another, more devastating error.

"Are you sure you feel good enough to go on?" I asked. He waved my question aside, but I saw his thin face take on a greenish tinge. I checked him. He looked at the board, then at me. In two moves I would checkmate. He struggled to get his handkerchief out of his pocket and brought it abruptly to his lips. I saw him go through a spasm of nausea and again motion to me, in a gesture between apology and dismissal, then run away down the hall. After that I saw little of him, and he never asked to finish his rematch.

As we approached New York harbor, the weather grew cold and gray. Even as I felt my extremities go numb, I was loath to leave the deck, my restlessness mounting as we came closer to land. America, after all, had been my idea. My mother had given in to my desire only after being warned off by relatives in Israel and seeing that the governments of Western Europe were most reluctant to let us take up permanent residence. The morning of our scheduled landing, I gazed about me and started jumping up and down with glee as I spotted the Statue of Liberty, a darker gray but unmistakable silhouette with the torch taking shape like an optical illusion amid the light gray enveloping us. People in the lounge saw me shouting and pointing, and they came out too to take a look. "I was the first to see it," I kept saying, "the first." As we floated so close to the New Jersey coast that store signs became visible, I was struck by the frequent appearance of a word that I thought I could fathom—one among the treacherous "*faux amis*" that would lead me into error for some years to come—in large, generally red letters, LIQUOR. "Liqueur," I mused. And already I felt that I would meet with strange obsessions in this new land.

After the customs officials processed us, asking in a familiar refrain, "Are you or have you ever been . . ." we found ourselves in the huge warehouse of the New Jersey port. A man with a tag of some kind approached us, identified himself as a member of the Jewish Federation, and said he would be escorting us to the train that would take us to Detroit. He communicated with my mother, the only one of us who knew English, although she found spoken American English almost unintelligible. "We don't get to spend even a night in New York," I nearly wailed. The man seemed huge, brisk, jovial, conforming to the stereotype that we had brought with us over the ocean. He drove us through tunnels and over bridges, too fast, I thought, since I was eager not to miss anything. In the tangle of Manhattan he had to slow down, and I gasped with wonder and joy at the skyscrapers, the promised metropolis with its crowds and glittering windows and animated advertisements. Over what must have been Broadway hung a billboard with a mouth outlined in lipstick and a cigarette; the mouth closed on it, then let it go, and a puff of smoke emerged. I was filled with enchantment, with a buoyancy much like that which had thrust the ship into the sky, beyond the reach of gravity. Even now, when I revisit Manhattan, something of that delighted wonder returns, and I walk the island tirelessly, happy to be released to the rhythms of my own locomotion from the automated prison in which I traverse my hometown, Motown.

The train that took us to Detroit—which, sometime in the late sixties, stopped service so that now to get to New York from Detroit one must travel to Chicago, four hundred miles in the wrong direction—was elegant, but that was nothing new to us. In the dining car, we had our first typical American meal of steak and baked potato and iceberg lettuce with Thousand Island dressing. Everything, most of all the salad, which I had never had before, tasted exotic, and I savored the crunch of the bland leaves, the strange sweetness of the dressing, the way in later years I would sample the peculiar blend of banana and lime that makes up the flavor of kiwi or the slight sting underneath the slimy sweet flesh of a mango. I willed myself to like it, as I would will myself to like so many other things that offended my palate or my soul in years to come, until something inside me would rebel and say, "Enough," curiously always in my mother's voice. For years now I've refused to buy iceberg lettuce, and I only had Thousand Island dressing two more times before deciding that I could not like that preposterous mix of tastes.

From the train window and then from the window of my great-uncle's car, the first sights of Detroit smote my heart. We arrived at the glorious Art Deco Terminal (now boarded up for at least two decades) and saw no one on the platform waiting for us. Bewildered, we walked to the end and discovered that people were not allowed to wait for passengers right on the platforms; my mother's aunts stood behind a rope, waving their handkerchiefs, applying them to their eyes. My mother's aunts and her uncle by marriage were not stereotypically American—they were tiny. My married aunt was dressed in black, with a little hat trailing a vestige of veil. My unmarried aunt wore a bright, royal-blue coat with a fur collar and earrings with red stones. Later, my mother said, "I knew right away which was which. Teresa, the sensible one, dressed as befit her age, and Golda, always inappropriately. Maybe it's because in a household of six girls she was the only one who was said to be just pretty. The others were all beauties." My great-uncle spoke no Romanian, though he remembered enough Yiddish to be able to exchange some words with Dick. My mother was of course immediately immersed in a flood of conversation with her aunts, especially as Teresa, when my mother asked about her two daughters, revealed for the first time that the younger had died two years before our arrival.

What was it in my mother's family, on both the maternal and paternal sides, that forced this reticence about death, as if it were obscene somehow? On her father's side, where the males were Cohanim, descendants through patrimony from the high priests of Israel forbidden to look on death, there was perhaps a shrinking to which they held as part of their genetic status as the only Jewish aristocracy. But here they were, all that was left of my mother's maternal side except perhaps for the sister in Russia from whom no one had heard in a long time, commoners all, with the familiar shame about having to speak of death. I saw my uncle, who understood only a few words of Romanian despite being exposed to it for over forty years in the private discourse of his wife and her sister, look sharply as he heard the name of his dead daughter, and then saw his wiry frame shaken by a brief sob. I began to love him at that moment. How different that naked, sudden pang from my step-father's elaborate preparations for grief, audibly revving up the motor of his emotions to the weeping point with a flood of words.

We piled into my great-uncle's unsafe-at-any-speed Corvair, for a time my ideal car because he drove one, and wended our way through the snowy city. City? I asked myself, feeling the whole fatigue of the journey sinking into the pit of my stomach. This was the small town against which I had been warned by all my reading of nineteenth-century French novels and more recently by *Babbitt*. It was the deserted provincial backwater that my physician uncle, who had never presumed to advise me about anything except germs, had brought himself to warn me against. In one of the few moments we had alone together in the feverish rush of our last days in Bucharest, he said, "Don't get stuck in Detroit. Go to New York, the center, where you can find your scope." I wasn't quite sure what he meant and didn't think much about it since all I dreamed about was severing myself from sick old Europe, but his words came back to me as I was forced to juxtapose the life and lights of Manhattan with the snowbound, empty landscapes along which we were driven. The view was incontrovertibly ugly, with unhandsome little houses on desolate streets and main thoroughfares on which all the build-ings looked flat, as if a plane had flown too low and its wings had razed the roofs on both sides. Their shabby, cardboard-looking façades looked like a theater set or a makeshift settlement in the mid-dle of the vast plain. Only rarely, when I'm in a particularly foul mood, can I recapture as I drive down one of Detroit's main arter-ies the aesthetic shock that benumbed me on my first ride through the city that would become my mental location for the remainder of my American life.

But I had not yet discovered downtown. For the first three weeks, we stayed at my married great-aunt's house, in a neighbor-hood that had already "changed," as people obliquely put it. Used to bodily freedom and now packed into the downstairs flat, we used every opportunity to take walks, to the amusement and alarm of our hosts. My great-uncle kindly offered to drive us wherever we want-ed to go, but we didn't want to go anywhere—we just wanted to get out for a while. My aunt would shake her head and say something in English to her husband, probably to the effect that he should let us learn from our mistakes, or that we should be given time to shed our European habits. Both she and her inappropriate sister remained slightly ashamed of us, as some families are of their mentally deficient children, especially after my mother's divorce. Whenever my mother indicated to her aunt that she found American ways retrograde, Teresa would dismiss her increasingly frequent and vehement critiques with stock phrases, no doubt inscribed on her own immigrant consciousness when she came to Detroit forty years before: "Don't act like you just got off the boat. Don't be such a greenhorn."

The first of these confrontations came early on, within the three weeks of our stay in that house. The man who had been an informer for the Jewish charity in Paris, whom my stepfather had known in Romania, came to visit us. I think he was trying to establish relations with all the recently arrived families in order to spread his network that spied and reported on who had gotten what job and didn't immediately declare it, whose relatives had bought them what stick of furniture that the Jewish Federation would not have to fund. He heard from my great-aunt about our penchant for perambulations, and no longer a greenhorn himself, he warned us that we should give up our wallets if a colored man with a knife approached us. Since he spoke Romanian, I understood him, whereas such euphemisms as "changing" remained incomprehensible to me for some time. I had never liked the man and couldn't wait for him to go so I could ask my mother whether she thought the same as I did, that only scum like him were racist, that all of that stuff about whites and blacks hating each other was just communist propaganda. "Communist propaganda?" my mother echoed, astonishment in her voice. "Is that what you thought? Didn't you know why I didn't want to come here? Didn't you see all the newsreels of police beating Negroes?"

The ground seemed to open up before me. I had spent my childhood decoding and hearing adults decode the lies in official news; now suddenly what I had regarded as the crassest of anti-Americanisms turned out to be real. "I thought they faked the newsreels," I said lamely.

"Look around you," my mother said. "Your aunt and uncle can't wait to move out of this neighborhood. Their neighbors are kind, educated people, but they're not white." I couldn't fail to notice that my mother had already begun the process of detaching herself from the only people on whom she might have had any claims on this vast continent. They had suddenly become *my* relatives, not hers.

From our first days in Detroit to my mother's last, much of our talk revolved around the insoluble. "Why?" I would ask about racial hatred. "There's no why," my mother would reply, and would remind me of the joke about the cyclists and the Jews. It goes like this: "Did you know that cyclists and Jews started World War One?" The common, all too common, response is, "Why the cyclists?" The teller then asks, "Why the Jews?" But she proceeded to alienate herself from various circles of people her age and older by her insistence on honesty about race relations. First, *my* great-aunts gave up on her, calling her a red, asking her if she hadn't learned anything from her sufferings, since they labeled all the civil rights fighters as communists. My mother would occasionally explode and tell them about the absurdity of a persecuted minority finding its place by persecuting other, more visible minorities. Embarrassed by our views and our readiness to express them, our relatives kept us from meeting their friends and relations and treated us as primitives.

The last time we saw our American relatives, they were about to move to Kentucky to be close to their remaining daughter, who had just married a rich appliance-store owner, painstakingly guarded from meeting my mother till the day of the wedding. Could they have thought that anyone interested in my exceedingly elegant, insipid cousin would be derailed from the course of true love by my mother? Were they motivated, once more, by their fear that in their ranks was a thinking, speaking, passionate woman with a daughter who also hadn't learned to govern her tongue? At any rate, our first intimations that our cousin was about to make a second marriage were invitations to the wedding.

Soon after, my great-aunt began spending my uncle's fixed income on several long-distance calls a day, timed when my cousin's husband was away so that she and her daughter could anatomize each word and gesture of the new marriage, as they had done the old, without a moment's reflection that no union can bear such intense scrutiny. In order to make sure that her daughter would find a refuge from marital discord should any arise, my great-aunt decided that she and her husband, and her sister, would move to Louisville and set up house together for the first time. Whenever my mother and I chanced upon my great-uncle alone, he would entertain us with stories about his eccentric sister-in-law that made us laugh ourselves silly but covered up the great bitterness of his marriage, the constant lack of privacy and harmony that my great-aunt Golda's daily visits had cost him. This planned move to an unknown city, though they were in their seventies, and the prospect of spending his last years in the unrelieved company of his sister-in-law made him visibly unhappy, but he had always honored his wife, and his respect for her made him unable to oppose her.

My mother and I arrived for our leave-taking, and to collect a cardboard wardrobe that my great-aunt had decided to bestow on us, as she had generously discarded other furniture that did not fit into the suburban house to which they had moved from their "changed" Detroit neighborhood. I hated the furniture, which followed us only as far as the hamlet up north where my mother and stepfather got their first teaching jobs. I hated its Victorian heaviness, its dark colors, its ornateness. I chafed at having to lift all eight of the chairs to vacuum under them. Only the credenza came back to the Detroit area with us. Objectively speaking, it is a lovely piece of old furniture, admired by my sister-in-law and left to her by my mother, now refinished in a lighter stain and standing in the foyer of her home. To all that I had always wished good riddance, my eye lusting for the irregular angles of the salt-and-pepper couch designed by my great-aunt's son-in-law, an interior designer who had had the misfortune to marry the cousin who died. From all accounts, especially those of great-aunt Golda's displeasure with this cousin, she was the one whose tastes we would have liked.

It so chanced that relatives of my great-uncle came to say goodbye at the same time as we. In our four years in and around Detroit we had never met these people. As we conversed, we found that the man worked in the production department of the local public television station, and my mother turned an inquiring look on my great-aunt, who had known that my mother's passion and trade were film editing yet had failed to connect her with this man of high position in the same profession because, she had insisted when we first came, my mother ought to start from the bottom, like everyone else. To my aunt's annoyance, my mother declared that at forty-five she had no time to start from anywhere but a professional level and refused a job as a cook's assistant in a home for the aged. She took the few documents that she had arranged to smuggle out of Romania to be evaluated at the Board of Education in Lansing, and she reluctantly returned to what had been her prewar career, teaching. My great-aunts took my mother's modest success as an affront—the green-horn making good despite the conventional wisdom they had dispensed.

Now, as the conversation meandered from jobs to politics, my mother and I for the first time found common ground with people in my great-aunt's house. The unknown relatives expressed the same opinions about race. When Golda said something about the colored and their ignorant ways, my uncle's nephew retorted, "Yes, and yet some highly educated people who appreciated Beethoven and Goethe sent our people to the gas chambers." In the meantime Teresa tried to keep a neutral face. She served them, and couldn't avoid serving us, a chocolate torte of fine quality. "Where did you get this?" I asked, mindful not to scrape my plate too obviously and much surprised because all we had ever been served at their house was store-bought sweets. "Teresa's famous in the family for her chocolate cake," my uncle's nephew said, at which my mother couldn't help but give me a wan smile. I had never known my great-aunt to bake anything, let alone something this delicious, but she undoubtedly judged that either we were not worthy of her labor or our palates were not fine enough to relish her specialty. My great-uncle's relatives left shortly after the cake was served, not before making it clear that they thought the move to Kentucky a grave mistake.

I don't exactly know what triggered the next events, for they seemed to happen at once, like an electric short circuit. Whether their own American relatives' disapproval of their views and alliance with ours had made our aunts feel once more out of step with the society into which they had tried so hard to fit, or whether they were saving all this up for the last time, I find impossible to tell. The moment their other visitors were out the door, Golda and then Teresa began their attack. They charged my mother with all sorts of crimes, from bringing me up as a "gypsy" who wore neither girdle nor lipstick and argued with boys and was never going to marry, to deep ingratitude toward them, who had sacrificed to bring her here.

The litany of wrongs went on and on, while my mother, stunned, tried to defend herself and I, stung by this trap set for my mother, told them a few home truths. My poor uncle, who had developed great affection for my mother and me, ran to the kitchen and then fetched me to help him take the cardboard wardrobe out of the basement. "Forget the wardrobe," I said. "I will not," my mother said, jumping up, and we were off, struggling to put the wardrobe on top of my mother's Valiant and tie it with rope, my great-uncle furtively wiping tears away, I sobbing openly, and my mother pale with anger. "Try not to let them get to you," my mother said as she hugged her uncle good-bye, and we drove off, never to see any of them again, since my grandmother's sisters made sure to write a last letter to my mother instructing her not to visit them in Louisville on our way to Florida, where we were planning to vacation.

As I learned on that journey, my great-aunts' move south might have actually helped them situate themselves more firmly within the American context, for in that brief time of the late sixties it had become unfashionable in the North and East to express racist views, and dupes like me thought that change would be irreversible. But I was awake enough to see, as we traveled down to Florida before Interstate 75 was completed, that unlike Detroit, where black people held government posts and even supervisory positions in stores and hospitals, the South still preserved the divide between "clean" and "dirty" jobs along the color line. The Dixie-flag bumper stickers all through Kentucky and the Wallace billboards in Tennessee and Georgia proclaiming white supremacy, five years before the 1972 primaries that made the governor of Alabama the great spoiler, made me afraid, as if we were traveling through a foreign country. Those feelings were compounded by my mother's inability to understand southern speech and southerners' inability to understand her, which I took as a sign of her profound antipathy toward them and theirs toward her as a foreigner, since in our motel in St. Augustine my mother had no trouble chatting at length with the maid, who was southern too but black. By that time, I had become so jumpy and ultrasensitized to matters of race that I could hardly behave rationally, and I worried that my mother's chumminess might appear patronizing, especially when she spent half a day looking for presents to leave for the woman's two children. Not for the first or last time, paralyzed by shyness, I misjudged the spontaneity of feelings between the two women, for on our last day Marcie came with a present for us; she and my mother had thought of each other, not of themselves as ideological symbols.

A short time before my mother's death, she once more went over her desires as to the disposition of her body. "Don't let me be buried here," she said. "I've never got used to this country." I would of course engage in futile arguments with her about the Constitution and the Bill of Rights. My mother said, "There is one thing I cannot get beyond—this country has made me a racist."

"You!" I exclaimed.

"Yes," she said. Then she reminded me of the episode in which a young black man had driven his car at her in a murderous manner, run out of it wearing a stocking over his face, snatched her purse, and driven away. "I'll not get over it," she said. "Now I'm afraid when I see groups of young blacks in the malls. I never used to think like this. But that's what comes of over twenty years of hearing little else than black and white, black and white. You begin to see things that way."

"But," I protested, "you'd be afraid of skinheads too if you saw a group of them at the mall."

"Yes," my mother admitted, "but people like that really hurt me. What's anybody black done to me? One man scared me and took my cash and caused me a lot of inconvenience, and look how it made me generalize. And I hate it, and I don't want to think that I'll be stuck here forever, in any shape or form."

As usual, I was frightened by my mother's honesty. It led me to

think back to how I perceived people when I first came and to contemplate how I have changed. I remember being asked, when I first
went to Northern High School, the only school in Detroit to offer
classes for immigrant students, "Are there a lot of colored at the
school?" and being unable to answer. I tried to visualize the people
in the hallways. I knew my classmates were Italian, Cuban, French,
Haitian, Greek, and I classified them according to whether I could
speak with them, but all the other students were American, the people with whom I could not communicate except through the most
inane phrases, "How are you," "Fine," and by gestures. I knew the
neighborhood where we rented an upper flat was white because my
great-aunt, who called classified-ad numbers for us, would cross out
ads and say, "No, coloreds," which incensed my mother: "How can
you tell, and what difference does it make?" "By the way they talk,"
my great-aunt would say, smiling at our naiveté. "And you can't rent
from coloreds." But the people on the buses that I had just begun
to use? The people in the Wrigley and the A&P supermarkets at the
diagonal intersection of Grand River and Oakman Boulevard? Were
they white or black? All I remember is that they dressed differently.
Shockingly, the women wore curlers in their hair. The children
chewed gum, which my mother did not allow me to do in public.
They were American, and we were not.

I do remember, however, that as soon as I learned a little English my teacher had me assigned to two "regular" classes at Northern High, and that both my teachers were black. One was an easy-
going man who taught world history. It was an easy subject for me,
and even in my linguistic and cultural haze I could see why: the
"world" we were studying was mostly Europe and its dreary record
of wars, subjects over which I had gone so many times before, the
scars of which I had seen and lived with all my fourteen years. Why
would these students, who smiled a great deal, did unthinkable
things like combing their hair and applying makeup in class, and
lived here, across the Atlantic divide, care about what my great-uncle
called the Old Country? The teacher was young and still eager, and
he made me horribly uncomfortable by holding me up as an example whenever I got a perfect score on a quiz. But he was truly kind
to all of us, helping one girl get out of a difficulty with another

teacher, keeping me a few minutes after class to enunciate for me the difference between *ear* and *year*, to which I had been deaf.

The other teacher was an older, bald man who taught art. Northern High had just refurbished its art room, and at the end of every class he went through a ritual drill during which we all ran around cleaning and scouring and putting things away while he shouted from the desk, "I want you to show them. We're gonna show them! They won't look at my room and say, 'Those Negro kids, it's no use spending money on them, they break everything, they dirty everything.' This room's gonna sparkle! I'm not gonna have them use *this* room to point to and say, 'What's the use of getting them nice things, they're like animals, they'll just destroy them.' " I had trouble understanding everything he said, just as I had trouble following his directions for class work. He took pleasure in intimidating me, which was not hard to do in those days, so after the first time he mocked me for not understanding him I gave up asking him to explain. I remember doing nearly everything wrong in that class. Even when I thought I did all right, as when I drew a pencil sketch of a little girl in heavy winter clothing going uphill against the wind, he looked at it, displeased, and said, "Where is this? It's nowhere. I don't have any sense of where this is."

But I also saw in his class young black men who bore themselves differently from so many other kids I saw in the hallways, with a quiet dignity, a seriousness of purpose in their work that I did not often see among the other boys, with their slicked hair and goofy ways. For it was the young men, not the girls, who heard that teacher's call clearly and distinctly. And for many years, when I talked about my former art teacher I would tell only the good half of the story—his success, not my humiliation. So, whatever your name (and I confess I've forgotten the names of my Detroit teachers, as I have the last names of all my international classmates at Northern High), I now break my silence because, though I did not always understand you, I sometimes did. In your wounded strength you needed me, my white skin, so you could enact your revolt against the oppressor through the one at hand, the figure for all those you could not reach. You saw in me not the bewildered, displaced child but the European invader who with half the effort would have more of a chance at the American dream than the young people you tough-loved, Americans if not by choice at least by four hundred years' birthright. And I, who in my childish need had to keep my heroes and villains unmixed, preserved for all those years only the righteousness of your fury.

Now, more than thirty years later, I too see in black and white. There are moments when I catch and shame myself, but there are others when I cherish my perception. Several times in the last ten years, I traveled to places that were represented in the media as the ideal American cities—Tempe, Seattle—or to others, back in sick old Europe, where there are more people of color now than at the time of my first sojourn, but not nearly as many as in my hometown. I remember landing from Seattle at Detroit's Metro airport and seeing a mass of faces of hues different enough from what we call white to be classified as partly African in origin. I remember the feeling of homecoming. I was back. When at the Munich airport, on what I vowed was my last trip to Germany, I was greeted on the plane by African American flight attendants who were to remain on board all the way to Detroit, I felt home again in an unprompted, spontaneous movement of the mind. I want my ashes scattered here, on the Detroit River or at the foot of a newly planted tree overlooking these straits on whose borders we are still learning to live. There is no escape from what we become, only consciousness, as long as we keep it, of what we are. And I know what my mother also knew, that only in death could she rest at ease in Israel because in life her fierce consciousness would not have let her be at peace with that country and herself.

SIXTEEN: *Where All the Lights Were Bright*

Had our Americanized relatives retained any Old World sensibility, they would have taken us downtown. We were left to discover it on our own, as we discovered the International Institute and Greektown and the Institute of Art and the campus of Wayne State University and the main Detroit Public Library, as well as the tiny jewel of the downtown public library, a triangle with softened sides taking up the median space between diagonally converging avenues. The downtown branch had books in foreign languages. Its Romanian collection was pitiful, but there were lots of books in French I was willing to reread or had not yet read.

I remember being issued a library card at the Main Library and walking the three miles or so to the branch downtown so as to get a card for it too. The librarian in charge seemed suspicious of my motives the moment I opened my mouth to tell her in extremely fragmentary English what I wanted. She told me under no circumstances would I be issued a card since I was not a permanent resident. This phrase puzzled me. I tried to say that we were planning to reside at our present address for a long while. I couldn't understand how anyone could claim permanent residence since they never knew when they might move. She said she would consider issuing me a card if I could bring a letter addressed to my parents at the address where I claimed to live. I tried to tell her that my own name differed from my parents.' By that point my lack of English had helped confuse the issue beyond resolution, for the librarian ordered me out of the library, and I left, tears in my eyes, muttering to myself, "But they gave me a card at the other library." The security guard, a large man, had been watching the scene. He put his hand on my arm, and I expected him to throw me out from impatience at my reluctance to leave, but instead he grabbed the library card out of my hand, ran heavily across the hall, and thrust it at the librarian. "I can't imagine why they gave you one," she said, over and over again, but she brought herself to inform me that the one card was valid for all libraries and that henceforth I'd be able to take out the books I could read.

But that was already in late spring, since for the first months in America even the simplest English remained a mystery to me. When I tried, for instance, to board the bus that would deposit me in front of Northern High, I went up confidently, handing the driver my red student card. He said something I could not understand, then gestured to me to get off the bus. I asked why, though I had no hope of understanding the reply, just as at the train station in Cologne I had asked directions in German that my mother had written for me and I had learned by rote, without ever grasping the answer. The bus driver got angrier and louder till I got off. When the next bus came, I was afraid to board it. At last, I got on the next bus, without incident, although for a while after I fully expected that each time I went up the steps of a bus the driver might start shouting and push me off. Later on, when I acquired the words with which to tell my teacher what had happened, she explained that I must have tried to get on an EXPRESS bus, which my student card did not entitle me to ride.

Yet the buses were our salvation. We took them everywhere. A person still could, in those days, go from one end of the city to the other on public transportation. The stories about people coming up to us with knives to ask for money, which my mother and I dismissed from the beginning, started fading even from my stepfather's mind as we waited, anywhere we needed to, for transfers to take us on the obligatory visits to hospitals to be checked for European germs, on more pleasurable errands to distant corners of a city spread out like the runny batter of a pancake, or better yet, downtown—to that small section where we could blend in with the crowds, where there were so many people different from one another that we could feel both American and cosmopolitan, those few blocks of skyscrapers and large department stores and side streets that felt like a city, full of secrets and surprises. On those unexpected, as yet uncharted streets, we found an Armenian watchmaker whom we patronized for the next two decades. We discovered a synagogue, at which we looked from the outside. My mother began frequenting little fabric shops that sold gorgeous woolens at prices much below those of department stores, which in those days had whole floors devoted to sewing. On Broadway we found a market that specialized in a dizzying array of ethnic foods *avant la lettre*, at a time when only the despised ethnics bought and ate the stuff, to the disgust or at least the distaste of true Americans, who when they heard we had lived in Paris would say, "But I heard they just hand you a loaf of bread, uncut and unwrapped, just like that, and that you carry it in your hand after the clerk touched it." Across from the largest department store, Hudson's, on a much reduced and narrowed Grand River, we discovered a sandwich shop that sold corned beef on real bread, not the spongy white stuff, untouched by human hands, in plastic bags at the supermarket, which we were convinced had been made of sawdust or shredded plastic.

And then, even on Ilene, the undistinguished street with the beautiful name on which we lived, spring came, and with it the ice shard that had entered my heart at my first glimpse of Detroit began to melt. Between Grand River and Plymouth Road, railroad tracks crossed Ilene. Most houses were two-story flats, but at the railroad crossing was a single-family home where an old couple lived. They had the land adjacent to the railroad tracks, which they gardened, and we watched spring announce each of its stages on their plot: first, crocuses, which in Europe I had only seen growing wild in the mountains; then tulips and daffodils; then irises. Suddenly, by mid-May, the whole street was suffused in flowers and blooms, and I lost my head in the happiness of inhabiting a city like the countryside. The provincial, mean look of Detroit's neighborhoods was camouflaged by the lovely greening umbrellas of the elms, the foliage and tenderer green of deciduous and evergreen bushes, the colors of annuals we watched women planting in almost every yard. "Look," my mother would say, pointing admiringly at children's tricycles, at bikes thrown onto lawns, "no one's afraid they will be stolen." As winter loosened its grip, we noticed that people left their front doors open to the sun. The first-floor windows, barless, gaped as if stupidly inviting robbers. By summer, when the moist midwestern heat lingered all night in our upper flat, we began to sleep out on the front porch, on a folding chaise lounge and a mattress, while all the windows in the flat stayed open since we too by then had become careless of thieves.

I was not to discover autumn in Detroit for two more years, for at the end of that first summer we moved once again, this time to a place to which I could reconcile myself only because I knew with all my concentrated desire that it would be temporary. Later, when we moved back to the metro area, to the northeastern suburbs I grew to loathe, I saw as I drove through Detroit the enchantment of gothic arches made by elms shedding gold. In later years the elms would die, exposing once more rows of cookie-cutter houses unsoftened by uniform rectangles of boring grass; as time passed, the meanness of those little houses began to break through at the seams as the "change" came over them. The whites living there no longer wanted to spend the money to keep them in repair, and the blacks moving in rarely had enough money, enough of a stake in the American dream to invest in paints and varnishes and aluminum trim. But for a while, when we returned to the city in 1965, everywhere in the old neighborhoods where trees had been planted for decades, where some had grown for a hundred years, the city was ablaze in its own beauty, the kind that in Bucharest we had to walk to parks or peek between wooden slats or metalwork into people's private gardens to see. Yet though I had longed for Detroit in my village exile and still longed for it in the crueler sterility of the suburb, I missed the leisurely walks in my European existence, the crunch of leaves underfoot in the public spaces of the parks, the promise of chance encounters with friends, with strangers—a possibility when one perambulates with the temporary but profound freedom of aimlessness rather than being condemned to the solitude and danger of the high-speed machine.

During our first Detroit summer I went to summer school and

mused over my almost-romance with Carlos. My mother worked for six weeks in a sweatshop owned by a man who employed only immigrant women. My stepfather stayed in our close upper flat, drank beer, and spun dreams of swindling large fortunes out of naive American jewelry-store owners. I remember my mother coming home in a state bordering total exhaustion, her hands and arms finely scarred from the rash induced by Fiberglas, the preferred drapery material of the sixties, which she had to hem and iron. For the first time in my life, at the age of fourteen, I took household work upon myself voluntarily, anticipating my mother's needs, looking out for her as my father had commanded me to do in my childhood so that dinner would be almost warm by the time she walked in the house. Not that the two of us wanted warm food in the midwestern wet heat, but Dick insisted that a cold dinner was no dinner at all, and we still were trying to propitiate him, thinking that when he got a job he'd calm down.

In the evenings, my mother would attempt to fill out applications for other jobs. One day, the notice from Lansing arrived. Both she and my stepfather had been granted equivalencies for their diplomas and other papers, and they were given temporary teacher's certificates. My mother immediately registered them with an employment agency and gave notice at her job. The women in the sweatshop, who had not befriended my mother despite their common East European Jewish background, tried to mask their envy with contempt: "You," they told her, to whom they had not spoken except to ridicule her as a newcomer, "You, a teacher?" But my mother told me that they had resented her precisely because they had smelled out the intellectual and had taken satisfaction in her "fall" to the same station they were bound to occupy. Besides, in the six weeks my mother had been there she'd already made a couple of vain efforts to organize the shop, and the boss had threatened to fire ·her.

On a late evening in August, a very American man, tall and blond, his face spattered with light freckles, came to our flat. He was the superintendent of a tiny school district in the rural Thumb area of Michigan, and he wanted to hire my stepfather since a teacher had suddenly married and quit, and the school was facing September

without a math instructor. To induce my family to move, he offered
to hire my mother half time as the French and German teacher. "You
understand," he told her, "we could only offer beginning German
and French since we've never had languages before, and there aren't
enough students in the high school to make up more than two
classes." I sat through the proceedings smiling every time the man
looked at me, my heart sinking within me as he described the glories of the countryside. "Do you like to hunt?" he asked my stepfather, who for once did not launch into a story of his days as a
big-game hunter in Africa. "Do you have any questions?" he
asked, finally turning to me. "Yes," I said. "Does the school have a
swimming pool, and is there a movie theater in town?" "No to
both, I'm afraid," he replied, smiling, and I could see that he
thought me a frivolous girl, something I cared about far less than
his negative answers. What point was there in moving to the desert
without the consolations of movies and year-round swimming that
I knew the high school kids in Detroit had?

When we left Detroit in the fall of 1963 so Dick could take the
job, there were movie theaters in every neighborhood, to which
people walked. My French friend and I went once to the one on
Grand River, a couple of blocks away from the corner of Ilene, where
we inadvertently landed in the middle of the kiddy horror matinee,
which she forced me to stay through and which gave me nightmares
for years to come. On my bus ride down Grand River I used to see
the marquees change, from *The Days of Wine and Roses* to *Where the
Boys Are*, which she and I saw in her neighborhood, at the Mercury
Theater. And there were still the downtown theaters, where our
Northern High class for foreign students had a brief reunion that
summer, arriving by bus from our different areas of the city—Juan
from the southwest, Liliane from the northwest, I from the west, the
Italians in a group from the east side, all made a bit shy by not having seen each other in a while, happy to roam the avenues full of people and then escape from the glare and heat of a true city's bricks and
streets into the cool darkness of the matinee, for downtown beauti-
fication had not yet started and the median on Madison Avenue and
the grass plots in Grand Circus Park were parched by the sun.

So much in Detroit comes too late. For instance, Alexander

Pollock, an urban artist with the same surname as my maternal grandmother and to whom I am perhaps related, created his marvelous, half-crazed visions of dizzy chicken and glandular vegetables at Eastern Market, sweeps of matching-color tulips on the medians of Madison and Washington Boulevards, and brickwork and fancy lampposts on Woodward just after people stopped coming to the city. Too late for downtown, where all the renovations, the elevated People-Mover rails, came long after the department stores had moved to suburban malls, where people mesmerized by free parking and newness and whiteness spent their weekends. That summer was the last time I saw any but two of those Detroit school pals, and one, my Italian friend, I met purely by accident a few years later in downtown Detroit, where she worked behind the cosmetics counter at Woolworth's, while I was a freshman at Wayne State.

Why is it that I hold American cities in my mind by virtue mostly of visual images? Is America so sanitized, despite the abundant refuse flying over the embankments of the freeways and nestling in the tall weeds of vacant lots, that it has no smell? Why don't the cities on this side of the ocean have their distinctive tastes, like the specialized delights of each continental town and even the awful blandness of London sausages? I remember reading *The Woman Warrior* and recognizing across cultures the narrator's mother's lament that flowers had no scent in America, food no taste. My mother came back from her visit to Romania in 1972 and said that despite the scarcity, the puny malformed fruit there had a flavor and an aroma she could not find here. Yet when I pick a handful of wild strawberries I ordered from Burpee's and planted by the front walk, my palm smells of the summers I roamed the Carpathian meadows, and the astringency hidden beneath the ripeness takes me back to those days. Exulting, I would bring back a half cup of wild strawberries for my uncle; he would refuse to eat them because he wanted me to have them all, and we would push them back and forth across the wooden table until I squashed them and mixed them with sugar and forced my uncle to eat at least a teaspoonful of the puree that held the savor of spruce and bracing air and wildness and the triumph of the find.

It's true that I lack the nerve to go mushroom hunting, that never again since my childhood have I tasted the earthy flavor, the biting succulence of wild mushrooms that my mother would bring from the market and grill on the stove. I would watch the various-sized caps, some small as a button, others large as the English roses I now grow, fill with their own juice as their undersides were seared by the high heat, and my mouth would fill with saliva as I breathed in the aroma of drying fungus. There are flavors and smells here too, but they come and go, like the people, who change residences on a seven-year average. Perhaps because my mother, driven by circumstances, could not stay put and I too, though I help lower the average of nomadry in the United States, have moved from place to place, the more subliminal olfactory and taste senses could not edge themselves on our subconscious minds, and we could never taste or smell our way home again.

SEVENTEEN: *Variations on the Pastoral*

My mother and stepfather left me for a few days to go to Harrisville, the place up north, in order to house hunt. It was more difficult than they had imagined. The town consisted of four or five blocks of houses, privately owned, and the adjacent farming community. My stepfather was the only one who could drive a car, or so we thought, but we didn't own one, so we'd have to live within walking distance of the high school. The house they found was up on a hill close to the main street, which was also the highway connecting Michigan's eastern city, Port Sanillac, to the mid-state industrial twins, Saginaw and Bay City. My mother came back relatively happy. She worried about yet another transition in my life, about my going to a high school where she would be the first language teacher ever, where moreover I would be taking math from my stepfather, whom I had tutored prior to his Lansing exams and would continue to tutor for the duration of his job at Harrisville High. She worried about transplanting me to a small town and thereby giving me over not only to an alien culture but to small-town mentality. So she returned like a general who had secured at least one victory though losing a war. "The house we're renting," she said, "is wonderful. It's brand new. We'll be the first to live in it. I got you the biggest bedroom."

But in fact I was excited about leaving. I had only been in the countryside for vacations before, and never in this country, so I was ready for adventures. I hadn't fallen in love with anything or anyone in Detroit since spring, and spring had passed. We left the city the

Sunday before Labor Day, crowded by as many of our things as we could jam into my great-uncle's Corvair, our furniture (consisting of my great-aunt's old dining room set and pieces given us by the Jewish Federation) having gone before us. I remember being disappointed by the three-hour drive. The landscape rolled monotonously along, flat cornfield after flat cornfield. Then, farther north, there were a few curves in the road, a couple of little towns with gingerbread houses, a few hills with apple orchards. "We're coming close," my mother announced. "The house is just beyond the hill," she directed her uncle.

"Where's the town?" I asked, like the straight man in a comedy act.

"We just passed it," my uncle said, and I thought he was joking, the same as when earlier, seeing a gigantic billboard in a field asking HOW DO YOU SERVE JESUS?, he had replied, "With a chicken sandwich." I turned to my mother and saw from her uneasy expression that the cluster of little shops on either side of the highway that whizzed by must indeed have been the town where we were to spend an indefinite but, I repeated to myself, temporary part of our lives.

Can I possibly write "Like Paris, Harrisville . . ."? Can any simile bridge the incommensurable gap between the capital of Western culture and the village, population 600, that even as a village lacked rustic charm, consisting of newish frame houses with no leaded windows, no weathercocks, no intricate wood trim and modern suburban ranch houses fronting the highway, hiding the truth of farm work behind them as if ashamed of its quaintness? And yet, there it is: as Paris had been my entryway into the West, Harrisville was my port to America. That was where we truly landed as inhabitants of this country, a family with regular paychecks and taxes to pay in a community to which we had to adjust and that had to reconfigure itself around our alien presence. No more minimal contacts with neighbors who remained insubstantial since we weren't going to be there long, no more dependence for all social intercourse on a small circle of Jewish-Russian and -Romanian and -Hungarian immigrants.

From the first, we lived within the web of Dick's lies. He decided that we would be Unitarians. Luckily for us, there was no Unitarian congregation around to test our faith, but I soon fell prey to competing attempts, by my Methodist and to a lesser extent my Catholic schoolmates, to recruit me. At first I didn't mind. The novelty of dressing up on Sunday morning, actually being sought by a classmate and her family who would come to pick me up and then take me home, reconciled me somewhat to the tedium of the proceedings. I even subjected myself to Sunday school one morning. After the teacher called on my expertise to tell the class, since I'd lived in large cities, what Jews were like ("They're very short, aren't they?"), I decided to absent myself from Sunday school. Then, one Sunday, when a guest minister of some renown took the pulpit from the mild-mannered local reverend, I heard my first fire-and-brimstone sermon and was so smitten by the cruelty of the man's vision that I told my stepfather I would no longer go to church. "But what will people think?" he asked. "They'll think that maybe we're not Christian," my mother said, and that was the end of my churchgoing, except occasionally with my Catholic friends to hear mass, still in Latin, and the rather decent choir.

For in Harrisville I made my first American friendships, which have not exactly withstood the test of time except for the rare postcard or Christmas note that appears like a bird straying outside its migratory path. But they were sustaining friendships, friendships with girls, unusual for me. To my surprise, I could not become friends with boys other than in companionable talk in school. Nor could I at fourteen play outside with the children in the neighborhood. First, there was no neighborhood—we lived on the open highway. The children next door, itself a quarter of a mile away, were all younger than I, but only the very youngest would engage in games. For the older boys, too close to my own age, I was the dangerous other; and the older girl, younger than I, affected a maturity that did give an aged cast to her features and actions. She was perfecting her domestic skills, partly out of necessity—in a family of eight, everyone needed to help out—partly out of great pride in her proficiency with the needle and the ladle.

This family was kind to us, with a brusque sense of what befitted neighborliness. They sent over sweet corn and other produce. They would give us rides to the next town, which had a supermarket, so we could stock up on foodstuffs at cheaper prices than in Harrisville. The parents were both well-read people who kept abreast of politics to a degree common in Harrisville but most unusual in suburban and urban areas, as we were to discover. Thus we had a skewed sense of the level of general knowledge in the United States. Nonetheless, when I naively told them once that *Le Monde*, to which my step-father insisted on subscribing even though it reached us with stale news, had editorialized that the election of Goldwater would be a disaster for American-European relations, they turned on me and said, "We don't tell the French how to run their country. They should keep their nose out of ours." "But Americans are always telling other countries what to do," my mother said, surprised, when I came back to tell her what the Glenns had said. One time, Mr. Glenn took Dick to get fresh fish. On the way home, my father lamented that there were no fish farms raising carp. "Oh," Mr. Glenn enlightened him, "in America only Jews and Negroes eat carp," thus silencing my stepfather the Unitarian.

Another time, the family left for vacation and asked me to give their new dog water each day. The older boys had mercilessly but effectively trained this pretty, red-gold dog not to go near the road. Once, as I burst into tears seeing them whip her, they said to me quite reasonably that it was better than letting the dog get run over by a car. This time, they tied her to a tree with a long chain and left for their usual camping trip, made educational by the parents' expertise in native flora and fauna. They would come back with samples of wildflowers and cones and seeds and shells and read up on them from excellent guides in their own library.

The dog howled with loneliness at night. I went to change her water a couple of times each day. On the first day I made the mistake of wearing shorts; the dog expressed such manic joy at my presence that she leaped up on me again and again, leaving claw trails along my thighs and shins that grew into welts by evening. The little girl on the other side of the Glenns' came to bring the dog's food. Between us the dog had some company, and she survived, even through the downpours that were bound to come during the two weeks that the Glenns were away. For some reason, of all our acquaintances in Harrisville, we could not bring ourselves to write to them after we left, and we heard years later that they'd been hurt by our silence.

As I contemplate this weirdly lit, humming text that constitutes itself before my eyes in seemingly no relation to what my fingertips are doing, I wonder at my reticence to write about Harrisville and its people. So many of them, unlike my own, are alive. If by some extraordinary chance this screen transmutes itself into the old-fashioned artifact, a book, and by some coincidence of fate someone from that past recognizes the odd name on the cover and picks up the book, what sting will it carry for people most of whom were decent and better to us than any strangers before or since? How would I like them to read my recollections? Perhaps as the refractions, split into distorting fragments, in the myriad facets of an insect's eye, the minute particulars that unlike fractals are not the whole picture contained in immutable patterns but only a slant glimpse from eyes as strange, as alien, as those of a remote species.

I think of our landlord, Mr. Allen, who kept in touch with the world long before the Internet, cyberspace, and virtual reality by fiddling with his short-wave radio, an intricate machine taking up a whole wall. A man with a lined, sunburned face lit up by uncommon intelligence and good humor, he listened patiently to my stepfather's tall tales. He made endless adjustments to our house so as to make us comfortable; he would drop in not to see whether we were taking care of his property, as other landlords would, but to make sure we were managing. Only in our second year, in a moment of solitude *à deux*, he smiled and said to me, "Your father's quite a liar, isn't he? And your mother works too hard." I was so shocked I couldn't speak, though my silence was eloquent enough. All this time I had thought Dick was fooling these naive Americans—after all, they were not confronted, as we had been, with the disparity between his claims to place and his getting lost in major European cities. And my mother of course did work too much. The suspicion struck me for the first time that perhaps Mr. Allen dropped in so often to interrupt her daily drudgery. His own wife, a tiny woman always on extremely high heels, was voluble and pleasant. I think she wanted to compensate my mother and me for what she saw as our deprivations—she'd cut half of a chocolate cake and wrap it for us, then push it into our resisting hands at the end of a visit. She'd insist on taking us shopping in Saginaw, and she introduced my mother to an elegant department store, where my mother of course found something to buy for me.

Another family, the Chalmerses, almost adopted us, inviting us over for meals, giving us vegetables from their garden, driving us around the country. I made my first American money babysitting for their two boys, who watched *Combat* every time I was there, it seems, and regarded it as a point of honor to fight going to bed. I couldn't care less about their bedtime—the Chalmerses depended on my good sense and left me with no instructions as to what to do, obviously a misjudgment—so I let the boys exhaust themselves trying to annoy me while I read. When they finally put themselves to bed, I would go in and keep them up longer by inventing weird fairy tales for them. Was it the incessant watching of war shows—not my tales, I fervently hope—that made the older boy rip out the lovely long, dark lashes, shadowing hazel eyes, he'd inherited from his mother when everyone teased him about looking like a girl? When the Chalmerses showed up at my wedding I was pleased that the son for whom I had babysat remembered me fondly and told a gathered group that I had been their best babysitter. The parents must have both been quite young when I knew them, but he was a teacher and they had a boy only four years younger than I, so I thought they were of my mother's generation. I was startled when my mother, who kept up a correspondence with them long after we left Harrisville, announced the birth of their third child, then of a fourth. I still use Ethel's marvelous fudge brownie recipe some thirty years after she, fully confident that a fourteen-year-old girl knew how to cook, gave it to me after blushing with delight at my compliments about the dessert. Ethel's recipe was my entry to one of my sustaining pleasures, competent cooking.

Tall and thin as a steel rod despite the twelve-ounce steaks he'd scarf down, John, who looked like a cowboy from a black-and-white movie, sold my stepfather our first car, a dilapidated old Plymouth, whose passenger door would swing open on sharp turns. Everyone in the village laughed at my stepfather being duped ("John's been trying to unload that junkheap on somebody for years"), but John did us a colossal service. It turned out that my stepfather had lied about knowing how to drive as well. He used that car as a battering ram for his driver's education—he knocked down John's mailbox in his attempt to back out of the Chalmerses' driveway; he plunged the car halfway into the ditch while gesticulating in an argument with my mother. He left indelible marks on both sides of the garage doorjamb by hitting it practically every time he backed out. He nearly killed us all on the way to Detroit once, and his stopping rush-hour traffic for two hours by insisting that cars turning left had the right of way is responsible for the no-left-turn sign still up at the northwest intersection of two Detroit main streets, Woodward and McNichols.

When he parked the car in front of my great-aunt's suburban house and we got out, people came out of their houses to stare at the ancient, dented black carcass of the Plymouth, with the manual, rotary passenger-door lock John had improvised after he saw me almost tumble out of the car during one of Dick's maneuvers. They asked in wonder, "You came down eighty miles in *that?*" *That* did expire on the road from Saginaw one evening, when we also found out that the prosperous German farmers of the rich Saginaw valley, where the corn grew twice as fast as the corn on farms in Harrisville, were not nearly as generous to strangers as our Americans, the ones we used for all our generalizations in letters back home. When at last my stepfather was moved to buy his first new car, I knew about it before he and my mother got back from the Ford dealership in the next town—Harrisville was abuzz with the news, and the next day I was teased by teachers and students asking whether my stepfather had already "put a dent in it."

For Harrisville was a village before cable TV, and its major source of entertainment was its people's doings—so-and-so getting some girl "in trouble," as they said in those days; star athletes perishing over the summer in traffic accidents; family cars totaled by collisions with deer; the antics of my stepfather's driving. One time I too provided an afternoon's entertainment. My adolescent horror of my body and my pathological shyness branded the incident into my memory; it took many intervening years to allow me to smile about it. I had got my long-standing wish, a bicycle, for my fifteenth birth-day, and had taught myself to ride it over the rough terrain of our backyard, a vast area of uneven sandy soil and rocks left over from the construction of the house. One warm spring afternoon I decid-ed to ride to town. I rode on the shoulder of the highway, then a mass of river rocks. Several cars honked as they went by, people wav-ing and laughing. I waved back, unconcerned, used to the friendli-ness of acquaintances and the expected sexual harassment of strangers, for which we had no such words then. When I got to town and went into the drugstore, I reached for my back pocket and real-ized I had forgotten to zip up the back of my shorts. My underwear had been in plain view for the whole ride to town; everyone heard and let me know about it for the next couple of days. I wanted to die instantly or to leave Harrisville forever that very afternoon for the grand, anonymous city where my social gaucheries would pass unnoticed or unremarked upon in my presence.

So as to dissolve her now forced union with Dick, my mother too was working toward leaving Harrisville. She had been unable to find any other place for rent within walking distance of the school, a fact of country living that condemned her to stay under the same roof with her nominal husband. But we were not to leave before my initiation in the great American ritual of separation, the prom. At the school's annual book fair, the most exciting event of the academic year for me, my two American friends told me about the prom. I had been instructing them in the rules of courtship European style, according to which a girl or woman is obligated to dance with any boy or man who asks, and conversely the boys and men at a dance make it a point to dance at least once with every girl/woman pres-ent, so that no one is in the category tactfully described in the film *Marty* as "dogs like us." "Wait," they said. "You think these dances are awful—wait till the prom." "The what?" I asked, and they enlightened me about the spring ritual designed to begin teaching women to work against one another for the distinction of being selected by men. While the prom may have served, as coming-out parties did, to put young women on the marriage block, in my American years it served merely—as Yeats uses it in "mere anarchy" to mean purely, symbolically, at a level transcending economics but inextricably meshed with politics—to separate women who please from those who don't.

Later in life I participated in, then retreated from efforts to institutionalize women's studies programs in the academy since so many seemed fated to repeat the patterns of prom selection. Directors, coordinators, heads, chairs—whatever the leading figures are called—start out as the women who were the smart, scary girls, the ones who didn't get asked. Then, as programs settle into administrative models, the "old girls" get edged out and the new, not always younger, women tend to be the kind of girls who please.

My own prom adventure in Harrisville belonged to yet another episode in the annals of aliens from outer space. In our second year in Harrisville, the school acquired a new principal, a vast improvement over the first, Mr. Zahn, who'd attempted to teach his ten-month-old daughter not to play with fire one afternoon in our own living room. He handed the fascinated baby a lit match. When she howled with pain, he chuckled. "That'll be a useful lesson to her." His wife, a Lebanese woman who, like us, felt terribly displaced in rural America and was subject to much village talk for her stylish clothes deemed too sexy for a matron, packed the screaming baby up and demanded to leave instantly. I hear that Mr. Zahn made his way up the political ladder to head the Republican Committee of an ultraconservative county in the Thumb of Michigan. He had imagined himself expert enough to give me an IQ test orally because, he said, he suspected I got good grades due to "good study habits, not intelligence." Our new principal, who taught chemistry, was the first good science teacher I'd had and the first who didn't condescend to girls. I thrived, having fought all the year before with the small-minded physics teacher who would not let me use my English-French dictionary during tests because "The other students don't need one."

That last spring in Harrisville, the principal asked my parents whether I'd consider going to the prom with his younger son, whom I had not set eyes on. "He's a good looker," he assured me when he saw me. I agreed, feeling highly amused by this arranged date and thinking that it could be no worse than staying home. I met Peter, who was downright handsome and much taller than I even as

I hobbled on spike heels, about half an hour before we were to go to the dinner given by the junior class in honor of the seniors. At least in Harrisville, all the juniors and seniors who chose could show up in evening dress at the dinner, to which all were invited. The dance for couples followed. At dinner, Peter and I sat with my two friends, one with a date whom she had accepted *faute de mieux* and over whose lack of manners she was in agony, the other truly the most attractive and popular of the three of us yet mysteriously dateless. The dinner was fun, but not knowing Peter and made doubly shy by my attraction to him, I was terribly apprehensive about the rest of the evening. My dateless friend looked forlorn and beautiful in her long white gown. I asked her and Peter simultaneously if they'd mind if we all went to the dance together. What could they say? We walked in as a threesome. As Hemingway would say, "We laughed a lot." I looked at the pinched face of my other friend as she sat next to the oaf, at the anxious looks of the other girls, fearful lest their dates, following Peter's example, would want to dance with other girls, and noticed that in contrast, all three of us were enjoying ourselves immensely.

A week later, as a group of us girls were eating lunch on a grassy slope outside the school, a few began to inquire about Peter. "Did he ask you out again, did he call, did he write?" they asked in succession, exchanging smirks whose significance was lost on me. "No," I said, surprised that anyone would have conceived of our seeing each other again since the circumstances of our going to the prom had been so bizarre.

My friend Lannea, who had accepted the date with the oaf, turned red. She dragged me away, pulling at my arm with unsuspected force. "They make me so mad," she uttered through clenched teeth when we were out of hearing of the others. "They've talked of nothing else since the prom."

"What?" I replied with my usual finesse.

"They think what you did was awful. I think it was great. They're trying to show you that he'll never ask you out again."

I was astonished. Mr. Sobchak, the principal, had called me to his office the Monday after the prom to mutter something about what a wonderful thing I had done, and I thought he meant my clever solution to the awkwardness of seeing my dressed-up friend go home before the dance and being left to spend the evening in the sole company of someone I had barely met. As a visitor from another planet, like the Americans we used to marvel at in Bucharest, I had not looked upon my spontaneous invitation to my friend as a breach of social norms that would generate such notice. My mother and stepfather too thought it a normal outcome of the situation. A week later, a letter arrived from Peter, in which he asked me in rather non-standard spelling to go with him to his prom and in which he described himself as having been the luckiest man the night of the Harrisville prom, spending it "with two beautiful young ladies." Lannea jumped up and down when she heard and filled the school with the news. Peter and I tried to keep up our acquaintance, exchanging a few notes after our second dance, but he wasn't much of a writer; then I moved away, and I don't know what's become of him. In my senior year, at last savvy in the ways of the New World, I deliberately crashed the prom as a social protest, but it wasn't nearly as much fun as when I hadn't known what I was doing.

EIGHTEEN: *Sub-Urban Skies*

No sooner had we escaped from my stepfather's reign of terror than I fell in the thrall, as far as my mother was concerned, of a German boy in my senior class. Not yet legally divorced but separated enough so that she'd become suspect to her American friends, my mother began to look forward to a renewal of the close companionship she and I had enjoyed in European adversity as we waited to come to the United States. But it was not to be. Perhaps I should call Max a man—he was a full year and a half older than I at a time in life when such differences matter, and far more sexually experienced. "He has to be German, of all things," my mother groaned. She thought I was becoming thoroughly Americanized, and did not understand that what attracted Max and me to each other was our common Europeanness in the brand-new, picture-windowed, flat-topped suburban high school populated by kids without our historical anxieties and our personal desolate oddities of speech and custom.

Max taught me to kiss, but even that he did too soon. He did everything too soon, and despite my passion for his company he must have begun to feel my abstractedness. Besides, when I questioned him about his previous adventures I found him eager to crow, but when he perceived the slant of my interrogation, "What did you do so the girl wouldn't get pregnant?" he got sullen. "Nothing," he said. "We moved here. I don't know what happened to her. It was a painless parting." This shook me. I'm sure my refrain, "I don't want to get pregnant," as he was concentrating on unhooking my bra or exploring the flesh above my stockings must have been disconcerting. Yet I must give Max his due; he did try to find out what might please me, even while fighting the conviction that girls take so long to feel sexual pleasure that they might as well not. He must have gotten hold of manuals about women's orgasms and practiced, somewhat fiercely, on me. I don't know how he managed to rub my clitoris so as to irritate the urethra, but I remember violently pushing his hand away and shouting, "You're hurting me." And still he tried. "Tell me what feels good," he said, "when you touch yourself." "I don't," I said, which was the truth, or partial truth, since I recollected dimly the winter of my father's absence, when I was four, feverish from the latest bout of childhood illness, and waiting for my mother to pick me up from the apartment of friends I didn't particularly like. I touched my clitoris and it seemed to soothe my ills and my loneliness, but in a crazy and enervating way that later made Moravia's oversexed TB wards and Proust's etiology of love resonate like familiar echoes. Max, however, knew my history better: "Everybody plays with themselves. Freud says so," he said. "Freud didn't know me," I said.

That, it would seem, spelled the beginning of the end. Actually, I had begun to suspect that we were not meant to last the one time that I went to visit him at his parents' apartment after he'd been in a car crash. While John, a mutual friend, and I talked to Max, who was confined to bed, his mother and father were in the living room watching wrestling. This pastime might not have shocked me had I not seen exactly the same look of deranged pleasure and heard the grunts of satisfaction that now emanated from Max's parents come from my stepfather each time the wrestlers did something unspeakable to each other. Perhaps I might have excused what I saw as the alien mentality of adult male creatures, of whose strangeness I had had ample warning during an adolescence shared mostly with male friends. But his mother was watching and registering the same pleasure, and this to me seemed beyond the pale.

For him, though, the signal may have been my detachment when, for instance, he placed my hand high up on his thigh. Suddenly my hand became an object severed from my body, without sentience, lying there like a dead thing so that I looked at it, then at him, in incomprehension. Not that I didn't want Max. I wanted him so much that I was afraid when we kissed of being electrocuted by the shocks of pleasure that coursed through me. But I also didn't want to get pregnant, and at that time I didn't have the courage or the right words to ask him whether he felt what I felt when I walked away from him—a slight shudder of disgust at the drying saliva, not mine, at the corners of the mouth. Because it was all too soon.

The way Max chose to break up, as we said in those days, with me taught me more than his kisses. Perhaps he only decided to do it after testing the limits of my tolerance for humiliation and finding them too restrictive. Perhaps he began to test only after he'd decided to drive me away. In any case, the ending followed a certain trajectory. It began with the personal and passed for insignificant at first. I told him I was thinking of growing my hair long. He looked at me as if sizing up the quality of my being and said, "No. Don't. It'll always look sloppy." Two years later my hair was halfway down my back. Another time, parked behind a closed gas station on the way to the basketball game we were supposedly attending, he said, "Your breasts remind me of a girl I used to know in Winnepeg." He laughed when I moved away, stung by the image I had conjured of his mind as a museum of female parts: here are the Detroit legs, in the glass display case the Munich rumps, on this wall the Winnepeg-type breasts. On the way home from the game—to which we had finally arrived (we were careful about our alibis in those days)—he moved from the personal to the historical assault. He first hummed, then sang out loud, with gusto, *"Deutchland, Deutchland, über alles."* I countered with "La Marseillaise," unknowingly replaying a scene from *Casablanca*, a film I was yet to see, then with the Communist International. We had never sat so far apart on the front seat of his dilapidated fifth-hand Cadillac. The next day, he gave me a note. It had been our custom to exchange notes as we passed each other in the doorway of a classroom, but I hadn't written him one this time; his was a redundancy announcing the end of his love for me and reducing me to tears in the hallway filled with people whispering and with too much light from those immense, energy-wasting windows. I can't recall why I had to drive my mother's car to the post office that day, but I remember Max insisting on coming with me. I kept repeating, "Don't worry. I won't kill myself over you," and brushing the tears away furiously.

My mother, who had liked Max less and less the more she'd seen of him and who had had plenty to say about what she felt was my general leave-taking of my senses, now breathed not an "I told you so." She even let me take the car for the weekend so I could visit my friends in Harrisville. I showed them the notes Max had written me, which outlined our brief togetherness, and they commiserated. At the end of the visit, I decided to come clean about my family's religion. I took my friend Lannea aside, the very same friend who two years before had looked me in the eye and said she could tell a Jew from anyone, thus anticipating a scene I would later watch in *Exodus*, and told her the awful truth. Here I was, observed yet undetected all this time. After my confession, she fell silent. Then she said, looking into space—the luminous spring morning disclosing, no doubt, how the disparate pieces of my past now fell into the symmetric and consoling mirage of stereotype like glass bits in a kaleidoscope—"That explains a lot of things." But somehow I went back to the loathed suburb lighter of heart. It's hard, at seventeen, to resist a splendid spring day even as you sing, teary-eyed, along with the Walker Brothers, "The sun ain't gonna shine anymore."

NINETEEN: *Endings, Continuities*

Postmonitions

We cannot help but see everything clearly only in retrospect; the future is always distorted as if viewed through the wrong end of the binoculars. In our anticipation, do we not merely project onto the blankness of the future the images of what we already know? At the American embassy in Paris I had dreamed up a tall, thin boy who would kiss me. Max was tall and thin, but his sensuous lips had a wolfish twist when he smiled, and he turned out to be the unimaginable in my future, a German with whom I fell in love because the city by the lake that I dreamed up happened to be four hundred miles west of the city where I actually landed, and the suburb where Max and I lived united us, or so I imagined, in a horror of barren flat land and barren lawns and flat ranch houses and stick trees that would take another quarter century to grow into themselves. Even then their rich crowns would not hide the segmented small thinking that inhabited the segmented small rooms of those flat, ready-to-wear houses.

I dreamed up a country such as I had not known and did not expect to find in sick old Europe any more than in the ancient, weary, seething countries of Asia, and farther south my imagination did not take me. I came to a country that took up almost a continent, where despite that vastness people could not give each other elbow room to live; a country that prides itself on its individualistic ideals, yet scrutinizes more intensely than the Communists what people do with their bodies in search of pleasure or freedom. Here charity wears a capital C, and people are moved by news stories to donate money, to volunteer services to those in need with a generosity unmatched anywhere else—but only in crises; and sustained systems of everyday safeguards against disaster are regarded with suspicion as inimical to the pocketbook and the American way of life.

Like anthropologists early in the century, my mother studied her immigrant life as if she were collecting data about a strange and impenetrable culture. She resisted adaptation with an intensity that seemed the antithesis of what "going native" meant in a book like *Heart of Darkness*. She watched me be seduced, corrupted, alienated by this same culture and tried to pull me back, only there was no shore onto which she could have rescued me, only herself, and she too was afloat. She clung to me more and more fiercely, as if fearing that either I would abandon her to the flood or she would lose me to the new element in which I swam with too much ease.

We ought to be careful of the advice we give anybody, especially the young, for the contingencies of history compounded by the intricacies of each person's genes and life make all advice another mere projection of "I've been there, I know how this will turn out," when in effect the "there" is yet to take shape through myriad chances. "Go to New York, the capital," said my uncle, his vision undermined by his weak geopolitical knowledge of the United States but accurate in some magical way about the American intellectual scene. Yet the advice was outdated—I was too late, Greenwich Village was already in the throes of premature yuppification.

"They're marrying without a solid future," said my mother, her heart aching from visions of a life of hardship when my husband's young sister married a young man without a profession. She could not foresee the drive of the young bridegroom, who took it upon himself to rescue his father's insignificant small business and make it into an extremely lucrative company. "Be aggressive in getting to know people. Hand them your off-prints; send them copies of your book," an older friend said to me, not imagining that in the world of conferences in which he'd found intellectual kinship a young woman would thus be exposing herself to unwanted advances from academic colleagues who chose to take her approaches as sexual permission. "I fear the aches and disability of old age," said a friend who would be hit by a train during her morning walk in her fifty-fourth year. And I too am seized by visions of times to come, remembering my father's blessing on each good meal, "When we hit hard times, let them be no worse than this," and thinking with a spasm of the heart that what lies ahead can be no better.

Yet so little of what I imagined as I moved from city to city, place to place corresponded to my envisionings that I am forever humbled by a reality that escapes my shaping. My uprootedness has kept me from becoming too securely anchored to happiness or success; yet webs of friendship, like nets stretched over the sawdust under trapezes where acrobats perform their flights, have let me bounce gently when I fall, have buoyed me so I could somersault and land on my feet and bow smiling. In a country where we decry distances and moves that break intimate connections, I've been sustained by ties of friendship that like arteries keep renewing my blood, my brain, my whole being. So many scenes—a car that rocked with our laughter as we looked for an address we couldn't find; the storm at sea when we went whale watching; a glass of kir in Barbara's garden in Surrey, during an afternoon of almost heart-rending beauty; taking the children somewhere, talking about the children, always; coffee and chocolate, consolations for absences; imagining an ideal lover for Jane at the beach, becoming so absorbed in the fantasy that we didn't notice the sun burning us; seedlings, volunteers, cuttings, exchanged so that our gardens, each so different, become a continuum of remembrance. And how shall I name those moments of plenitude when friends did something so unexpectedly selfless as to take away my breath? Lore, whose review of my book earned me tenure, unbeknownst to me was asked to write, again, for my promotion to professor. She called to tell me she'd be undergoing major surgery for an illness that would in two years' time take her life. She said, "You'll probably hear that I went in for this procedure, and I want you not to worry about the letter I'm writing for you. It will go out before I have my operation." So unmerited, so unpredictable has been my fortune.

And the cities that began constituting my consciousness? Bucharest lies before me in a tangle of walks unrelated to compass

points or the layout of a map, merely slack heartstrings crossing continents and oceans but connecting only to dust and ashes. The Paris
I dreamed materialized sometime after I left it, when Malraux
ordered the massive cleaning of black soot from its façades, which
surfaced gray-green and detailed like a mermaid in an Ingres painting. Detroit, the archive of my Americanization, still has the power
to smite my heart with a past and present that resist the most modest dreams of recovery; and yet, and yet, the white-throated sparrows and the juncos with their Japanese fantails still pass through the
inner city each spring. In the open space called the Mall at my urban
university, small children that Claire and I watched in our chance
meeting—she between classes she was taking, I having just given a
lecture—were caught by the weird light of a near-total solar eclipse,
just as I had been in my childhood by what I was told would be the
last eclipse of my life. How could I foresee the change in my global
perspective that would allow me yet another, one that will not be
seen in these parts again in sixty years, they say, those undaunted sci-
entists who cannot tell whether the city itself will stand, let alone the
race, but who can read infallibly beyond their own mortality the
movement of the stars?

Writing History
"Haven't you imagined them saying to their wives in the evening . . .
Haven't you imagined those prudent people saying to their wives in
the evening . . ." The phrase is repeated in Joseph Brodsky's
reproach to Havel, published February 17, 1994, three days before
what would have been my mother's seventy-fifth birthday. If I now
address the writer, Joseph Brodsky, the Nobel prizewinner for literature, I am addressing someone beyond reproach, another of the
hallowed dead. Yet I cannot imagine a Czechoslovakia, any more
than a Romania or a Soviet Union, made up of the categories "people," prudent and otherwise, and their "wives." It is these somno-
lent rhythms of beautiful prose that I fear most: with a stroke of the
pen or the light tapping of fingertips on a keyboard, a famous figure
can overwrite history without risk, for the "people" and especially
their "wives" have no equal access to readers. The discourse has
already been shaped by those who should have learned better from

their past. For I remember a different history, anecdotal but no less true than the encounters Brodsky imagined between "people" and the renegade Havel on the streets of Prague, the moral choices he imagines them having to face—whether to greet Havel or to pretend they didn't know him, then to recount to their "wives" their choice when they got home.

My childhood was populated by women who lived with daily choices between integrity and survival; they might have wanted husbands to whom to delegate those choices, but life under communism allowed few to be "wives" of the kind imagined by Brodsky, the stay-at-home waiting for her husband to bring her news of the world. When I was nine or ten the husband of my mother's friend Hetta was arrested on a political charge. Hetta was instantly expelled from the Communist Party, to which she had belonged since before the war, and demoted to the same work for half the pay. Hetta's laughter and beauty were equally remarkable, but now her laughter was heard less often and her beauty grew gaunt, and my mother would look at her with concern and ask, "Can't you get a pass to the sanitarium?" At sixteen, Hetta had watched the Nazis hang her father. Herded in line with the other Jews of Iaşi, she had stepped out to reach for her father's hand. An Iron Guard hit her in the back with the butt of his gun. The thin, cold rain, the act she'd witnessed, and the blow to her back made Hetta susceptible, and she succumbed to tuberculosis.

Now in her thirties, still loyal to her husband though she had long ceased to love him, she took care of her demented mother and of her brother, who suffered from a degenerative spine disease. Her husband was condemned to five years' hard labor, working on the canal that was to provide a quicker route to the Black Sea from the Danube; it was one of the half-baked plans that my father had opposed publicly and vehemently, thus digging his own grave. Thousands of political prisoners died in the sands of Dobrogia digging by hand a trench that due to the nature of the soil could not hold against erosion and would have disastrously diverted the waters of the Danube from its delta. One of the richest wetlands in the world, the delta is now so polluted from unproductive heavy industry that chances of its recovery are slim.

Hetta cleaned and shopped for her mother and brother. On a household budget that barely allowed her to pay the rent on her one-room, closet-sized kitchen apartment with a shared bathroom down the hall, she had to collect food and clothing to send to her husband, who without them would have died. The most precious gift people could give her during his imprisonment was a chunk of hard salami. I remember my mother religiously putting aside non-perishable foodstuffs for Hetta's husband. I also remember Hetta coming over for coffee at our apartment, talking for hours with my mother, striking in her beauty and gaiety, and, yes, her singleness, this wife made widow by the government.

Then there was Dora, my mother's greatest friend, who in her sixties would be murdered in a terrorist attack in Jerusalem in the fall of 1979. Dora was not a beauty, but she was solid as rock. Even my serious mother appeared scattered by comparison to this woman. Her husband was incidental to the friendship—they had known each other before she married him, and my mother along with many others felt that he was unworthy of her, but then, after her first husband had been put on a train for a labor camp by the Iron Guard and shot with all the other inmates at the end station, did the world hold another match for her? Dora gave me the birthday presents that changed my intellectual life, such as the complete set of Molière's plays I received on my tenth birthday. Despite distance and many years when Dora, under surveillance in Romania for "ideological" reasons, simply could not afford to correspond with someone in the United States, she remained my mother's moral anchor. I recall this woman of calm and even temper, in a rare moment of despair, telling my mother when we visited in Israel in 1978 that, as usual, the responsibility of providing for the household had fallen to her and that she'd had to accept employment in the office of a crooked lawyer, who made a living off the compensations he obtained from the German government for victims of Nazi crimes. "I never had to compromise to this extent," she said, "even working in Romania. After a day at the office, I feel a pain settling into my chest. I can hardly breathe on the bus home."

Not all the "wives" I knew were Jewish. There was Milka, the Bulgarian who through the vagaries of genetic mixing resembled my mother and me so much that we would trick people by showing them infant pictures of each other and pretending they were our own. Every time Milka entered a shop with me, everyone said, "You can't hide it. That's your little sister," to which we giggled acknowledgment. At the office, people would often leave messages with my mother meant for Milka and vice versa. Once, I naively asked Milka, "When did you apply for a passport?" since everyone we knew seemed to have done so, and she laughed. "We Christians are lobbying for equal rights with the Jews. We're not allowed to apply." I was shocked, and shocked again by my surprise, so deeply had I internalized the anti-Semitic notion of the Jewish look. Married to the son of a famous national painter, Milka made no bones about training her husband into equality. He, like many other men, refused to stand in line for food. Milka began making dinner for herself alone and told him that if he wanted to eat, he had to bring home some of the staples. For years, they would both kneel on the bathroom floor and wash linen in the tub, a standard procedure in most families but one performed by precious few men.

There was Marguerite, a Transylvanian colleague of my mother's. A high-ranking Communist Party member at the office, who had befriended Marguerite and seemed to be genuinely interested in her, her child, and her ailing husband, had actually "infiltrated" her household so as to denounce her to the authorities. My mother had watched the friendship between the two women with apprehension; she'd even warned Marguerite that her newfound friend had a reputation as a stool pigeon. One Sunday Marguerite was crying in our living room, by turns trying to justify herself for having trusted this woman and berating herself for her stupidity. "What am I going to do?" she kept saying, for now that her husband's past as a bourgeois exploiter (he had owned a small manufacturing company employing eight people) had come to light, he would lose his ration card, and only she could buy flour, sugar, and oil—for one person's consumption—in a family of three. In the next years, I saw Marguerite occasionally, more rarely after my mother herself was fired for having applied to leave the country, each time visibly more aged. She somehow made ends meet so that neither her sick husband nor her daughter went without, only Marguerite herself.

One choice brought up by Marguerite when she came to my mother that early Sunday morning was divorce. "They're telling me to dump him," she said, "now that he's so sick and would die without me."

My mother reassured her, "Yes, I know. No, you don't have to do it." She did know. Shortly after my father's disappearance, one of her bosses got wind of his arrest. Solicitude for my mother, he said, prompted him to advise her to divorce my father. My mother's response was similar to Marguerite's: "Now when he needs me most? What do you take me for?"

Her boss, who had changed his name from Horowitz to Moraru, said, "You and I know the Yiddish saying: If somebody's drowning, you have an obligation to jump in and save him—but only if you know how to swim."

"I know how to swim." My mother shrugged.

"I could denounce you, you know, though I probably won't," he said, and she, turning on her heel to leave, replied over her shoulder, "That *probably* is very reassuring." When I was older I understood that there must have been some sexual bartering in that exchange, for thereafter my mother never referred to Moraru other than as "that vile man." To illustrate the vagaries of fate, she would point to the two brothers, Horowitz, the gentlest, most righteous man (who became my pediatrician while my first pediatrician did time for "Zionist" activities) and Moraru, lackey of the occupying Soviets. "Born from the same womb," my mother would muse, "raised in the same household. Horowitz, you couldn't ask for a better friend; then there's that vile man."

There was also my aunt, my father's sister, who for all her flaws was an impeccable head nurse, then hospital administrator, positions that sapped her of vitality and made my uncle's congenital inability to fight for advancement, for payment from patients, for responsible work from repair people almost impossible to bear. I remember one time, when my mother was out of town and I was between two trips, my aunt met me at the train station to keep me overnight. I had gotten my period while at the seacoast, and since all of us students used one common bathroom I had been deathly embarrassed about washing my pants and hanging them out to dry where the boys could see them. The blood was dry and set in the crotches of about five pairs of underpants. I told my aunt I had to wash them that night, otherwise I'd run out of clean underwear, and she surprised me by urging me to bed. I could hear her for at least an hour afterward swishing and rinsing, working on getting the stains out, voluntarily binding herself to me in that loyalty of blood and its secret traces.

The history of women—their daily acts of heroism—is so easy to write over in imagining them as homebodies, passive receptacles for the world's news, as if the men's world did not press them, whether they wished it or no, into the crucible of moral crisis. Why talk of revolution, the rise of nationalism, ethnic wars, the new world order, when in none of the countries newly escaped from tyranny is there a woman visible, a woman audible? Do the political essayists and theorists think to ask the other half how *they* live, how *they* manage in the new economy? Who bears the brunt of skyrocketing inflation, of finding food for each day, shoes for the children's growing feet, medicine for aged parents whose pensions have evaporated? Must speculations about a new Europe be protected from these mundane concerns by the buffer that women have so often made of their bodies, their minds, their ambitions? And is the West free of this collective amnesia about who cooks the dinner that allows the writing of essays into the night?

In looking back over my mother's life in America, I can understand why she thought she'd failed to win appreciation for her remarkable intellect and moral rectitude in a profession occupied at the time by people a generation younger, in the all-white, homogenized, all-hetero-coupled brand-new suburbs. She represented just what they'd fled in the city, a reminder of origins, of their uncertain possession of the continent, of parents and uncles and older neighbors still going on about the war and labor struggles and, in Detroit, the 1943 riots, of age, of loneliness. From people my age, though, I expected a salute of some sort for these women, whose heroism lightened our load. As I made my way from university degree to university degree, from promotion to promotion, I kept looking for that moment in which at least the women would recognize Brodsky's "wives" as capable and willing to make moral choices. And of course there have been such moments: a colleague surprised by a conversation with my mother, whom he regarded as belonging to a reactionary generation, quoting her dismissal of a local group as fascists; the young student at my friend Lore's memorial celebrating her ardent commitment not just to teaching but to daily political acts; another woman my age turning to a woman my mother's age and saying, "You were the only woman professor I had in my entire graduate career, and I was so lucky I had you as a role model."

When I was five months pregnant, women's groups in Detroit organized a "Take Back the Night" event in Palmer Park, a lovely island of greenery in the city. Ironically, the demonstration was scheduled in the afternoon since the park became dangerous after dark. The Detroit mounted police came, purportedly to protect the demonstrators, although no counterdemonstrators showed up. I had no qualms about attending the event—after all, I walked around the pond in the park daily, schoolmarming children into not throwing rocks at the Canada geese, wandering into the grove of old trees where I could spot the high nest of the wood ducks.

My mother wanted to come with me. She believed in the cause—she'd long railed against the poor quality of life in a city where a woman alone was not safe, and I knew without her saying it that she wanted to keep an eye on me in what she thought was my vulnerable condition, since she harbored as deep a suspicion of the police as of any counterdemonstrators. The event went off without a hitch. As we broke into smaller groups after the speeches and began to hold pleasant conversations in the mild May afternoon, a colleague of mine, a well-known writer, came toward us. "Ah," she said to me, "I see you brought your mother. You're raising her consciousness." I was so surprised I could not reply soon enough for her to hear before she walked on, "No, rather the opposite." Years later, when she came to give a lecture from her own retirement and I was directing the Women's Studies Program, she asked me in the department secretary's office, "How's your mother?" I had to tell her my mother had died three years before, and as I tried to control a brief burst of tears, she said, "It must be hard for you. You two were a team."

How and where can I rewrite the history of anonymous women?

My very act of writing without fear I owe to my mother, who left her own habitation of language to give me voice. Only now, in middle age, can I appreciate her courage in parting at the age of forty-five with all she'd been at home with, in embarking on a perilous and most lonely adventure so that I would be preserved from what with her usual prescience she felt would come—a Ceaușescu regime under whose surveillance my urine would be examined for evidence of pregnancy monthly, my most intimate functions becoming duties of the state; my mind would be a negligible defect to be corrected and possibly erased.

Let me imagine, then, my mother in the streets of Prague, meeting the outcast Havel. She knows him at a glance. They look at each other. They shake hands. They go their not so different ways.

Broken Shade

When I came across Meursault's observation that we have all desired a loved one's death, it cleaved my conscience. I recognized it with a recoil, as one instinctively starts at the sinuous movement parting the grass. Later, as a mother, I thought, no, not children, not grand-children, we surely exclude them, and Camus knew nothing about that, but I wondered if beneath our anxieties for their safety there lurks a germ of that imagination preparing us for loss.

This morning I woke up having touched my mother. I had a vivid dream that I was massaging her neck and back, and my finger-tips remembered with an accuracy sharp and sudden as a splinter the texture of her body, the petal-softness of her skin and the muscles beneath, so taut that often the joints of my hands would hurt as I tried to work out the knots. Vainly I fought to get back into the dream. My hands still possessed my mother, kept for themselves the recollected back of her neck and shoulders, while my mind's eye was incapable of reconstructing her face except in flashes, like film frames moving through a hand-cranked projector, fractured in their still-ness yet too fast for beholding.

At the time of my mother's death, I didn't have the heart to call up all my friends to let them know, so when I heard Margaret's voice over the wires from Boston and she asked me how things were going, I began to sob. I felt foolish, unable to speak, but she, who had lost a sister under terrifying circumstances, understood. Later, I got a note from her saying that my mother would remain a living presence in my life, as her sister had in hers. I was adrift in clichés at the time, unable to dig out the few nuggets of truth from the platitudes with which people were snowing me under. Now, three and a half years later, on the balcony of the Howard Johnson's in Tempe, Arizona, I contemplate the mixture of the familiar and the alien in the vista, fauna, and vegetation before me, and ask myself, how is memory distinct from imaginings?

Just as in late adolescence I populated every solitary landscape fleetingly glimpsed from moving cars or buses with the presence of my beloved so that our imagined erotic togetherness suffused the terrain with an aura of shimmering intensity like a desert mirage, so now I reconstitute my mother's presence in every new locale, every new film that I see—she being so intimately connected for me with the screen; I can no longer remember with any precision what was the last movie we saw together, and whether she also saw and loved the stark asymmetries of the American Southwest.

My mother died sometime in the night between the fourth and fifth of October, 1989. I remember trying to call her as I did every day, then trying again with increasing frequency from morning to late afternoon on the fifth, letting the phone ring longer and longer. The last half of the day seems to have been made up of a web of voices connected by phone lines: first, my husband at work, apprised that something might be wrong; then, him talking with my daughter's school, first being told that she had been picked up by her grandmother, and his relieved anticipation of our teasing my mother later about worrying us to death; the school calling back to say that our daughter was in day care, my mother not having come for her; me calling him and finding out, and knowing right then that my mother must have died, but clinging to the hopes, now monstrous to my mind, that she might have had car trouble and been away from a phone, or that she'd been in an accident and was recovering in a hospital, unable yet to speak.

I remember the darkening October day that started out with dazzling sunshine and ended in violent rain, thunder, and wintry winds; the first large, warm drops fell intermittently on me as I rushed from a building at the farthest corner of the campus toward the parking structure, registering the flock of kinglets fluttering in a locust tree, wishing with all my will that what I knew had happened the moment I found out my mother had failed to pick up Olivia would somehow come out differently, would somehow take the implausible plot turns toward a happy ending. I remember gliding from lane to lane in the rush-hour traffic in what must have been the most skillful and reckless bit of driving of my life, arriving I don't know how on the street and parking across from my mother's apartment building. The first thing I saw was her car in its carport, a repellent omen. She had not gone anywhere. Then I saw my husband's car, and then, outside the building door I saw him and his father, waiting. They had no key. I remember thinking we'd have to cut the chain inside my mother's door, but the door opened smoothly and fully, without the abrupt jerk and stop of the chain lock, as if—perhaps because—my mother had intended to remove one last barrier for me. The outside hallway smelled like cooking, and for the briefest second I let myself be lulled by the fantasy that my mother had forgotten about fetching Olivia, that she was home preparing the quince stew she had promised, a dish from my childhood that she made every fall as a treat especially for me.

Inside, the apartment was still and cold and smelled of nothing, not even the underlying odor of stale tobacco smoke that would so often filter through the ventilating system from the neighbors in the apartment below. But the silence did not last. I remember hearing a rush of deafening sound that made me run frantically from the living room, from where I could see all but the rooms giving onto the hallway to the left, into the bathroom, then the bedroom, where I glimpsed the top of my mother's honey-colored hair above the comforter. I ran to touch her right arm, stretched out beyond the covers, in what I knew was the most futile gesture I'd ever made, trying to find a pulse and feeling only an icy coldness. My mother always had warmer hands and feet than I, and from the time I was little she'd warm my hands between hers. The utter cold of her skin felt like the most complete abandonment, and I gave way to my own voice, trying to still the insistent, hokey pounding in my ears that seemed nothing more than an imitation of the score at the climax of a cheap horror movie.

In civilized society, we are not allowed even a breath's span of solitude with death. My mother used to tell me the story of her maternal grandmother, condemned with her family to Siberia for being Jewish at some point in the war when anti-Semitism was in vogue among the Soviet troops. She knew she would die soon and her daughter would be left alone with the body for quite some time before the authorities would permit her to begin procedures for interment. She instructed her daughter not to be afraid of her mother's corpse, that the same love she'd borne her daughter in life would prevail in death. Before my mother's body was removed, before the police traipsed through, before the seemingly endless series of calls, official and personal, began, before I succumbed to the siege of decisions about funeral arrangements, announcements, timetables, the business of tidying up, I went alone only for a brief moment into my mother's bedroom. I caressed her cheek, which did not have the same frightening iciness as her wrist, and tried vainly to close her lids. My mother's eyes never fully closed in sleep, a physical peculiarity that often encouraged my cruelty when a child. I would convince myself she was only pretending to sleep and would pull one of her eyelids open, to make sure. Now I was powerless either to prolong or to interrupt her sleep, and surely that is how she died, in an untroubled dream, her left arm bent and her wrist turned in, the back of her hand supporting her left cheek, her right arm stretched in complete abandon beyond the covers.

I draw a breath that cuts sharply between my ribs on the less and less frequent occasions when I look in on my sleeping daughter and see her arm curled to support her cheek and her other arm flung out over the bed's edge. There was a time when I looked in amusement at this astonishing replication of sleep habits that had skipped a generation. Now that the borderline of sleep and death has vanished for me, I tiptoe to my daughter's bed and in a needless gesture, given the gently rising and falling covers and the almost traceless yet audible rhythm of her breath, I touch her wrist.

My mother died in the same month she gave me life. In retrospect, I interpret her melancholy every year at the approach of autumn as a premonition of the permanent sadness with which she would endow the season for me. I, the eternal student-teacher, would protest, "But the new year really begins in fall. But that's when I was born—wasn't that a beginning?" My mother's eyes would nevertheless film over as she watched the splendor recklessly burning itself off in the deciduous trees of this northern clime, and she would sigh, and she would fret at the small death of light each day. Like her father, who died sometime during the eight days of Passover, she was said to have died a holy death, between Rosh Hashanah and Yom Kippur. She died six days before her granddaughter's birthday, leaving presents beautifully wrapped, ready to be delivered.

At the last dinner we had together, on the eve of Rosh Hashanah, my mother delivered before us and our friends the following judgment on her own father, her only parent since she was two years old, as she was to be my only parent for thirty-two of my then forty years. She said that since coming to America she had resisted but been drawn in by the constant psychologizing going on everywhere, in newspapers, talk shows, countless books, and had begun reconstructing her childhood and adolescence. Her father had sinned much against her, she had concluded, first by mourning too long over her mother and living a bachelor life, thus denying her a home, then marrying for the wrong reasons a woman as ornamental as his first wife but with neither her intellect nor her heart, thus again denying his daughter by making her into an intruder in the home he briefly had. Yet, my mother declared, after much reflection she realized that he couldn't have behaved otherwise, hedged in by constraints of his time and circumstances. "I blamed him," she said, "for not knowing how to raise an infant girl on his own, for not being two, three generations ahead of his time. After all, he did all he knew how to do; he spent most of his money on the best education money could buy me, and at the time, like now, a lot of money bought the kind of education that would give a person professional independence for life." She sighed, "He did the best he thought he could do for me," and added that her resentment, induced by psychologizing, had melted away.

My mother, whose hopes became more and more restricted by

age and her own circumstances as well as by a history that had repeatedly attempted to obliterate her being or at the very least her spirit, in her last years clung fervently to one wish—an easy death. It would be comforting to think that in that holy week when Jehovah records the deaths to come in the next year, my mother's impulse of love toward the father who had in the best-meaning ways blighted much of her youth earned her that border crossing without a trace of pain or struggle. Does God really mind, as my paternal grandfather thought, what comes out of our mouths?

When the concept of death first made an impact on my consciousness, my father was still alive. I don't remember asking him about it, but I do remember him, voice breaking, telling my mother about an accident he'd witnessed in which a streetcar had cut off a woman's legs. As she, visibly in advanced pregnancy, lay bleeding to death, she kept asking, "But what about my baby? What about my baby?" Shortly after, perhaps because my father'd noticed that I overheard the story, perhaps because my parents ran into our dayroom when they heard me sobbing uncontrollably over the death of the heroic ant in my storybook, my father in the offhanded way that made him a brilliant teacher told me about Lavoisier and the law of conservation of energy and matter. Even in death, he said, nothing is lost. Every part that makes us up becomes energy and matter, no longer in the configuration under which we know it but still the same in terms of the immutable laws of the universe. And, seeing me stare off into space as if I had begun to see departed souls peep out from leaves and stars, my clear-eyed father, not wanting me to transform a piece of scientific information into antihistorical mysticism, added that as an aristocrat the discoverer of that law was guillotined during the French Revolution.

Due to insalubrious houses and poor nutrition, my father's bones had begun disintegrating long before his death, while he was still in his twenties. Did that breakdown release the extraordinary energy and turns of his mind? As a student, ever hungry, he devoured his way through a law degree, then a degree in economics, then a degree in math. He and many of his friends, most of them Jews, most from provincial towns and without relatives and resources in the capital, were on a predictable regime of starving and bingeing. They would not be able to buy food for as long as four or five days; then one of them, though almost never my father, would get a package from home, or another, often my father, would get paid for lessons, and they would feast on bread, salami, cheap wine, olives, feta, and they would keep eating while the food lasted, into the night, often into indigestion. My father's digestive system never quite recovered from those years.

In the damp, unheated jail cell where my father spent a year, his bones sped up their crumbling. He had been arrested sometime in July, shortly after his thirty-eighth birthday. The men who came for him simply marched him out of the house in his summer clothes. My mother was not even allowed to mention his disappearance, let alone attempt to visit him, but despite all advice to the contrary, she began to post herself daily at the Ministry of Military Justice until an older man, to whom she always referred as her guardian angel, took pity on her and acquiesced to her outlandish request to send my father a package of clothing. To allow this, the authorities had to acknowledge that he had been arrested, so her insistence probably brought his case to trial sooner than the long years such cases usually took.

Accompanied by Herczog, my mother set out for the jail in the middle of nowhere and arrived there at dawn, in a field of snow up to the knees. They waited for hours outside the gate until my mother, maddened by the thought that the risks she had taken would be in vain and that she and Herczog might die of hypothermia in that field, waved the permission letter from the Military Tribunal before the guard's startled eyes and shouted with all her might that she would report to the very people who had signed the letter about his refusal to comply. The guard, a sadist from pleasure rather than principle, became frightened and let my mother enter the jail and deliver her package, while Herczog changed color several times, from pallor at certainty of death by cold to a purple hue at the thought of being shot by the guard because of my mother's threats. Later I heard my father say that the B-complex vitamins and the sheepskin vest, the only two items that made it through the guards' and supervisors' "inspection," had saved his life. But he also talked about seeing my mother's signature, faint but still legible on the quadruplicate carbon of the obligatory form. He had been told during interrogations that my mother had been arrested as well and I had been placed in a state orphanage. Was it the vitamins, the vest, the ocular proof that his torturers had lied and we were free that kept him going and saw him out in the world once more, though not for long?

In the Greek Orthodox rituals the bones of the dead are not allowed to rest undisturbed. After seven years, they are disinterred and ceremonially washed in wine, then replaced in the casket and reburied. My father's bones, which clamored for his attention when the weather was about to change and made his face contract with pain, were disturbed not once but twice, perhaps more, for all I know. Some years after we left the country, my aunt his sister moved his remains to a cemetery closer to her house, right next to their mother's grave. My mother expressed great displeasure, insisting that my father, who because of his mother's brutal reference to his infirmity had stopped calling her "mother" at fourteen, would have never wanted to be this close to her. I tried to appease her anger. "He doesn't live in his grave," I reminded her.

My mother's people are Cohanim, high priests of Israel, and therefore have troubled relations with death, which they perceive as a fluke, a sign of failure, and thus a pollutant before the Almighty. From them all of us, even we women, have inherited an unhealthy aversion to last rites. I cannot recall the name of the cemetery where my father was first buried, though I went to the gravesite once. I either never learned or promptly forgot the name of the cemetery convenient to my aunt's house, where now she and my uncle lie, I suppose, in the vicinity of my father's and grandmother's graves, tended by no one, their bones perhaps pitched to make room for the dead relations of people committed to permanent habitation there, where I was born but will most likely never return.

As for my mother's remains, they too had to have their adventure, since my mother could not rest easily without having tried to breach the most impenetrable boundaries. She wanted to be cremated but made it clear she would be loath to lie in a country that ultimately remained inimical to her. She told me more than once that though she could not live in Israel, she would like to be dead there. The two wishes are contradictory—cremation is not permitted in that theocracy. But all rules are made to be broken, as my mother never tired of proving, so I carried her ashes over the ocean through German customs to Israel's shore. Surely my mother does not live in the orange grove where her ashes were scattered. Yet the thin strip of sea visible from the hill and that fragrant orchard make me feel as if something of what she cherished continues, as if the bitter yet consoling nearness of my young cousin's grave in the cemetery close by keeps her from being too lonely.

After my mother's death, I could not touch soil for two years. My garden fell quickly under the law of the survival of the fittest. The entrance to our house was barren of color all summer long. Then, having moved to the first place that has not known my mother's presence except in our intense dreams of her, I began a program of compulsive gardening. I plant pansies for Phil, butchered in 1984 for being gay, because he taught me to love my talent for making things grow and said once, after I'd wondered about the staying power of seemingly fragile things, "Honey, pansies are tough." I plant carnations, to which I'm allergic, for my father, who favored them above all flowers. I try to find the blackest hybrids to plant for my husband, in love with that unnatural hue that begins and ends each of his affairs with the flickerings on the screen. I plant tulips because a former student I much cared for said she wanted no other flowers. I plant berries and sugar peas for my daughter to extract for her the sweetness and flavor of the earth, forget-me-nots and bellflowers for my childhood rambles in the Carpathians, and the rest, all for my mother, whose admiring glance and bursts of pleased wonder made my garden live. So much of it for my mother, snowdrops and violets and lilies of the valley, yet mostly the roses, with their quaint names, the pitiless hooks they leave in you, the permanent scars, the attention they demand, prey to bugs and molds and harsh treatment and rough weather; roses, of which some survive even under the unbroken shade of the oak, where they should not be planted, where perversely, to prove common wisdom wrong, they bloom once, twice a summer, surprising the jaded sight with their recklessness in chancing such beauty in the relative dark of so brief a time.

Between the fall of 1972 and the summer of 1997, I visited Paris many times, all of them in my mind. Under these circumstances the city remained surprisingly unchanged over a quarter of a century, though here and there a corner, a street sign, the hand-lettered name of a shop fell into the disrepair of forgetting, crumbling, fading quietly away almost undiscerned from my stock of images. How clever of the Revolutionaries to name the months after the weather: Brumaire that clothes the quays and the mottled trunks of sycamores in grayish-lilac tulle as if all of Paris had become a Degas backstage, Pluviose with green lashes of rain, or, as I remembered from my returns to Paris, Thermidor with chalky powder rising from the limestone gravel of parks, carried onto the pavement, into subway tunnels, all the way into houses and hotels on shoes and sandals and bare ankles and cuffs of pants.

I could count on Paris, bank on it, bet on it, time after time: the smell of machine oil on the tracks of the metro; the inexorable hiss of pneumatic doors barring rushing passengers from the metro cars pulling out of a station; the fragrant bakeries at street corners; the frantic pace; the undiscriminating rudeness of the locals sometimes honed to cutting wit; the food invariably delicious, whether an omelet served at the sidewalk table of a neighborhood café, the steak-pommes frites of the self-serve places, or a more leisurely three-course meal in an unpretentious neighborhood restaurant that would have earned five stars and snobbish waiters in tuxedos elsewhere.

I could count on Paris to remain where it was, what it was, I thought, even after the shock that it had given my nerves as my first Western city had stopped reverberating. The smells, the dust, the tempers would be the same. So, in the summer of 1997 I traveled with my sixteen-year-old daughter to Paris, for her first time. And yes, everything was more or less where I had placed it in my mental museum. Not once did we get lost. But this newfound clarity cut off my present middle-aged self from the adolescent, then just adult, who had acquired that older Paris, dark in the early sixties, brilliant and white-washed in the seventies. I could no longer get lost in Paris or in London, or, I suspect, in Bucharest the way I used to, so desperately, so magically that the strangeness opened a portal into another world, a parallel, sometimes an altered universe. What has happened to me in the twenty-five years between my short trip to Paris with my husband of two months and my return with my nearly grown child? I know that to some extent I have become my mother, taking my daughter to Place Vendôme to gawk at the jewelers' absurd windows (she finds the displays unimaginative), going up to Rue St. Honoré to the Godiva shop to buy liqueur-filled chocolates not sold in puritan America, wanting to buy her all the Paris I can possibly afford, having her settle for a modestly priced silver moon-stone ring in an underground shop, one of the myriad surrounding the metro exit leading to the Pyramid, the new entrance of the Louvre. Next time there'll be yet another entrance, to relieve the congestion, the ceaseless stream of people so thoughtfully directed by icons placed from the metro exit through the museum to the three must-see exhibits, *Winged Victory,* the *Venus de Milo,* and the *Mona Lisa,* which one can also "visit" at the Louvre via the Internet. It is impossible anymore to get lost looking for a small museum like the Marmottan, the way my husband and I did—or rather, we took the long way round, saw more than what we expected to see. Paris is mapped out; road signs direct tourists with the authority of an eighteenth-century signpost toward the proper destination.

What has happened to Paris since my last time? And by extension to the West, that monolithic myth, that contradiction to everything the communist East stood for? As we ramble through the still-medieval streets of the Marais, we notice the old signs inscribed in calligraphic characters, BOULANGERIE, CRÈMERIE, hanging high and fading above shops now neon-lit, lettered in black computer font on display windows. Versace, Gucci, Dior, Comme les Garçons have taken the place of neighborhood markets. At the corner of St. Antoine and St. Paul, a Monoprix proudly announces, with large painted vegetables, sausages, and fish, its supermarket on the lower level. I am skeptical. A supermarket is a supermarket, after all. Following my investigation, I come up the escalator dizzy and heart-weary. This market, by U.S. standards small, has every imaginable variety of cold meats, seafood, alcohol, breads, chocolates, jams, cheeses, fresh produce, all at slightly lower prices than what's sold above in the specialty shops.

How long before the shops on St. Antoine become clothes and shoe boutiques? There's already a Pier 1 in sight. Another house-wares shop sells products I see advertised in Pottery Barn and Smith & Hawkins catalogues. How long before the supermarket, having garnered the trade, stops carrying all the varieties of cheese it has now? After all, some don't move very fast. The irregularly sized plums might not sell as well as the beautiful ones. Perhaps they should be dropped. A buyer for Monoprix will be pressured to think of the bottom line, no, not now when there's still a bakery across the street and a fish shop and a butcher shop next to each other three steps down from the glass doors, but once they go. The disgruntled customer will only have another Monoprix by another name to which to take her trade, only a clothes boutique and a Pier 1 and a Crate & Barrel to console him for not finding the right ingredients for the right sauce for the right meat. Already the ham in sandwiches is saltier, less tasty than I remember. Already the open market in Place Maubert, where I take my daughter one morning so she can photograph a true French market, is crowded into one small space by the machines excavating Paris everywhere, and reduced to "eth-nic" foods for the most recent immigrant wave to make the Latin Quarter its first stop. And despite the ethnic flavor, the butcher shops have long stopped carrying the marvels I saw when I first came—the innards of animals, clusters of perfectly formed yet unshelled eggs that had been waiting their turn down the oviduct inside the hen when she met her end; her ovaries were still pushing out those strings of yellow pearls of increasing size, marshaled directly to the frying pan. Perhaps I'm wrong, and the French won't easily give up the food, the way they won't give up their civilized day care and vacation time, even if they need general strikes to make their point with whatever government tries to move them into American-style capitalism.

No, it's not the Americanization I find shocking. London in 1986 had already driven home to me the Dunkin Donuts and Kentucky Fried Chicken phenomena, and in 1997 I found it comforting to have a scoop of Belgian chocolate ice cream from a Häagen-Dazs shop in Rue des Rosiers. It's the sameness. The tarama salad available in supermarkets of small Surrey villages, that pinkish mash produced by food processing and altogether different from the real thing, is everywhere on entree lists in Paris, as it is on appetizer lists in the United States. My father's people have conquered their old enemy, the Roman Empire, at a cost. They have gone farther than the emperors dreamed. Their food, adulterated for mass production and tastes, has taken over the West, including a good deal of North America. There's a whole street of Greek restaurants in Paris, and even when not designated as such, restaurants are owned and run by Greeks. In Germany or England the Mediterranean influence, however inauthentic, might be thought an improvement over local cooking. But in Paris?

Along the Champs Elysées, where I take my daughter to look at elegant cafés and shops, the movie-theater marquees show the familiar proliferation of titles, indicating the multiplex, postage stamp-sized screens inside. Of the three we pass, not one shows a French film—all feature American imports. The old cafés are pizza places. The designer boutiques, the ones that have not taken over neighborhood bakeries in the Marais or the Latin Quarter, have moved over to Avenue Montaigne, in a deadly quiet of wealth and custom that turn it into a cemetery this afternoon, when all the action takes place along the Elysées as the Tour de France passes by. If we're not willing to settle for hot dogs/pizza or a $150 meal, there's nothing in between. A little hole-in-the-wall convenience shop run by a francophone African sells ice cream bars; the man also has a small gas pump in front, on the sidewalk, a sight reminiscent of those all-in-one stores of the American desert scape, as in *Petrified Forest*. Beside this makeshift gas station there's a small table with two chairs. We sit there, slurping ice cream and smelling gas fumes. It is so quiet we hear the rumble of the throng an avenue away, but it's not calm for long: we look good there, eating; we advertise well. A few people, then a crowd, push into the shop for ice cream, for biscuits, for soft drinks. As said of people marrying those they don't precisely love, this is settling—nothing between a hugely expensive meal and hot dogs but ice cream mixed with gas fumes. I hope the African will strike it rich. He certainly exhibits more drive and enterprise than other shop owners in this elegant sector.

As we head back to the hotel, I realize that the metro cars too have been replaced with smoothly running, modern open wagons, well lit, less noisy, altogether more comfortable. The pneumatic doors are gone, replaced by photoelectric cells overseeing entrances and exits, making them unlikely to crush passengers who rush in at the last second. The ticket punchers in their little kiosks on the platforms are gone. Everything is automated; machines stamp incoming tickets. The scent of burnt grease no longer lingers along the tracks, smacking the returning traveler with an olfactory reminder of times past. But inside the modern wagons there's something new, a drama of our moribund century played in all great cities now, giving us the same reassurance of inhabiting one planet as the golden arches of McDonald's in every port: the homeless, the crazed, the street people who perform, annoyingly enough to force the reluctant hand into the pocket so as to put an end to the music. On one long trip underground a middle-aged woman with a decent haircut and old clothes twirls around and around the metal poles, improvising a song that sounds like nothing so much as "Misery, oh, misery." Around her rises an odor of long unwashing. Another time I hear Romanian barely discernible to my ear, spoken fast and choppily by a group of musicians, Gypsies, who play, talk fast, make rapid sweeps of the cars, and are gone before official notice can be taken.

Everywhere in Paris there are foreigners. The man selling me a silk scarf in Rue St. Honoré is Vietnamese. The woman directing us toward clothes our sizes in a small shop on Ile St. Louis is African American. The waitress in the café of the Tuileries gardens is Swedish.

The taxi driver who takes us to the hotel is North African, the one with whom I get into a shouting match on the way to the bus for De Gaulle Airport, Italian. The infamous Parisian temper has been replaced with indifferent good will; everyone speaks some English; none of us can be really lost in this largely friendly, accessible, recognizable locale. I am so much at ease that it makes me uncomfortable, for I wonder, is it that Paris is so thoroughly cosmopolitan as to make me feel, despite its architectural splendor, that I haven't left the States? Or is it that I have become part of the strange, often inimical, West without realizing it, have discovered myself at home at last in the world, and find the feeling uncanny? Except for tempers, Paris now mirrors Manhattan more than it does European cities. There's one exception, perhaps, one that sticks in my throat: there is no preponderance of Jews here, where after all at least one Final Solution was tried; it almost worked, and the demographics have not recovered. The face of Europe will never be the same. I take my daughter to the Church of St. Roch, where there is a chapel dedicated, the plaque tells us, to Nazis' and bigots' victims, whose ashes regardless of their faiths commingle. Here too renovation has closed down most of the nave and played tricks with the interior of my own St. Roch, so that what I see is a dis-membering. But the side chapel is open, and I light a candle, here in a Catholic church where my mother over a quarter of a century ago stood next to me and read the moving inscription, for my mother, for my daughter whom I am able to bring to this place for the time being, while the memory and these stones last.